The Crown of Thorns
Humble Gods and Humiliated Kings

Faith Tibble

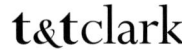

LONDON • NEW YORK • OXFORD • NEW DELHI • SYDNEY

T&T CLARK
Bloomsbury Publishing Plc
50 Bedford Square, London, WC1B 3DP, UK
1385 Broadway, New York, NY 10018, USA
29 Earlsfort Terrace, Dublin 2, Ireland

BLOOMSBURY, T&T CLARK and the T&T Clark logo are trademarks of Bloomsbury Publishing Plc

First published in Great Britain 2025

Copyright © Faith Tibble, 2025

Faith Tibble has asserted her right under the Copyright, Designs and Patents Act, 1988, to be identified as Author of this work.

For legal purposes the Acknowledgments on p. xi constitute an extension of this copyright page.

Cover design: Gita Kowlessur

All rights reserved. No part of this publication may be reproduced or transmitted in any form or by any means, electronic or mechanical, including photocopying, recording, or any information storage or retrieval system, without prior permission in writing from the publishers.

Bloomsbury Publishing Plc does not have any control over, or responsibility for, any third-party websites referred to or in this book. All internet addresses given in this book were correct at the time of going to press. The author and publisher regret any inconvenience caused if addresses have changed or sites have ceased to exist, but can accept no responsibility for any such changes.

A catalogue record for this book is available from the British Library.
A catalog record for this book is available from the Library of Congress.

ISBN: HB: 978-0-5677-1323-0
       PB: 978-0-5677-1322-3
       ePDF: 978-0-5677-1324-7
       eBook: 978-0-5677-1325-4

Typeset by RefineCatch Limited, Bungay, Suffolk
Printed and bound in India

To find out more about our authors and books visit www.bloomsbury.com and sign up for our newsletters.

The Crown of Thorns

To Steve

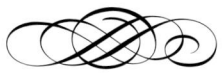

Contents

List of figures ix
Acknowledgments xi

Introduction 1

1 The wreath of acanthus—a humble and humiliated god 3

   Historical context—the making of the Crown of Thorns 4
   The wreath of acanthus 14
   Jesus the failed general 18
   A sarcophagus' story retold 24

2 The triumph of humility 25

   Triumphal imagery and the Roman military 27
   Early significance of the wreath 31
   The crowning of Christ and the importance of demeanor 34
   The Enthroned Christ 37
   Imitating the gods of Rome 39
   The wreath and the cult of martyrs 42
   Martyrs as imitators of the passion 52
   The triumph of humility 55

3 The Crown in transition 57

   An image divided 57
   The Carolingian development of the Mockery scene 60
   The lone wreath 70
   The rise of the Instruments of the Passion 74
   Wreaths and undertaking the world's sin 87

4 The Crown of Thorns—a humble and humiliated king 89

Establishing innovation 90
An Ottonian Mockery 93
Imagery united—the Enthroned Mockery 96
A humbled and humiliated king 106
Coronation and enthronement of the Ottonian and Salian kings 115
The Mockery solidified 122
The Crown's audience—patronage and media 126

5 The Crown revived and revered 145

Byzantine influence—or not? 150
The Sainte-Chapelle and the return of enthronement 152

6 Medieval or modern? The Crown of Thorns today 161

The Crown of Thorns makes it to the big screen 162
All is transitory—the modern artist's Crown of Thorns 164
A story for the ages—the Crown of Thorns in literature 168

Conclusions 173

Bibliography 177
Index 185

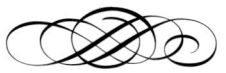

Figures

1	Passion Sarcophagus, Rome, c. 350, Museo Pio Cristiano, Vatican City. © Photo Faith Tibble.	3
2	Tree Sarcophagus, Rome, c. 360, Museo Pio Cristiano, Vatican City. © Alamy.	26
3	Judaea Capta Coin of Titus, Rome, 80–81 CE, The Jewish Museum, New York City. Gift of the Samuel Friedenberg Collection.	30
4	Sarcophagus with Victories, Rome, c. 210 CE, Walters Art Museum, Baltimore.	30
5	Twelve Apostles Sarcophagus, fifth century, Basilica di Sant'Apollinare in Classe, Ravenna. © Alamy.	38
6	Sarcophagus of Beato Rinaldo fifth century, Cathedral of Ravenna, Ravenna. Courtesy of Arcidiocesi di Ravenna-Cervia.	39
7	Aureus of Diocletian and Jupiter Coin, Rome, c. 284–305, The British Museum, London. Courtesy of the Trustees of the British Museum.	40
8	Mosaic of Saint Lawrence, c. 424–425, Mausoleum of Galla Placidia, Ravenna. © Alamy.	43
9	Procession of Saints, c. 557–70, Basilica di Sant'Apollinare Nuovo, Ravenna. © Alamy.	46
10	Gospels of St Augustine, MS 286, fol 125r, Monte Cassino, c. 600, The Parker Library, Corpus Christi College, Cambridge. Courtesy of The Parker Library Corpus Christi College, Cambridge.	58
11	Stuttgart Psalter, Cod.bibl.fol.23, fol. 73r, St. Germain-des-Pres, c. 820–830, Psalm 61, Württembergische Landesbibliothek, Stuttgart. Courtesy of Württembergische Landesbibliothek.	62
12	Utrecht Psalter, Ms. 32, fol. 12r, c. 816–835, Reims, Utrecht University Library, Utrecht. Courtesy of Utrecht University Library, Ms 32, fol. 12r.	71
13	Carolingian Ivory with Scenes of the Passion, Metz, c. 850, Louvre, Paris.	77

14	Crucifixion, c. mid-eighth century, Theodotus Chapel, Santa Maria Antiqua, Rome. © Alamy.	80
15	Irish Evangelary, Cod. Sang. 51, p. 266, c. 750, St. Gall, Ireland, Stifsbibliothek, St. Gallen. Courtesy of St. Gallen, Stifsbibliothek.	81
16	Pericopes of Henry II, Court School of Charles the Bald, c. 840–870. Courtesy of Bayerische Staatsbibliothek München, Clm 4452, cover.	83
17	Codex Aureus of Echternach, Hs156142, fol. 111v, Echternach, c. 1020–1030. Courtesy of Germanisches National-Museum, Nürnberg.	91
18	Saint Peter Gospels, MS M. 781, fol. 83v, Salzburg Abbey, second quarter of the eleventh century, The Morgan Library & Museum, New York. Purchased on the Lewis Cass Ledyard Fund, 1933.	97
19	The Golden Alter of Aachen, The Aachen Cathedral, Fulda, c. 1020. © Alamy.	99
20	Gospel Book of Otto III, Clm 4453, fol. 24, Reichenau Abbey, c. 998–1001, Bayerische Staatsblothek, Munich. © Alamy.	102
21	Bamberg Apocalypse, Msc.Bibl.140,fol.59v, Reichenau, c. 1010, Staatsbibliothek, Bamberg. Courtesy of Staatsbibliothek Bamberg, Msc.Bibl.140,fol.59v, Photo: Gerald Raab.	104
22	Vysehrad Codex, MS. XIV A 13, fol. 42r, Bohemia, c. 1085, National and University Library of the Czech Republic, Prague. Courtesy of the National and University Library of the Czech Republic.	125
23	Codex Eyckensis, MS 185, fol. A. 1v, Echternach, c. 760, Saint Catherine Church, Maaseik.	132
24	Codex Aureus of Echternach, MS 156142, fol. 20v, Echternach, c. 1020–1030, Germanisches National-Museum, Nuremberg.	133
25	Bay 7, Legends of Charlemagne, Chartres, c. 1210–1220, Chartres Cathedral, Chartres. © Alamy.	148
26	Sinai collection (Princeton) image 535, Sinai, c. ninth century, St. Catherine's Monastery, Sinai. By permission of Saint Catherine's Monastery, Sinai, Egypt. Photograph courtesy of Michigan-Princeton-Alexandria Expeditions to Mount Sinai.	151
27	Sainte-Chapelle, Paris, c. 1241–1248. © Alamy.	155
28	Crown of Thorns, 1939, Albert Houthuesen 1903–1979. Tate, Presented by Lady Matthews 1940. © Tate, Photo: Tate.	165
29	Crown of Thorns, 2012, Jane Morgan. Courtesy of Jane Morgan.	167

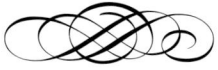

Acknowledgments

There are few of us who, when we walk through the halls of our most esteemed museums and art galleries, could miss the religious iconography. We shuffle by the subtle, the charming, the heartfelt, and the ostentatious. Depictions of Jesus and his earthly life continually catch our eye. More often than not, particularly as the artists delve into the most tortuous moments of Jesus' days, we find depicted the Crown of Thorns. Sharp and painful, it brings to mind suffering, sacrifice, and death.

It seems pointless to write a book about the Crown of Thorns. Considering its near ubiquity in Christian art, why bother confronting the issue? We all know what it looks like, but it is striking how evocative this small item can be. Why does it appeal to our sense of empathy and horror? Perhaps because this particular feature in Passion iconography is so very recent—and one that came bursting forth onto the Christian art scene already steeped in theological and political sentiments. We see it for the first time in the mid-fourth century, but then it disappears almost entirely. For 700 years. We must know why.

This project began with two questions: where did the Crown of Thorns go and why did it change so dramatically? The foundations of this book came about from my PhD dissertation thanks to the guidance and relentless enthusiasm of my supervisor Professor Anat Tcherikover. Alongside her, the Art History department at the University of Haifa, particularly Dr. Emma Maayan-Fanar, Dr. Gil Fishhof, and Dr. Sonia Klinger were unstintingly supportive - they never saw this project as anything but fascinating and were unquestioning in its ultimate success.

Many thanks go as well to Dominic Mattos, Senior Publisher at Bloomsbury T&T Clark and Katherine Jenkins, Editorial Assistant at Bloomsbury T&T Clark for their support, faith, and calm optimism in this study. Dominic and the team's careful consideration and encouragement helped this book become an even better version of itself. I am grateful as well to the anonymous reviewers of the manuscript whose invaluable critiques gave this study the well-roundedness it needed.

I do not believe that much in life is as rich, or even possible, without the support of one's "little village" of friends and family. I am grateful to the unwavering encouragement of my friends who saw me through, especially Professor Jonathan Harris, Professor Kristen Poole, Professor Martin Brückner, Dr. Kate Mesh, Dr. Lluís Vilanova, and Dr. Eric Kondratieff. And to my delightfully multifaceted family who continue to celebrate my triumphs and are constant in their love and positivity.

This book, however, is dedicated to my husband, Dr. Steve Tibble, who above all has been by my side every step of the way—keeping me steady when I stumbled, rejoicing in my every discovery, and loving me with all his might. You are, and always will be, my true inspiration.

Faith Tibble
London and Herefordshire, UK
March 2025

Introduction

When anyone mentions the phrase "Crown of Thorns," a near-universal image spring immediately to mind: a bloodied, beaten, bearded Jesus adorned with a makeshift crown, woven with sharp, painful thorns, pressing viciously into his brow. His expression is pained. He is a man sentenced to death, cruelly mocked by his oppressors.

Derisively bestowed upon him by a merciless cohort of Roman soldiers prior to his Crucifixion, the Crown of Thorns is widely seen as one of many instruments of torture that Jesus endured—a pitiful decoration meant to cause humiliation and pain.

The story is as powerful as the image. The Gospel of Matthew tells us that the Roman soldiers undertook a ruthless taunting of Jesus, who was just condemned by his community for claiming to be the Son of God, and sentenced to die by crucifixion by the Roman governor, Pontius Pilate. But before he could die, the soldiers would have their grotesque form of fun:

> Then the soldiers of the governor took Jesus into the governor's headquarters, and they gathered the whole cohort around him. They stripped him, and they placed around him a scarlet cloak, and after weaving a crown out of thorns, they put it on his head. They put a reed in his right hand and knelt before him and mocked him saying, "Hail, King of the Jews!" They spat on him, and took the reed and struck his head...[1]

---

[1] Mt 27:27–30. The episode of the Mockery of Jesus is also found in Mk 15: 16–20 and Jn 19:1–3.

The Roman soldiers' horrid torment of their prisoner has inspired imagery without which the scenes of Jesus' Passion would seem to be lacking something crucial. But in fact, this seemingly timeless imagery of the Crown of Thorns—sharp and cruel, placed on him during his Mockery—came shockingly late to Passion iconography.

It is not until the eleventh century, and after hundreds of years of depicting Jesus' arrest, trial, flogging, Mockery and Crucifixion, that thorns of any kind even begin to make an appearance on Jesus' head—let alone streams of blood or agonized expressions.

This book tells the extraordinary story of when and under what circumstances the Crown of Thorns developed the familiar artistic attributes that we recognize today.

The depiction of the Crown of Thorns, and everything it represents, is an organic, dynamic process, rather than a single, fixed point. Its development is instead set within three distinct eras. The first development occurs in the fourth and fifth centuries, when Romano-Christian art began to render it as a wreath. The second major development occurs in the ninth-century art of the Carolingians, where two lines of innovation are introduced concurrently: the scene of the Mockery, which creates a narrative context for the Crown of Thorns but excludes its depiction; and a singular suggestion of the Crown of Thorns within the so-called Instruments of the Passion. Third, and lastly, significant changes take place within the Ottonian and Salian art of the eleventh century, where the Crown is both finally depicted with distinguishable thorns and is also included within the Mockery scene.

The rendering of the image of the Crown of Thorns and the Mockery did not, of course, spring forth devoid of context. The artistic analysis will therefore necessarily ask what significant cultural, theological, and political undercurrents influenced the depiction of the Crown of Thorns in each of those three periods. We also examine the implicit ideologies that have become associated with the Crown of Thorns and the Mockery in the different periods, and trace a changing balance between notions of victory, humility, perseverance, and imitation.

Most importantly of all, however, is our new understanding of the Crown of Thorns—what it is, what it represents, and how that meaning has shifted over time. And what that tells us about the peoples and societies that continually reframed it—reshaping it in line with their own, generally unspoken, spiritual, social, and political needs.

As we shall see, that which is supposedly timeless is actually often surprisingly transient—and that which, superficially at least, has obvious meaning is often not at all what it seems.

1

The wreath of acanthus—a humble and humiliated god

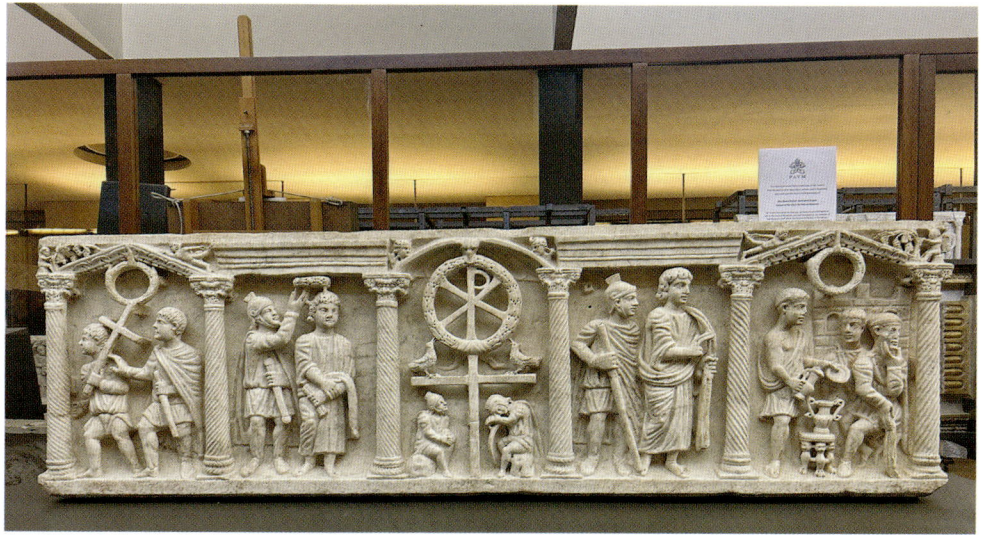

Figure 1 *Passion Sarcophagus, Rome, c. 350, Museo Pio Cristiano, Vatican City.*

A sarcophagus dating to around 350 AD that now resides in the Vatican Museum, contains a twisted-pillar colonnade holding up a series of lintels (Figure 1). Within the colonnade a story unfolds. To the far right, Pontius Pilate, the fifth governor of Judaea and the man who sentenced Jesus of Nazareth to death, is seated on a special, cross-legged seat, called a "curule chair." He turns his body away from the man before him, deeply contemplating his choices. Two attendants are by his side, offering Pilate a bowl with water with which to wash his hands of the death of Jesus.

Before Pilate, a curly haired, clean-shaved, youthful Jesus stands with one hand on his cloak and the other outstretched in blessing towards Pilate. An unmistakable Roman soldier stands guard behind him.

On the left side of the sarcophagus, we see Pilate's decision has been made. Here we find Simon of Cyrene, the man in the Gospels who was pulled from the seething crowd to carry Jesus' cross when he no longer could. We see his leg muscles visibly strain under the weight of his burden. Another soldier pushes him along, sheathed sword in hand.

Next to them, we see Jesus again. With the same curls and robe, he holds a scroll in one hand and serenely stands calmly clasping his own wrist, patiently waiting. Behind, a third Roman soldier—complete with sword and *paludamentum*, a small cloak worn by Roman soldiers—gently lifts a leafy wreath, bound with flowers. We catch him in the moment he begins to softly adorn Jesus' head.

This is the first known depiction of when, during his Passion, Jesus was crowned by Roman soldiers. And it is the last time we will see it depicted for another 700 years.

This is not the scene we have come to expect.

Where are the thorns? Where is the agony and beating? Why does Jesus not suffer from brutal spikes piercing his bloody brow?

Why is it that we find Christ so early in Passion iconography crowned with a leafy wreath, and not the vicious thorns we have come to expect? The answer lies in three seemingly disparate reasons: first, a typical Roman soldier's experience of messianic leaders; second, the connotations of a plant known as "acanthus"; and third, the immense importance placed on wreaths in early Christianity.

This book is an art historical one. But we cannot hope to understand the earliest art of the Jesus' Passion and his time with the Roman soldiers without appreciating why the Crown was made and why Jesus would have been derided in the way he was. An understanding of the world and circumstances in which he lived, preached, and was killed will help us better appreciate the motives of the Roman soldiers, Pilate, and Jesus' contemporary and subsequent followers.

The key to unlocking the death of a Messiah lies in an unlikely place: the career trajectory of an insensitive provincial governor on the brink of losing his job.

Historical context—the making of the Crown of Thorns

Pontius Pilate, the governor of the province of Judaea, had a decision to make. In 36 AD an armed crowd of pilgrims was gathering. Hundreds of Samaritans throughout the region were rushing to Mount Gerizim—their sacred mountain. A messianic leader promised they would witness the revelation of the sacred vessels which Moses had buried there. But Pilate was wary. The crowd was growing by the hour, and he worried there was a chance that the pilgrimage could morph into a violent riot. He decided to send heavily armed soldiers and a squadron of cavalry to investigate the situation. It did not end well. Pilate's troops soon came to blows with the pilgrims when they blocked their path up the mountain. They killed many, dispersed the rest, and Pilate had the leaders of the group executed for good measure—lest other religious upstarts get any ideas.[1] It was, by all accounts, an unnecessary slaughter by a nervous leader.

Even by Roman standards, this seemed an extreme action. But it does provide us with enormous insight into the political climate of first-century Judaea.

It is within this context that the Crown of Thorns and Mockery first—historically—is begotten.

At the time of Jesus' ministry, Judaea was a province of the Roman Empire and firmly under imperial control. The region had previously enjoyed semi-autonomy under the Herodian Dynasty, who acted as the vassal rulers of Judaea, but incompetent leadership by King Archelaus (son of Herod the Great) led to a subsequent revolt in 4 BC.

After Herod the Great's death in 4 BC, his final will handed his kingdom over to his son, Archelaus. There was, of course, some dispute over this among the rest of his children. Archelaus needed to get to Rome quickly and asked the emperor Augustus to approve his claim to the throne—especially since his siblings and other anti-monarchic Jewish contingents were already on their way there to challenge or protest his claim.[2] In his haste, Archelaus left his region in utter turmoil, having had to use sudden and ferocious force to quell a riot that had sprung up just before the Passover. Killing an astounding 3,000 people and sending the rest of the crowds packing, he then departed for Rome. Even the procurator of Syria, Sabinus, who was left in charge of the region during Archelaus' trip to Rome, ended up being cornered in Jerusalem by an angry, vengeful Jewish army, incensed by Sabinus' own insolence and provocation. Sabinus was forced to call on the Legate of Syria, Publius Quinctilius Varus, for assistance.[3]

Varus swept through the region, starting in the Galilee, with two of his legions and several calvary regiments and crushed the revolts that had sprung up throughout the

---

[1] Josephus, *Ant.*, 18. 85–87.
[2] Josephus, *War*, 2. 80–94; *Ant.*, 17. 224–228, 299–314.
[3] Josephus, *War*, 2. 4–79, *Ant.*, 17. 210–219, 254–285. The same Quinctilius Varus of the Battle of Teutoburg Forest fame, later in 9 AD, where he lost three legions to ambushing Germans.

entire region—and did so brutally. Once Varus stormed and occupied Jerusalem, he ended up crucifying 2,000 Jewish rebels.[4]

All this, occurring so soon after Herod the Great's death, reveals the highly discontented and unstable nature of the region—one which sees any significant transition of power as an opportunity to fight to dispel their overlords. Augustus—understandably perhaps—was wary of allowing Archelaus to rule Judaea, as he had demonstrated an utter lack of control over his people. The emperor, mostly out of respect for Herod the Great's wishes, did give Archelaus the chance to rule briefly, but after several subsequent complaints about Archelaus' blunders and his irritatingly stagnant economic progress, Augustus lost faith in his ability to rule properly. He therefore stripped the Judaeans of their privileged status of semi-autonomy, exiled their king to Gaul, and appointed the first in a line of Roman prefects, or governors, to control Judaea in 6 AD.[5]

Considering how little time had lapsed since the death of Herod, and the number of riots and rebellions that had since erupted, these prefects had quite a job on their hands. They would be all too familiar with the reputation of the Jewish people in the region and would constantly have been on their guard—poised to strike viciously, and occasionally overreact, at the slightest scare.

The prefects of Judaea, as with most prefects of the first century, were mostly military men who oversaw smaller provinces. They were headquartered in Caesarea, which was well-situated for the best transport and communication links with Rome and the rest of the empire.[6] While much of the local administration of the province would have been left to the native authority, it was the job of the prefect to lay down the law, particularly for political offences, and administer capital punishment.[7] Religious offenses, which were potentially incendiary and not of particular interest to Rome, were left in the hands of the Jewish religious leaders.[8]

The prefect of Judaea did not have command of any legionary troops, as these soldiers would sit with the Legate of Syria, but he would have six or seven auxiliary troops, the vast majority of whom were from the local Gentile populations of the region,

---

[4]Josephus, *War*, 2. 66–75; *Ant.*, 17. 250–253, 286–298.
[5]Josephus, *War*, 2. 117; *Ant.*, 17. 317–320, 339–344, 354–355; Mary Smallwood, *Jews under Roman Rule: From Pompey to Diocletian* (Leiden: Brill Academic Press, 2001), 113–17. It is worth noting that we are discussing only the region of Judaea itself, not those of Galilee and Peraea, and Auranitis, Trachonitis, Bataneae and Paneas. These regions continued to be ruled by tetrarchs, Herod's sons Antipas and Philip, who died in 33 and 40 AD respectively.
[6]Josephus, *War*, 2. 111; Smallwood, *Jews under Roman Rule*, 145–147.
[7]Josephus, *War*, 2. 117–118.
[8]Smallwood, *Jews under Roman Rule*, 149–150.

taken from amongst the Greeks and other communities in places such as Caesarea and elsewhere in Syria, as well as a few from farther afield, such as Italy.[9]

These troops, who would certainly have had no fondness for the Jewish population, assisted the prefect in keeping the peace in Judaea. They certainly had a tough job of it in the first century.

Particularly during this sensitive transition of power, and especially around the time of Jesus' ministry (c. 30 AD), the region of Judaea was a tinderbox—still sore from the lost opportunity of shaking off Roman rule after Herod's death. It was a region prone to riots, dissent and disturbances—all of which were met with a swift and brutal response by the prefect and Roman soldiery.

There are multiple examples of prophetic or dictatorial leaders rising up against Rome in the first century around the time of Jesus' ministry. Governors tended to be wary of crowds, as with the example of Pilate's response to a gathering crowd of Samaritans consumed with religious fervor in 36 AD.

There were long-standing precedents for such suspicion. For example, under the first prefect Coponius (who governed from 6 to 9 AD, only a few decades before Pilate's rule), the region needed to conduct a census. As Judaea was now a newly annexed province, Rome needed accurate, up-to-date information about the population in order to tax them accordingly. This inevitably meant an increase in taxes. A certain amount of grumbling was understandable, but the resulting fury from the population was more concerning. Resistance came particularly from a small, newly created, religious sect led by Judas of Galilee. He and his followers felt that paying an additional tax—or any tax— to Rome assumed you had another master other than God. Their subsequent revolt was swiftly quelled, but the simmering fury remained.[10]

Even from the outset of direct Roman administration and control, the Jewish people were dissatisfied and frustrated to the point of open rebellion.

Again, under Cuspius Fadus, governor of Judaea in 44–46 AD, a rebel and self-described prophet named Theudas persuaded a huge number of his followers to go to the Jordan river where he claimed he would part the waters and let them cross more easily. Fadus sent a cavalry detachment to intercept them. They killed and captured most of the followers and sent Theudas' head back to Jerusalem.[11]

---

[9]Adrian Goldsworthy, *Pax Romana* (New Haven: Yale University Press), 212, 228; Smallwood, *Jews under Roman Rule*, 147.
[10]Josephus, *Ant.*, 18. 1–10, 20. 102–103; *War*, 2. 118; Smallwood, *Jews under Roman Rule*, 151–154.
[11]Josephus, *Ant.*, 20. 97–99; Goldsworthy, *Pax Romana*, 227.

Then under Felix, procurator from 52–60 AD, a messianic, Egyptian Jew and yet another self-proclaimed prophet, gathered thousands of followers and led them to the Mount of Olives. From there he said he would easily make the walls of Jerusalem crumble before storming the city and proclaiming himself tyrant. Felix wisely met the frenetic quasi-army in the open country outside Jerusalem with his infantry and ordered a massacre. Felix had every right to see this armed group as an insurrection and acted accordingly.[12]

These small uprisings were much more frequent occurrences in Judaea, compared to the entirety of the Roman empire. In addition, however, there was a far more sinister threat bubbling under the surface of the Judaean urban areas such as Jerusalem. The threat came from politically inclined, violent terrorist gangs, such as the well-known sicarii—so-called from the Latin *sica* or dagger which many of them carried.[13] These, and others like them, were small groups of armed young men who carried concealed knives and targeted high-profile victims, usually political figures. Like the Assassins almost a thousand years later, they would stealthily dispatch their targets on a busy urban street and then dissolve, unnoticed, back into the crowd.[14]

Motivated by pure hatred and bitterness for the Romans, any attack was a threat to Rome. The local leaders of the community (such as the high-priests or wealthy, influential members of society), who were also charged with keeping the population calm, were inevitably seen as collaborators by these gangs.[15] This simmering unrest, this far quieter but more deadly rebellion against Rome during the early part of the first century, could strike without notice. It left a strain and feeling of anxiety equally on the population of Judaea as well as on its rulers—all fearing that they or their loved ones would be next.

Herod, his heirs, and the prefects and procurators who ruled after them, all sought to wipe out these gangs. They were occasionally successful at flushing out one terrorist group but were soon frustrated by new ones cropping up in their place.[16]

Indeed, even during Jesus' trial, he is lumped in with them, and his crime is considered equal to that of these sorts of criminals. Not only is it assumed that Jesus had several political thugs amongst his disciples, but Barabbas, the criminal in the Gospel narratives who is released from prison instead of Jesus, is described as an insurrectionist who committed murder, likely recently, while the men who were crucified on either side of

---

[12]Josephus, *War*, 2. 261–263; Josephus, *Ant.*, 20. 169–172; Goldsworthy, *Pax Romana*, 227.
[13]Josephus, *War*, 2. 254–257.
[14]Goldsworthy, *Pax Romana*, 235–238.
[15]Goldsworthy, *Pax Romana*, 240.
[16]Goldsworthy, *Pax Romana*, 239.

Jesus are described as *leistas*, a specific type of rebel who murdered political opposition.[17] While perhaps misplaced, Jesus, in the eyes of the crowd and likely the Roman soldiers, was perceived to be part of this problem—a quiet, threatening, murderous subversive who must be brutally snuffed out.

The Roman prefects may perhaps then be forgiven for their wariness when any popular, preaching leaders emerged—or when crowds came from all over to hear them speak. Judaea had a reputation for the combination of political violence and large crowds gathering to protest or cause trouble. This was the world Jesus was preaching in. One filled with violence and sedition.

Little is recorded of the state of Judaea during the period of its first four prefects. Valerius Gratus (15—c. 26 AD) was the fourth prefect of Judaea and lasted about eleven years, whereas each of his predecessors had held the post for only about three years each. Gratus' only dealings in the region that were deemed worthy of mention were the four appointments of High Priests that he made in quick succession at the end of his tenure.[18] This could suggest some unrest from the population and Gratus' attempts to assuage a full-blown revolt. He stuck with his final choice, Joseph Caiaphas, the same man who was still High Priest at the time of Jesus' Crucifixion. Whatever simmering discontent Gratus left behind him was likely ready to express itself. Transition to a new ruler after a lengthy stint with the previous one, as we have seen, almost always provoked unrest among the people of Judaea.[19]

It was in this febrile climate of change, tension and instability that Pontius Pilate arrived at his post.

Josephus, whose record is one of the only truly detailed sources we have, describes Pilate's time in Judaea from 26–36/37 AD, as being more troublesome than the last few years which had preceded it.[20] As we have seen, resentment and discontent had been brewing in the area. This, combined with a less patient, less conciliatory governor, was like a lit match getting precariously close to already smoking kindling.

---

[17] Mk15:7, 27; Goldsworthy, *Pax Romana*, 238–239.
[18] Josephus, *Ant.*, 18. 34–35.
[19] Smallwood, *Jews under Roman Rule*, 159–160.
[20] It is important to note this fact and therefore take Josephus' record with a grain of salt. Tacitus' cursory nod to the region before the Great Jewish Revolt is simply "under Tiberius all was quiet" (Tacitus, *Hist.*5.9), which suggests anything that happened in the region prior to the Great Revolt was considered relatively unimportant. The vast majority of local politics in the provinces are unworthy of mention to many chroniclers. The time before 66 AD is unusually well documented due, not only to the survival of Josephus' accounts, which are likely biased with little to corroborate his claims, but also the New Testament, whose historical records, while helpful and fascinating in their own way, are largely accidental.

There are four episodes that cause consternation in the region and speak to the environment in which Jesus was preaching and crucified. The first happened early in Pilate's governorship. As was customary, one of the six or seven units garrisoned in Judaea was stationed in the Antonia—the palace in Jerusalem close the Temple. By this time in Roman military history, each century would have its own standard, or a decorated shaft, that identified them. The standard was also treated as the physical representation, or indeed, the soul, of the unit of men. They were deeply revered and worshipped by the soldiers. It was the soldiers' duty to protect the standard as its loss during a battle was profoundly humiliating and considered a defeat if left unrecovered. The standards, unique to each unit, were brought with them everywhere. Some perhaps had depictions of animals, gods, wreaths, the emperor or similar on them.[21] In Judaea, the prefects tended to pick units stationed in Jerusalem whose standards did not have any depictions of the human form out of respect for the Jewish laws, which prohibited such imagery.

Pilate, as was his prerogative, likely in the first year of his governorship, switched out the unit stationed in Jerusalem, and replaced it with fresh men. The unit he was bringing in, it seems, happened to have medallions on their standards with the image of the emperor on them. As such, Pilate decides to take the soldiers into Jerusalem at night, veiling the standards as he and the soldiers make their way through the city. He did this, perhaps hoping to get away with the indiscretion, or possibly so as not to offend any of the resident Jews who might see them, while also respecting the standards—as items of worship in their own right—of his men by allowing them to accompany them into the city.[22]

Pilate walks a fine line. But even with these attempted precautions, once the Jewish population found out that these standards were in the city, they were shocked and disgusted. Furious, a crowd rushed to Pilate in Caesarea and demanded he take the offending standards down, which they felt were deliberately put up as a provocation to insult their laws. Pilate held his ground and refused out of respect to his soldiers, and the emperor they served. The crowd, not to be put off so easily by their new prefect, sat outside Pilate's residence in protest for several days. Eventually Pilate gathers them all into the stadium in Caesarea, surrounds them with his troops who draw their swords awaiting Pilate's signal to cut every last protester down. In response, the Jews beg to be

---

[21] For more information on and depictions of standards and *signum*, see Adrian Goldsworthy, *Roman Warfare* (London: Cassell, 2000); Adrian Goldsworthy, *The Complete Roman Army* (London: Thames and Hudson, 2003); Kevin F. Kiley, *An Illustrated Encyclopedia of the Uniforms of the Roman World* (Wigston: Anness Publishing Ltd., 2012); Peter Connolly, *The Roman Army* (London: Macdonald & Company, 1975); Raffaele D'Amato and Graham Sumner, *Arms and Armour of the Imperial Roman Soldiers* (Barnsley: Frontline Books, 2009); Graham Webster, *The Roman Imperial Army* (London: A&C Black, 1979), especially 133–140. Please note this list of references is not exhaustive.
[22] Smallwood, *Jews under Roman Rule,* 160–161.

killed, saying they would rather die than give up and leave the standards in their place. Pilate, impressed by their devotion and determination, immediately removes the images and presumably switches the soldiers for a unit without medallions of the emperor.[23]

The Judaeans now had their first taste of their new governor. More brutal and less accommodating to the people he was ruling. Not what this frustrated population was used to.

In the next incident, Pilate, keen to start works to improve an aqueduct into Jerusalem to provide a better water supply, finds the funds in a readily available, though extremely controversial source. He uses the Corban—or the sacred funds of the Temple—to build the aqueduct. Using this money—which was protected by law—for something secular, was met with understandable uproar.

But Pilate's patience was starting to thin. He expected the resulting clamor that came rushing to him in Jerusalem the next time he visited. As such, he decided to intersperse his own men in the crowd, disguised as civilians. At his signal, the soldiers began to beat the unsuspecting rioters to death.[24]

This had the desired effect. The riots were subdued, with more dead than perhaps was necessary (or intended), and left the population with a growing, festering wound.

But Pilate was not done trying to honor his own Roman traditions, even at the cost of irritating the local population. Taking a lesson presumably from the incident with the standards, Pilate makes a dedication of shields coated in gold with no images on them—only a small inscription stating he had dedicated the decorations to the emperor Tiberius—and put them up in his residence in Jerusalem. Though attempting to politely adhere to local customs, the shields represented a dangerous precedent. They were just shy of outright emperor worship. The imperial cult was forbidden from the Jewish cities, especially Jerusalem, where, as a compromise, they made sacrifices in their Temple praying that God might maintain the health and well-being of the emperor and his empire—rather than worshipping the emperor himself. The shields, if accepted in the holy city, were one small step away from flagrant disregard of their customs.[25]

Conscious of Pilate's proclivities towards violence in the face of rioting and insolence, the Jewish leaders sent a small diplomatic embassy to plead their case. They begged Pilate to take them down and not disturb the peace that was hanging on by a thread in the region. If he did not, the embassy requested, could he please produce the written

---

[23]Josephus, *Ant.*, 18. 55–59; *War*, 2. 169–175.
[24]Josephus, *War*, 2. 175–177; *Ant.*, 18. 60–62.
[25]Philo, *Leg. Gai.*, 38. 299–300; Smallwood, *The Jews under Roman Rule*, 166.

letter of Tiberius' permission to put the shields up in the first place, and thus dishonoring the ancient laws.

Pilate was backed into a corner. He had no such permission. The Jews therefore took their case to Tiberius, outlining their argument to take them down. A furious Tiberius sent a strongly worded letter to Pilate ordering him to remove the shields and place them in a far less controversial location, like, say, the temple of the imperial cult in Caesarea. Pilate does so and avoids yet another riot that was clearly about to erupt.[26]

Indeed, the corroborating archaeological evidence of a dedicatory inscription bearing Pilate's name as dedicator of a *Tiberieum* (presumably a building dedicated to Tiberius) may confirm that Pilate did have some sort of decoration put up, as proof of his loyalty to the emperor.[27]

Philo, who relays this episode, describes Pilate as "naturally inflexible, a blend of self-will and relentlessness" with a flawed character of "vindictiveness and furious temper." His conduct as governor was defined by "the briberies, the insults, the robberies, the outrages and wanton injuries, the executions without trial constantly repeated, the ceaseless and supremely grievous cruelty."[28] While certainly no great fan of Pilate's, Philo's description may again allude to simmering bitterness towards Roman rule. Feelings of animosity were palpable.

The final incident brought a swift end to Pilate's career. It is perhaps understandable that when it was reported to him that a large, armed, group of Samaritans was gathering at Mount Gerizim, as described above, he took the precaution of sending part of his auxiliary unit to investigate the situation, then executed their leaders in the aftermath. Large crowds of armed civilians were dangerous at the best of times and very rarely led to mild-mannered revelry. Pilate, who had already overseen several more revolts and protests than his predecessors, likely wanted to make sure he did not have a full-blown rebellion on his hands.

However, the soldiers' response, possibly at Pilate's command, should things get out of hand, was seen as a heavy-handed overreaction even for the Romans. His actions were the last straw for the Judaeans. A delegation of Samaritans and Jews took their complaint, as was their right, to the legate of Syria, to whom Pilate reported. Vitellius, the legate at the time, wisely seeing that Pilate's long stint as governor was coming to an end, swiftly packed Pilate off to Rome to plead his case to Tiberius. It seems Pilate's

---

[26]Philo, *Leg. Gai.*, 38. 299–306.
[27]Smallwood, *Jews under Roman Rule*, 167.
[28]Philo, *Leg. Gai.*, 38. 299–303.

reaction to the crowd was regarded in Rome as less measured than it ought to have been and it is significant that Vitellius felt the matter was too egregious for him to handle. After ten years in the same post, Pilate's nearly frayed patience and jumpy overreaction needed a final say from everyone's boss.

Pilate left as commanded to Rome to answer to Tiberius. It took him several months to get there and by the time he arrived, Tiberius had died (on 16 March 37 AD), with Pilate no doubt thanking his lucky stars.[29]

After this, Pilate disappears from the annals of history.

All of which provides us with some perspective on Jesus' own dealings with Pontius Pilate. Jesus' trial, which chronologically would have happened before Pilate's over-step with the Samaritans, took place amidst a froth of tensions between the Jews and their governor. And it is a superb example of Pilate's tight-ropewalker act.

Jesus' trial came at the time of one of the biggest, holiest festivals in the Jewish calendar: Passover. Jerusalem would have been swelled to bursting with pilgrims who had made their way there from throughout the entire region, not just Judaea. During big religious festivals, the governor was expected, and indeed had every reason, to leave Caesarea and also descend on Jerusalem with even more soldiers to help maintain tranquility during the high tensions of the festivities. For Pilate, the charges brought against Jesus were less than ideally timed.

As will be discussed in more detail below, Jesus was accused of claiming to be the King of the Jews. In very recent history, the King of the Jews, for the Romans, meant Herod—a vassal king who ruled the region on Rome's behalf. It was a privilege that was, in Jesus' own lifetime, taken away from Judaea. To claim—or even be proclaimed—as a king was a direct challenge to Roman rule. Kings were no longer allowed in this province.

As governor, Pilate was expected to listen to the local leaders in this province—what they wanted and needed to quell any disturbance in the area. Especially considering the time when Jesus' charge was brought against him, with large, excitable crowds already on edge, denying the demands of the people alongside the demands of the elite would spell certain uproar and disaster for Pilate. It was exactly the sort of thing Pilate was instructed to avoid at all costs. The Gospels also allude to existing tension from political terrorists. As mentioned, Barabbas, and the men crucified with Jesus were being sentenced to death for just such criminality.[30]

---

[29]Josephus, *Ant.*, 18. 88–89; Smallwood, *Jews under Roman Rule*, 171.
[30]Goldsworthy, *Pax Romana*, 306–307.

We can also see how, in the eyes of the soldiers who beat, mocked and crowned Jesus, he had all the signs of being the kind of troublemaker they were used to dealing with. He had prophetic characteristics, made wild promises about salvation, claimed he could summon angels to battle, drew enormous crowds wherever he happened to be, and even rubbed shoulders with known terrorist groups. From a Roman perspective Jesus looked like yet another political upstart, and only served to make their lives more difficult. It is little wonder they would act the way they did towards him.

For Pilate, and in line with Roman punishment and treatment of prisoners, a flogging and public humiliation by his soldiers—including crowning him in a mock wreath and making jeers about his failures—would have been enough. Pilate was also likely conscious that if Jesus did have many followers in the city, killing him might start its own riot. But Pilate, with the seething crowds before him and the hissing of the priestly class in his ear—not to mention the thinly veiled threat of being disloyal to Rome—relents. He deems Jesus' death the least problematic of two possible bad outcomes. The Gospels, however, describe Pilate as still conscious of how this episode might come back to bite him. As such he very publicly, in front any of Jesus' followers in the crowds, and those who called for Jesus' death, washes his hands of the guilt of any subsequent trouble. He places the blame squarely on the shoulders of his subjects and their community leaders.[31]

It is in this time, and in this place, that the Crown of Thorns was made. We will next explore why the Roman soldiers fashioned the Crown, but it is important to understand the boiling discontent and hatred that almost visibly frothed, not only from the masses, but also from the soldiers stationed in Jerusalem during the Passover. They had seen their commander backed into a corner, they had trouble day and night from the unhinged frivolity of the festival-going crowds, and not unexpectedly, we find them unleash their frustrations—and somewhat, though not entirely, mis-placed assumptions—on Jesus.

The wreath of acanthus

With this historical context in mind, we can shift back to our Passion Sarcophagus. As we have seen, Jesus is depicted as calmly crowned by a Roman soldier with what is

---

[31]Mt. 27:24.

unmistakably a leafy wreath. Why then was this a wreath when what we have come to know is a thorny crown?

Wreaths had a profound importance for both the Romans, and the Romano-Christians. But to understand why wreaths would be important to our discussion of the Crown of Thorns at all, the reader must briefly endure a digression into the original languages of the Gospel texts.

The scene of the Mockery and Crowning, as we described in detail above, in the original Greek texts is found in the Gospels of Matthew, Mark and John.[32] Each of the Gospels describes the Roman soldiers as weaving and placing a "wreath of acanthus"—ἀκάνθινον στέφανον—on Jesus' head. Jerome of Stridon, more popularly known as St. Jerome, in the fourth century translates the Gospels into Latin and writes that the soldiers' craft a *spineam coronam*—a wreath (or crown) of thorns. It is from Jerome that the modern translation of "crown of thorns" arises.[33]

Wreath and acanthus. Two small, but underappreciated, words. Both imbued with small differences in inference that can have significant consequences for interpretation over the succeeding centuries. As we shall see, the wreath is a powerful decoration. It is used to portray greatness on many levels both during life and beyond the grave. But let us first examine the word "acanthus."

Jerome was of course not incorrect in his translation of the word "acanthus" from the Greek into the Latin word "spina." "Acanthus" can just mean a spiky plant. But the acanthus plant itself has such profound implications in the ancient world, it is hard to believe the word was used without significance in the Gospel texts.

The acanthus is a large-leafed, low growing plant. The leaves spread widely outward from its base and in the early summer, tall stocks of delicate purple and pink flowers dramatically shoot up from the center. Acanthus, which has not changed significantly in its many thousands of years of existence, grows ubiquitously throughout the Mediterranean and even into northern Europe. The most common variety has soft, delicate leaves that shimmer pleasantly in the sun. In rougher, drier terrain—such as that of first-century Judaea and even nowadays in the Middle East—while still a very common plant in the wild, with lovely purple blooms, it also has a more sinister side. Each large leaf is edged entirely in tiny sharp thorns. Not only do these thorns immediately draw blood when a careless, bare-legged, walker might rub up against them, but the minute amount of poison in each thorn will leave an agonizing ache for

---

[32] Mt. 27:27–31; Mk. 15:16–20; Jn. 19:1–3.
[33] *Corona* can be translated into English as either a "crown" or a "wreath."

hours after the encounter. Rubbing, washing or any form of sanitation will not dull the pain.

This is clearly not your delicate desert flower. The acanthus plant leaves that the Roman soldiers had access to in Jerusalem to fashion Jesus' wreath would likely have been just as painful as the sharp thorns with which we have become familiar. But it is the acanthus plant itself—regardless of how much injury it might cause when worn—that evokes profound connotations.

Acanthus plants have deep and long-spreading root systems that are incredibly difficult to eradicate. When the plant is pulled up, even if an infinitesimally small piece of the root remains, the acanthus will fully regenerate itself in the next season.[34] It then seems as though the plant cannot die and will always return on a seasonal basis without assistance. This gives the plant an "anamorphic quality," that is, it can "form anew" and has the ability to change back into its former state. The acanthus plant thereby has a quality of "eternal return."[35] The acanthus is thus a plant that lends itself well to metaphor: it seems as though it is undying and will always return without assistance.

It is probably due to this aggressive regrowth that the plant attracted connotations of regeneration and immortality, both of which, of course, resonated strongly with the Romano-Christian audience. It is a plant with eternal qualities, everlastingly renewing itself even when faced with eradication.

In the Greek and Roman world, the acanthus had strong associations with spiritual healing and resurrection. Coupled with the plant's medicinal properties, it was closely associated with Apollo and Asklepios, gods of healing and resurrection. Acanthus wreaths and garlands decorated Asklepios' Tholos interior at Epidaurus, for instance, to emphasize the theme of healing and rebirth. The acanthus plant is also strongly seen in Apolline representation due to its regenerative symbolism. The sun, for example, which is reborn each day, is often depicted as rising out of an acanthus plant to represent Apollo.[36]

Closely aligned with the connotation of resurrection and rebirth is the chthonic nature and symbolism of the acanthus. It is a plant with power in the underworld and is considered to be a mediator between the living and the dead. The acanthus is traditionally planted on Roman, Greek, and Jewish city limits so as to delineate the

---

[34] John Pollini, "The Acanthus of the Ara Pacis as an Apolline and Dionysiac Symbol of Anamorphosis, Anakyklosis, and *Numen Mixtum*," in *Von Der Bauforschung Zur Denkmalpflege*, edited by Martin Kubelik and Mario Schwarz (Vienna: Phoibos, 1993), 184.

[35] Pollini, "The Acanthus of the Ara Pacis," 185.

[36] Ibid., 202–209.

boundary between life in the city from that of the dead in their graves just outside the city's walls.[37]

It was therefore also common to depict acanthus on funerary monuments, either as the plant, or as garlands made from acanthus. Many funerary monuments depict the leafy stock of the acanthus plant with vines growing and spiraling outward from it.

While many of us may not be familiar with ancient Roman and Greek funerary monuments, most will have seen the acanthus depicted regardless. It is most popularly seen on the capitals of Corinthian columns. At the top of the column, the distinctive broad leaves burst forth around the capital. According to Vitruvius, the architect Callimachus, who was credited with the invention of the Corinthian column, was so impressed with the beauty of the acanthus leaves and their ability to grow around any obstacle, that it led him to place them on what would become one of the classical world's most widely used capital decorations.[38]

It is, however, perhaps the emperor Augustus' Ara Pacis, the Roman temple dedicated to the goddess Pax and built in 9 BC to celebrate the new era of peace brought by Augustus' rule, which best captures the nature of the acanthus plant. The exterior walls of the Ara Pacis are copiously covered by plants, all of which grow outward from the central acanthus plant. At first glance, the vines and plants which grow from the acanthus may seem disordered, random, and unrestrained, but upon closer inspection, they form an intricate and constant pattern; the abundant chaos is, in fact, orderly and calm. The central acanthus plant produces a plethora of fruits and houses animals and insects within its dense foliage, providing for them both a peaceful home and food. This fantastic display and use of the acanthus, evokes Roman values such as order, peace, and dignity through its symmetrically balanced representation of nature. The acanthus of the Ara Pacis also conveys unity. All animals and plants, different aspects of nature which represent the different gods, are all unified and all one under the foliage of the acanthus. Acanthus represents all the powers of the Roman world and balances them.

The ancient world—from the Roman pagan to the Christian cult—knew that the acanthus plant represented resurrection and immortality. The Gospel writers were undoubtably aware of the plant's resurrective qualities and its connotation with eternal life.

Jesus, so the Gospel writers believed, would save people from death and grant them immortality. His wreath was a carefully and consciously crafted symbol of rebirth and

---

[37]Ibid.,184.
[38]Vitruvius, *De Architectura*, 4.1, 9–10.

eternal life—here in the acanthus plant was a living, growing symbol of the central message of Christ's life.

There is a good chance that even the Roman soldiers who tormented Jesus during his trial knew of these connotations with the acanthus plant—and likely they also knew about the salvific nature of Jesus' ministry. After all, he was a messianic leader, and they were all too familiar with these often-troublesome messiah figures. Why then bestow on him this wreath? What was so delightfully cruel about this style of Mockery, which actually seems rather an apt adornment? The Mockery and style of crown has much to do with the type of honors these same Roman soldiers might even strive for themselves: the military decoration.

Jesus the failed general

Decorations were an essential part of Roman military life. One reason for the success of Roman army was that it paid as much attention to rewarding the success of their soldiers as to punishing their misdemeanors. As well as handing out the more traditional spoils of war to their soldiers (cash, slaves, and other booty), generals also gave out prestigious honorary decorations as rewards. These decorations were usually in the form of a wreath. They were given to individual soldiers in honor of their bravery—for saving a fellow soldier, for instance, for storming an enemy camp, or for other significant acts of meritorious conduct. Each honor had a specific plant attached to it, such as the laurel or the olive.[39] But the greatest and most prestigious of these honorary decorations was a crown fashioned simply from the plants of the battlefield: the *Corona Graminea*.

Pliny the Elder (d. 79) describes the *Corona Graminea*,[40] or "grass crown," as the most esteemed decoration that anyone could receive, and one that was only bestowed upon generals. All other crowns, Pliny explains in his *Naturalis Historia*, were given by officers to individual members of the army, but the *Corona Graminea* was voted "only by the whole army and only to him who rescued it."[41]

It was a wreath given only to a commander by all of his soldiers. There were few (and very specific) reasons why the army would give this crown to their general, and few ever received it. A general could gain the crown "when a whole camp has been relieved and

---

[39] See especially Valerie Maxfield, *The Military Decorations of the Roman Army* (Berkeley: University of California Press, 1981), 67–100.
[40] Also known as the *Corona Obsidionalis*.
[41] Pliny, *Naturalis Historia*, 22.4: *nulli nisi ab universo exercitu servato decreta*.

saved from awful destruction."[42] If an army, cornered in a place of hopelessness and facing impending death by their enemy, is saved by the leadership, persistence, and endurance of their general, the army might vote to bestow upon their general the most revered crown. Pliny praises the extraordinary virtues of those who won this crown since it was only given to an individual who single-handedly saved his entire army, and therefore his entire people, country, and all of Rome, from death and destruction.[43]

Critical for our understanding of the "Crown of Thorns," Pliny also explains that the *Corona Graminea* was specifically fashioned from the grass of the site of the battle. The original symbolism was that the conquered people would present a crown made from the grass of their own land to the conqueror as a symbol of their submission. When the crown was later used to represent the salvation of an army and nation, Pliny states that no special plant was used, simply the plants that populated the site of the victory.[44]

While the *Corona Graminea* was not awarded to generals during the Principate, it was nevertheless highly prized and continued to be widely known. Since generals such as Octavian and Fabius Maximus had received such a crown, the *Corona Gaminea* would likely still have been embedded in the memory of the lower soldiery and common Roman citizenry in the first century CE.[45]

For those who wanted to do this, it would therefore not be difficult to conflate Jesus' supposed military activities with those of famous generals—to mock, from a Roman's perspective, the risible efforts of a presumptuous and irritating enemy leader.

Jesus, as a messiah, was supposed to save his nation, his people, from destruction and death. Many of the Jews, including some of Jesus' own followers, thought that the messiah would unleash the army of heaven to end the Roman occupation, and obliterate its armies, after which he would restore order and re-establish the sovereignty of the Jewish people. The role of "messiah" was thus both practical as well as spiritual, and encompassed military and political skills as well as those of religious leadership.

The evidence suggests that Jesus was seen as a military commander, a kind of general, by both the Roman soldiers and by his own followers. As we examined above, the

---

[42]Ibid.: . . . *liberatis obsidione abominandoque exitu totis castris.*

[43]The *Corona Graminea* could also be given to a general on behalf of the people of Rome by the Senate; for instance, when a general stopped a siege or an invasion that would have spelled doom for Rome. See Maxfield, *The Military Decorations,* 67–100.

[44]Pliny, *Naturalis Historia,* 22.7. It should also be noted that the *Corona Graminea,* unlike other wreaths, takes no absolute form and cannot be accurately identified on coinage or statuary. One can only imagine what it looked like through the descriptions of the ancient authors.

[45]The last general to receive the *Corona Graminea* was Octavian/Augustus. No other general could afterwards receive a higher honor than the emperor. Pliny, *Naturalis Historia,* 22.5–6.

political climate of the time was such that it would have inevitably led the Romans to perceive Jesus automatically, whether grounded in fact or not, as a rabble-rouser, a potentially violent terrorist and a quasi-military leader. Indeed, the Gospels themselves portray Jesus in many instances as a military leader, thus giving credence to the idea that his wreath was similarly conceived.

It was not uncommon for the Jewish communities in first-century Judaea to find a messianic leader who proclaimed impending Jewish victory over their perceived tormentors, assisted by their powerful and vengeful God. Even in our brief historical overview above, we encountered a multitude of examples of messianic leaders attempting to overthrow Rome: the prophetic Judas of Galilee in 6 AD preached that paying more taxes to Rome was heresy, causing a short-lived rebellion; the messianic Theudas around 44 AD claimed he could part the Jordan River, thus drawing crowds to his side who encouraged him to wield his God-given power against Rome; and again in 52 AD, a self-proclaimed prophet and messianic leader was in the process of militarily organizing his followers on the Mount of Olives where he would besiege Jerusalem and set himself up as tyrant. And these were just the higher profile candidates. In this time and place, messiahs were abundant and even expected.

Even in the Gospels, the desperation for a messiah figure is palpable, with the people of Judaea looking anywhere and everywhere for one. Before Jesus enters the scene, everyone from the common crowds to the Jewish leaders assume, or desperately hope, that John the Baptist is a messiah. Though a preacher of impending winnowing and chaff burning, with loyal disciples of his own, John denies these claims.[46] The Jews' desperate need for a savior during the time of Roman occupation caused many self-proclaimed messiahs to reveal themselves and start uprisings among the discontented masses. Such movements were often violent, as all of the above turned out to be. The Roman response, as we have seen from the actions of the first few Roman prefects, could be substantially more violent. After several messianic uprisings, Romans became intimately familiar with the characteristics of messiahs and undoubtedly assumed the same of Jesus.[47]

There were no immutable boundaries between religion, politics and warfare. Messianic leaders were often considered to be prophets. Being "messianic" was synonymous with being eschatological, political, or both. Their movements were led by

---

[46] Lk. 3: 1–22; Jn 1:19–42
[47] Horsely, "Popular Prophetic Movements at the Time of Jesus; Their Principal Features and Social Origins," *Journal for the Study of the New Testament*, 8:3 (1986): 6–14.

active, politically inclined, men. These leaders encouraged the belief among their followers of the necessity to participate in several crucial campaigns. First, they were to partake in the redemption or liberation which God not only mandated, but initiated. It was God, the messiahs proclaimed, who started Israel's redemption and the onus fell upon God's people to make that redemption real. Second, such movements—often more numerous during times of immense suffering and violent submission—were directed towards their alleged oppressive foreign rulers. As we have seen, the first century's social unrest and the simmering resentments of suppression among a large portion of the Jewish communities, resulted in several major revolts against Roman authority. These movements—messianic or otherwise—were seen by the Judaean population as attempts to reclaim the liberty of the Jewish people and save their nation from oppression. In turn the Roman authority, true to Roman form, combated insolence with brutality.[48]

In assuming that Jesus was a military figure, the Roman soldiers were making an understandable mistake. It was based on damning, predictable, and consistently provocative, patterns of behavior within the community over which they were instructed to maintain peace.

Even Jesus' own followers clearly saw him, to some extent at least, in this same light. The Gospels often describe Jesus in a similar way and certainly suggest that Jesus' own ministry and actions fulfilled the assumptions Roman soldiers had about the militaristic, messianic leaders of the Jews. Given the atmosphere and tensions of the time, this was perhaps inevitable. The following episode, for example, was recorded by the Gospel writer Mark, and, if the Romans had heard of it, would have been a matter of great concern. To the Jewish followers of Jesus, on the contrary, it would have been an impressive demonstration of Jesus' purpose and power as a messiah:

> Then Jesus asked [the unclean spirit] "what is your name?" He replied, "My name is *Legion* (Λεγιὼν); for we are many." He begged [Jesus] earnestly not to send him out of the country . . . and the unclean spirits begged him "send us into the swine; let us enter them." And he gave them permission. And the unclean spirits came out and entered the swine; and the herd, numbering about 2000, rushed down the steep bank into the sea and were drowned.[49]

---

[48]Horsely, "Popular Prophetic Movements at the Time of Jesus," 6–14
[49]Mk 5:9–13.

Λεγιών, or "Legion," is a transliteration of a uniquely Latin and specific Roman military word, *legio, legionis*.[50] The name of the demon is therefore explicitly and intentionally Roman, and not merely an abstract word for an army. The not-so-subtle implication is the "demon" represents the Roman army, together with, perhaps, the entire Roman occupation. The unclean spirit named Legion begs Jesus not to "send him out of the country." The Jewish people hoped a savior would expel the Roman legions from Judaea, and both Jews and Romans alike expected the messianic military leaders to attempt, or at least preach about, such action.

In this episode, Jesus demonstrates that he not only has the power to command Legion, like a general, but can cause the spirits to destroy themselves through creatures considered unclean by the Jewish people. The Legion, so the story goes, would rather throw itself off a cliff and die than face the power of Jesus. This exorcism implies not only Jesus' superiority over a "Legion" but also his ability to demolish all 2,000 of them with a nod. This was the power the Jews were looking for, and which the Romans were inevitably working hard to suppress.

Similarly, when Jesus was arrested in Gethsemane, Judas arrived with an armed guard.[51] Those seeking this new messiah's death arrested him as they would any other upstart: as if he were a militarily inclined leader, seeking to send his followers against the authorities with violence. Indeed, Jesus' disciples not only carry swords themselves, but attack the guard, thus confirming a stereotype which the Romans had come to assume when dealing with proclaimed messiahs.[52] Jesus even boasts of his ability to summon "more than twelve legions of angels," approximately 61,440 soldiers, implying his vast military capabilities—should he have felt the need.[53]

As discussed above, during his trial before Pilate, the texts of both Mark and Luke mention that Barabbas, the alternate man whom the Jews could have chosen to set free instead of Jesus was "in prison with the rebels who had committed murder during the insurrection."[54] Barabbas had been, it would seem, part of an insurrectionist group who had recently committed murder, probably targeting the Roman authority. He had been caught and sent to prison where he was more than likely awaiting crucifixion himself.

---

[50]By the first century CE, a Roman legion consisted of ten cohorts and 120 cavalry, totaling approximately 5,120 men. See Goldsworthy, *The Complete Roman Army*, 50–54.
[51]Mk 14:43; Mt. 26:47; Lk. 22:52; Jn 18:3.
[52]Mt. 26:51; Mk 14:47; Lk. 22:49–50; Jn 18:10.
[53]Mt. 26:53: "Do you think that I cannot appeal to my Father, and he will at once send me more than twelve legions of angels?"
[54]Mk 15:7; also Lk. 23:19.

Jesus is considered an equal exchange for Barabbas. It seems the Romans felt that their crimes were not so very different.

Prior rebellions made it easy for the Romans to associate Jesus with the same type of unrest. They were also aware of what the followers of Jesus would have considered appropriate behavior for a messianic figure. Jesus displayed the qualities of a general—and one bent on lethal subversion—both to the Romans and to many of his followers.

If the Roman soldiers who mocked Jesus knew anything about him and the apparent purpose of a messiah figure, they would undoubtedly have connected Jesus' messiahship to the deeds performed by generals who received the *Corona Graminea*. This action by the soldiers, then, more realistically could be seen as a brutal parody of a failed general, in which they bestowed upon the beaten Jesus the most prestigious and honorable military crown in mock ceremony.

The Roman soldiers, to create their *Corona Graminea*, naturally adhered to custom by choosing appropriate material from which to fashion the crown. Parody, after all, necessarily requires reference to actuality. As Pliny describes it, the crown would be constructed, not from precious metals, but from the plants which grew around the battleground, or the place where salvation had occurred. What better plant than the abundantly plentiful, probably painful, and highly symbolic acanthus?

For the Romans, Jesus could not save himself, let alone his people, from the might of Rome, from destruction, or from death. For the writers of the Gospels and their early Christian audience, however, the irony of Jesus' sacrifice, and the belief that he did in fact save humanity from death, would not be lost.

It seems likely therefore that Jesus' "Crown of Thorns" was a crudely fashioned mock *Corona Graminea*. Jesus' ministry took place in a Judaea fraught with unrest; a Judaea that had produced a succession of messianic figures who incited the people against the Roman regime. The Roman soldiers who handled Jesus would assume the same characteristics of this new messiah and treat him accordingly. To them, Jesus represented yet another militaristic savior who intended to rescue his people from death. To the soldiers, Jesus was a joke. In mock ritual, they present the failed general with a crown of his failed victory over them and the failed salvation he brought to his people.

Ironically, however, this Mockery had a dual resonance. Jesus' followers and the later Christians would see their own truth in this Mockery. They believed they saw the restrained military might of Jesus during his ministry and believed that, through his own death, Jesus saved his people from death and from oppression. Little did the soldiers know that they gave this messiah a crown that his followers thought he truly deserved; one that represented victory over death and salvation from destruction. Though the intention was mockery, the soldiers unwittingly honored Jesus appropriately.

Critically, the Gospels state that the soldiers fashioned this mock crown out of the acanthus plant, a weed common throughout Judaea. The plant furnished the traditional material used to create such a crown: the flora of the battlefield where the victory was won. For the Gospel writers and Jesus' followers, the plant's significance reached far beyond that of a persistent weed. Instead, it held chthonic, liminal, and resurrective significance. It was a wreath of victory made from the leaves of a plant of eternal life—the ultimate triumph of life over death.

A sarcophagus' story retold

The Vatican Passion sarcophagus' message is loud and clear. In a single image, the fourth-century Christians have managed to turn the entire Mockery on its head. The calm crowning by the Roman soldier, the audience knows, was incredibly humiliating. But what they portray here is victory. Jesus is appropriately crowned—not with cruel thorns in mock ceremony—but with a proper, dignified leafy wreath. One that belongs on the head of a victorious general. Jesus, the image tells us, is recognized for the salvation he brought to the viewers, to the deceased inside the sarcophagus, and to the entire Christian people. It does not need to be violent or bloody. Instead, it portrays what the Gospel writers intended all along: Jesus' wreath was unwittingly one of absolute triumph.

2

The triumph of humility

The wreath as a symbol of triumph sticks. Jesus' wreath-crown represented victory over death and destruction. It also represented rebirth and resurrection by virtue of the plant from which it was made. Wreath-crowns have a special significance for early Christians. For this reason, it is imperative to follow the progression of the representation of the wreath-crown in Romano-Christian art. While still far from the Crown of Thorns we all would recognize today, the wreath itself contains significant associations with the Crown of Thorns, particularly with those of Jesus' Passion, of death, and of victory.

In the Gospels, Jesus' Crown of Thorns was a representation of a military-style victory over death, destruction, and sin. This idea is not only discussed in the Gospel texts but also in early Christian commentary which in turn manifests itself in the depictions of the wreath and the wreath-crown on Romano-Christian funerary art. The use of wreaths and military insignia can particularly be traced through two types of Christian sarcophagi of the fourth and fifth centuries: the Triumphal Wreath type of the fourth century, and the Enthroned Christ type of the fifth century. These sarcophagi demonstrate the idea (well-established amongst his followers) that Christ defeated death and that all Christians would similarly be able to overcome death through their belief. As we shall see, these two types of imagery will also prove highly influential later on when the scene of Jesus' Mockery assumes a more familiar form.

The Triumphal Wreath type is characterized primarily by its central decoration (Figure 2, 3). In the center typically stands a cross-shaped standard, resembling a Roman military trophy adorned with a wreath enclosing the chi-rho monogram. Birds perch on the arms of the standard and eat the fruit of the wreath, while two soldiers sit beneath. This type falls into two categories in the fourth- and fifth-century depictions:

the Triumphal Wreath with scenes from the Passion and the Triumphal Wreath with the twelve apostles. Both bear the central motif of the wreathed monogram and soldiers.

The most important example of the Triumphal Wreath type for our purposes is that same Vatican Passion Sarcophagus mentioned above. Usually, these so-called "Passion sarcophagi," depict the contemplation and hand-washing of Pilate and the arrests of Peter, Paul, or Jesus. They do not generally include the Crucifixion, the Mockery, or any indication that Christ suffered during his Passion.[1] This Passion sarcophagi type includes themes from the Old Testament as well. On the Tree Sarcophagus of the Vatican, c. 360 (Figure 2), for example, on the far right panel, Job is confronted by his wife, while on the far left Cain and Abel present their sacrifices. The respective arrests of Peter and Paul are depicted on two further panels, one each on either side of the central Triumphal panel.

It is significant that the central image of the cross and wreath appears for the first time on the Vatican Passion Sarcophagus (Figure 2).[2] Its presence is deliberate and full of meaning. It is in the most prominent location on the sarcophagus, under the central arcosolium-style arch. Representations of Sun and Moon peak out from above the arcosolium and look down on the standard. An eagle clasps the wreath in its beak. The purpose of this central scene is to represent Christ as the triumphant victor over death and the calculated use of the wreath and especially the military imagery on the

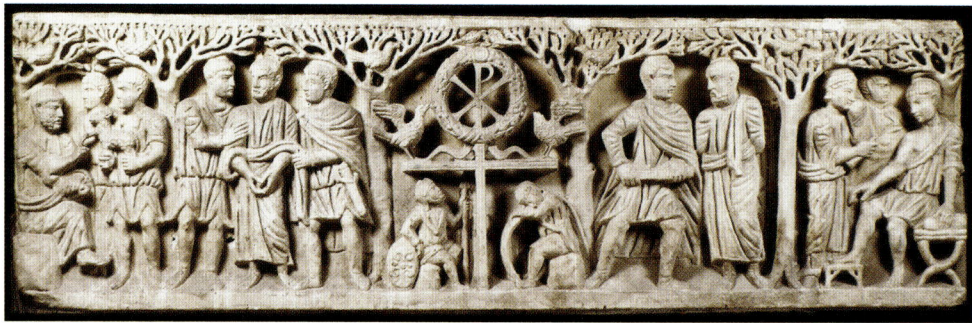

Figure 2 *Tree Sarcophagus, Rome, c. 360, Museo Pio Cristiano, Vatican City.*

---

[1] Gertrud Schiller, *Iconography of Christian Art*, trans. Janet Seligman (London: Lund Humphries, 1972), 4. For the lack of the suffering Christ in Romano-Christian art see Robin Margaret Jensen, *Understanding Early Christian Art* (New York: Routledge, 2000), 131–136.
[2] Schiller, *Iconography of Christian Art*, 5.

sarcophagus speak to this theme of victory and identify Christ as a militaristic conqueror. As we shall see, the Crowning scene will eventually be explained in relation to this "military victory."

Triumphal imagery and the Roman military

Indeed, the entire central scene of the Triumphal Wreath is supported by what appears to be a Roman military standard. There is a general assertion that this scene depicts triumph or the Resurrection. This is presumably expressed by the resemblance of the central image to Roman military decorations.[3] The central image is perhaps a combination of Constantine I's *vexillum* and the Roman *tropaeum*. The *vexilla* were cross-shaped armatures that bore a banner of the legionary insignia, used to designate different units of the army.[4] Eusebius reports that Constantine's *vexillum* was adorned with the chi-rho and images of himself and his sons. Constantine's particular *vexillum* was known as the *labarum*.[5] While Eusebius is the only, and perhaps a dubious, source for this information, there is enough evidence to show that the chi-rho was used by Constantine.[6] It was traditional for legions to decorate their standards, helmets, and shields with symbols that illustrated the loyalties and cults of their legion.[7] The chi-rho would do this sufficiently.

This central image on the Triumphal Wreath sarcophagi, however, is more reminiscent of the *tropaeum*, or "trophy" standard. The *tropaeum* was a makeshift Roman monument

---

[3] Schiller, *Iconography of Christian Art,* 5; Robert Milburn, *Early Christian Art and Architecture* (Aldershot: Scolar Press, 1988), 72; Jensen, *Understanding Early Christian Art,* 148.
[4] Yann Le Bohec, *The Imperial Roman Army* (London: Batsford, 1994), 148; Goldsworthy, *The Complete Roman Army*, 134.
[5] Oliver Stoll, "The Religions of the Armies," in *A Companion to the Roman Army,* ed. Paul Erdkamp, (Oxford: Blackwell, 2007), 451–476.
[6] It is possible that, instead of the *vexillum*, the chi-rho was placed on the *laurata*, or the imperial images that were placed on a standard in the form of an *imago clipeata*, or "portrait shields." These portrait shields, which were round shields with the image of the emperor or imperial insignia encased in the shield, were hung on a standard, like the banners of the *vexillum*. These standards were taken into battle while smaller versions were hung around the necks of high-ranking military personnel in the form of a *bulla* (Hans Belting, *Likeness and Presence; A History of the Image before the Era of Art*, trans. Edmund Jephcott (Chicago: University of Chicago Press, 1994), 107). The image on the standard represented the emperor, his leadership, and his protection of the army. Supposedly Constantine may have also attached the chi-rho to the *imago clipeata* of his military, replacing his own image, or adding to the images already adorning the cross-shaped standard. *Imago clipeata* were also common on Roman sarcophagi, where the bust of the dead is encircled with a shield, shell, or wreath.
[7] Stoll, "The Religions of the Armies," 458.

set up on the battlefield where they had defeated their enemy. It was a simple pair of stakes set crosswise upon which the armor of the defeated foe was erected as a sign of victory over the enemy.[8] Not unlike the *Corona Graminea*, which was woven from the plants native to the land of the defeated nation, the *tropaeum* used the armor of the defeated nation to represent the victory of the Roman army and the abject humiliation of their enemy. Several third-century Christian theologians, such as Minucius Felix (d. c. 250), noted the parallel of the Roman standards to the cross as well: "For what else are your military standards and banners but gilded and adorned crosses? Your victory trophies not only imitate the simple shape of the cross, but even a man affixed to it."[9] The "man" is in reference to the shape created by the armor that was fastened to the *tropaeum*.

Tertullian (d. 240) also unravels how the Romans unwittingly worship the cross of victory, writing:

> You celebrate your victories as you would deities with religious ceremony ... the frames on which you hang your trophies must be crosses ... thus in your victories, the religion of your camp makes crosses the object of worship ... the standards are adored, the standards are worshiped as gods, the standards are preferred to Jupiter himself ... the banners and ensigns which the soldiers guard with sacred care, are dressed with robes.[10]

Justin Martyr (d. 165) expresses similar sentiments. In his Apology One, Justin states that, without knowing it, the pagans use the form of the cross on their "own symbols on what are called standards and trophies ... using these as the signs of your rule and power." That is, the shape of the cross is even used to represent government.[11] They see their own sign of victory in the Roman victory trophies and

---

[8] Beat Brenk, "The Imperial Heritage of Early Christian Art," in *Age of Spirituality: A Symposium*, ed. Kurt Weitzmann (New York: Metropolitan Museum of Art, 1980), 43.

[9] Minucius Felix, *Octavius*, 29.6–7: *Nam et signa ipsa et cantabra et vexilla castrorum quid aliud quam inauratae cruces sunt et ornatae? Tropaea vestra victricia non tantum simplicis crucis faciem, verum et adfixi hominis imitantur.*

[10] Tertullian, *Ad Nationes*, 1.12: *Victorias ut numina et quidem augustiora, quanto laetiora, veneramini ... cruces erunt intestina quodammo do et tropaeorum; itaque in Victoriis et cruces colit castrensis religio. Signa adorat, signa deierat, signa ipsi Iovi praefert ... Sic etiam in contabris atque vexillis, quae non minore sanctitate militia custodit silphara illa vestes crucum sunt.*

[11] Justin Martyr, *Apology One on behalf of the Christians*, trans. Leslie Bernard (New York: Paulist Press, 1997), 62–63. For the Greek text see Migne 1841–1865b, vol. 6, col. 411–413A: Καῖ τὰ παρ' ὑμῖν δέ σύμβολα τὴν τοῦ σχήματος τούτου δύναμιν δηλοῖ ἅλωμεν (55) καὶ τῶν τροπαίων δι' ὦν αἴτε πρόοδοι ὑμῶν πανταχοῦ γίνοντι: τῆς ἀρχῆς καὶ δυνάμεως τὰ σημεῖα ἐν τούτοις δει χνύντες, εἰ καὶ μὴ νοοῦντες τοῦτο πράττετε.

state how the soldiers worship the true victor merely through the shape and style of their trophy.

The imitation of the Roman *tropaeum* in the Triumphal Wreath sarcophagus becomes still more pronounced when one observes the soldiers seated below the standard. One of the soldiers usually looks up at the cross and monogram, while the other rests his head on his shield. It is entirely possible to assume this to be a representation of the soldiers who guard the tomb after Christ's death. Though described in the Gospels as having become "like dead men,"[12] they are usually depicted asleep in representations of the Visit to the Sepulchre following the Resurrection. If this were the case, then the central scene would indeed represent the Resurrection.[13] The placement of the soldiers, however, is much closer to that of Roman depictions of imperial victory. This was popularly depicted on Roman coins, as with the imagery on the *Judaea Capta* coinage. After Vespasian's, and ultimately Titus', quelling of the Jewish revolt and the ultimate destruction of the Temple in 70, a variety of coins were minted with the expression: "*JUDAEA CAPTA*" and an image of one or two male or female figures seated beneath a palm tree or a *tropaeum*. Often the figures sit with their head clutched in their hands, mourning their loss (Figure 3). This was a common Roman motif of victory over a nation. The captives represent the defeated people and the *tropaeum*, complete with the armor and shields of the enemy, celebrates the glorious Roman victory.

The same image of victory in fact persists on Roman sarcophagi into the third century. On the so-called Sarcophagus with Victories, for instance (Figure 4), the central Gorgon's head depicted inside a shield is set up on a cross-beam made of grape vines. Two female figures sit defeated below the cross, one looks up at the Gorgon, the other mourns with head in hand. The Victories on either side of the Gorgon shield carry *vexilla*. This early third-century sarcophagus displays many similarities to the Triumphal Wreath sarcophagus: the central motif, the cross it is set upon, and the defeated pair of figures beneath. The associations with the military are seen on both sarcophagi. The central image on the Passion sarcophagi of the defeated soldiers under the *tropaeum*, explicitly indicates Christ's triumph in military terms. In the middle of the sarcophagi Christ's trophy stands victorious over his defeated captors: the Romans, the enemy, the pagans.

---

[12]Mt. 28: 4.
[13]Schiller, *Iconography of Christian Art*, 5.

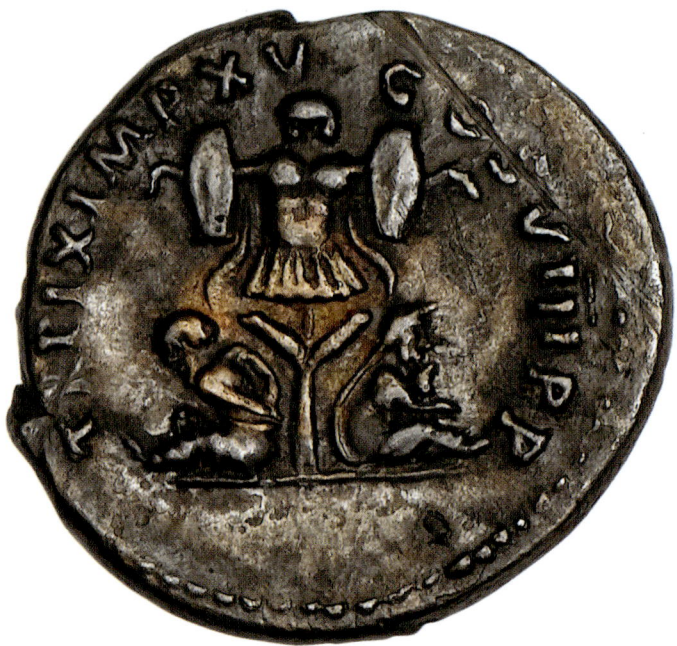

Figure 3 *Judaea Capta Coin of Titus, Rome, 80–81 CE, The Jewish Museum, New York City.*

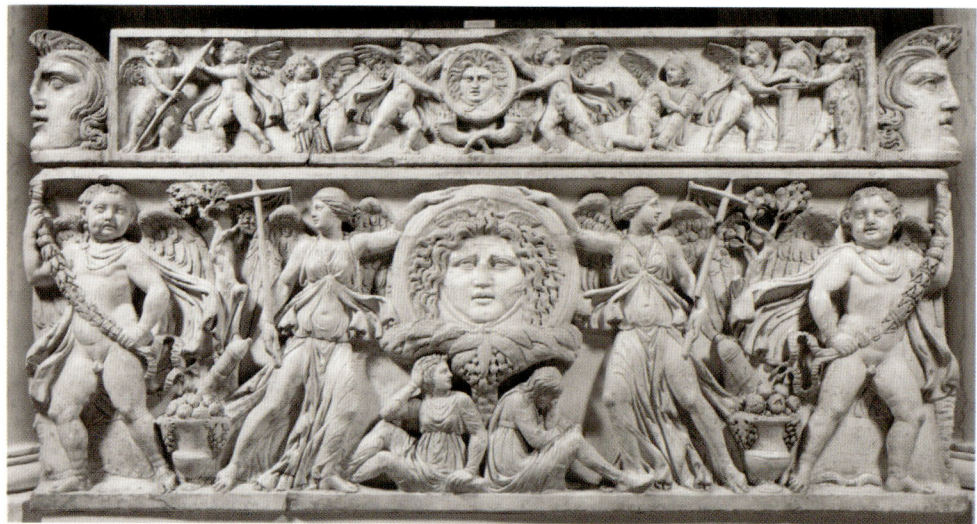

Figure 4 *Sarcophagus with Victories, Rome, c. 210 CE, Walters Art Museum, Baltimore.*

Early significance of the wreath

While the Triumphal Wreath sarcophagus is certainly reminiscent of military standards of victory, the wreath enclosing the chi-rho adds another dimension of meaning to the image. As we have seen, the chi-rho may well have been a prominent symbol in Constantine's army, but the wreath also bears even more significant ritualistic associations for the Roman and Christian cultures. Wreaths were a fundamental part of Roman society and religious ceremony, especially that of sacrifice: sacrificial victims were crowned with wreaths; cult statues were bedecked with wreaths; wreaths and garlands (which are essentially extended wreaths) were hung around altars and temples; suppliants could not pray to the gods without first offering them a fresh wreath. Wreaths were particularly used as apotropaic devices, warding off evil and purifying victims and those performing sacrifice. Soldiers were even crowned with wreaths upon their return from battle for purification purposes.[14] This association of wreaths with sacrifice and purity, as we will see below, was especially important to the Romano-Christians. Since the art of the Romano-Christians did not explicitly portray the suffering of Christ, the wreath, already embedded in their society, was adopted to specifically portray Jesus' sacrifice, as well as victory through implied suffering.

The wreath, however, was also an object of contention for the early Christian theologians because of those deeply pagan links. It was therefore important to the early leaders of the Church that Christians used wreaths appropriately or preferably not at all, due to their intrinsic associations with secular and non-Christian society. Christians were told that it was inappropriate for them to wear crowns for two main reasons: first, that it was against nature and second, that it was inherently a part of idol worship and therefore forbidden.

Tertullian's *De Corona* particularly features some of his more nature-based theology. For Tertullian, nature dictates "divine command," and nature represents the foundation of divine laws. That is to say, that which conforms to nature therefore conforms to divinity. This idea that nature is interpreted by the help of the Spirit will, for Tertullian, often supplant arguments that come from Scripture.[15]

---

[14] Thomas Mathews, *The Clash of Gods* (Princeton: Princeton University Press, 1993), 163.
[15] Tertullian, *Christian and Pagan in the Roman Empire*, trans. Robert Sider (Washington, D.C.: Catholic University Press, 2001), 116.

It is with this fundamental argument that Tertullian seeks to demonstrate how wearing wreaths is inherently unnatural and therefore contrary to divine law. Flowers, or any material that would make a wreath, are naturally on this earth to be enjoyed by sight and smell. When they are plucked from the earth to weave them and put them on our head, the natural senses of sight and smell are no longer engaged in the purpose of the flower. Flowers and plants on the head put the flower in an unnatural state, and one should "consider it as a sin of sacrilege against God, the master and author of nature."[16]

Clement of Alexandria (d. 215) also makes use of the nature argument. He, like Tertullian, wrote that humans can best glorify God by using nature as God intended. That is, flowers are beautiful, and because of their beauty, were meant to be looked at. When flowers are placed atop heads, they no longer give pleasure and so the action is only harmful.[17]

Perhaps the strongest case against using wreaths was their close, and very public, association with idols and pagan ritual. For people like Tertullian, the Roman religion was considered to be "pagan," that is, profane and worldly. The gods of the Roman world, says Tertullian, are not real gods. They were deemed to be gods by humans, but are not in fact divine. Christians, says Tertullian, who are dedicated to the true God, should therefore not participate in Roman wreath-culture because wreaths were invented to honor these profane beings. They are unsuitable for true divinity and those, such as the Christians, who, he asserts, follow true divinity.[18]

Yet another reason Christians should not wear wreaths is exemplified by the Crown of Thorns. For Tertullian, the Crown of Thorns was made from thorns (*spinis*) and thistles (*tribulis*) that represent our sins, which Jesus' death on the cross removed.[19] The Crown of Thorns was humanity's death, placed on the head of Jesus, which he bore, single-handedly, for the sake of all. If Christ, says Tertullian, was given on earth a crown made of something as base and wretched as thorns, then mere humans should not wear crowns made of some better material, such as laurel or olive branches. Nor should they wear wreaths of thorns, since thorns represent Christ's sacrifice of bearing humanity's sins.[20]

---

[16] Tertullian, *De Corona*, 5.4: *Penes nos vero etiam elogium sacrilegii in Deum, naturae dominum et auctorem.*
[17] Clement of Alexandria, *Christ the Educator,* trans. Simon Wood (Washington D.C.: Catholic University Press, 1954), 146–159. For the Greek text see Migne *Series Graeca*, vol. 8, col. 465–490.
[18] Tertullian, *De Corona*, 7.2–3; 8; 13.
[19] Ibid., 14.3.
[20] Ibid., 14.4.

Tertullian, Clement of Alexandria, and Cyril of Jerusalem (d. 386) all concede, perhaps because the use of wreaths was unavoidable in Romano-Christian culture, that wreaths do have relevance for Christians, albeit limited. In their commentaries, wreaths were most strongly encouraged in terms of their relationship with death, victory, and martyrdom.[21] All of these topics are, of course, related.

As shown above, Christians saw the greatest triumph as Christ's victory over sin and death, and that the crown made of thorns or acanthus is closely associated with victory. Wreath-crowns were synonymous with victory long before the Christian era. Athletes most significantly gained wreaths for their achievements. Soldiers were given crowns for their success and victory over enemies. Emperors wore wreaths during triumphs, and so on. The Christians borrowed and, as so often, syncretized this idea into their own cult.

Jesus' Crown of Thorns thus became an object of victory. It is a symbol of Jesus' own victory over death. By the very act of believing in Jesus and his salvific victory, Christians too became victors over death. Because they too were victors, who had struggled on earth to believe in Christ, face adversaries, and promote the faith, they would also receive crowns in heaven. They believed that these wreaths, unlike the wreaths that heathens received in their profane rituals, would not wither or fade. They were eternal wreaths, everlasting flowers, fit for Christ's athletes of faith. Wreaths, then, in Romano-Christian society became closely associated with death. Christians only received their eternal wreaths after they died, since truly they had conquered death by being Christian. So, according to Tertullian, Christians should:

> Keep untainted, therefore, for God what is his; he will crown it if he wants. And he will, in the end, invite us to be crowned. To him who conquered he says: "I will give to him the crown of life."[22] Your destiny is to wear a diadem. For Christ Jesus has made us to be as kings to God and his Father, so why do you bother with a flower that will die? You have a flower from the branch of Jesse, upon which the grace of the divine Spirit has rested, a flower unspoiled, unfading and eternal.[23]

---

[21] The wreath's ubiquitous use in association with martyrs will be discussed in detail below.
[22] Cf. Rev. 2:10; Jas 1:12.
[23] Tertullian, *De Corona*, 15.1–2: *Serua Deo rem suam intaminatam. Ille eam si volet coronabit. Immo et vult denique invitat: "Qui vicerit inquit, dabo ei coronam vitae"... Nam reges nos Deo et patri suo fecit Christus Iesus. Quid tibi cum flore morituro? Habes florem ex virga Iesse, super quem tota divini Spiritus gratia requievit, florem incorruptum immarcescibilem sempiternum.*

It is perhaps not surprising, therefore, to find a plethora of wreaths in many forms on Romano-Christian funerary art, particularly ones which overwhelmingly pertain to victory over death.

The crowning of Christ and the importance of demeanor

As we have already determined, the scene to the left of the central triumphal standard of the Vatican Passion Sarcophagus depicts a serene and gentle crowning. The Roman soldier carefully and almost reverently places a wreath-crown, woven from flowers and leaves, on the head of a calm Jesus. He stands in a relaxed pose, hands crossed, holding a scroll. They are the only two characters that face completely towards the central image of the standard. This scene alludes to both the Crowning and Mockery of Jesus from the Passion.

The scene on the sarcophagus is peaceful rather than the violence found in the Gospels. Jesus does not suffer in any way. The soldier is not obviously mocking him. Instead the crowning scene is shown as it was meant to be understood by the Christian audience of the time—one of the soldiers rightfully bestowing upon the victorious leader a wreath-crown that represents his single-handed victory over death and destruction. This spiritual and moral victory is emphasized by their position facing towards the central image, which is here a trophy of Christ's victory. The general Jesus is rightfully crowned for his success and he looks towards the trophy, a further indication of his triumph.

The depiction on the sarcophagus is indeed the Crowning scene, but it is depicted as one that more closely exhibits not the Mockery or suffering of Jesus, but the implied victory. The soldiers mocked Jesus for his failed military success, but in a double irony, the Christian audience understood that he actually did, on a far more profound level, succeed in saving his people from death. The scene on the Vatican sarcophagus thus turns the "Mockery" on its head, showing both the crowning scene and the implied irony of the soldiers' deed.

By the time this sarcophagus was carved in the fourth century, the crowning episode in the Gospels was understood by many Christians as one of the soldiers rightfully paying homage to their leader. Cyril of Jerusalem contends that although the soldiers appear to be mocking Jesus, they are nevertheless on bended knee—and that is precisely where they should be. The placing of a crown on his head makes perfect sense in this context. As Cyril wrote, "for what it is made of acanthus? Every leader is proclaimed by soldiers; it became Jesus too in a figure to have been crowned by soldiers."[24] It is fitting for Cyril that Jesus be crowned in this manner by soldiers—not by the mob, but by the military. It suits his role as ruler, general, and king to be crowned by the soldiers, just as any legitimate ruler would be. Jesus, both in Cyril's understanding, and in how he is depicted on the sarcophagus, is placed in the position of successful general and uncontested ruler, assured by the support of the soldiers. Cyril and the Vatican sarcophagus unmistakably place Jesus in a military context where he is rightfully crowned by the soldiers, disguised in mock ceremony, as a victorious leader.

Christ's demeanor in the panel also reflects popular contemporary commentary on the episode of the Crowning and Mockery. Here Jesus is calm, with hands folded, accepting humbly what is happening to him. Several commentators, including Origen and John Chrysostom (d. 407), use the episode of the Crowning as an exemplar for Christian behavior. In his long anti-apology, quoted by Origen in his *Contra Celsum* (c.248/9), Celsus is made to say that the Christians could have picked any other man to worship who died a noble death; one who was already distinguished by myth, and one who was already known to be like the gods, such as Orpheus, Anaxarchus, or Hercules. Instead, says Celsus, the Christians "assert that a man who lived a most infamous life and died a most miserable death was a god."[25] Celsus argues that the Christian god uttered absolutely nothing during his punishment, which, according to Celsus, deems him unworthy to be worshiped as a god.

Origen counters this argument by suggesting that Jesus' silence was far more profound and significant: "By his silence," he wrote, "under the scourge and many other outrages he manifested a courage and patience superior to that of any of the Greeks who spoke while enduring torture..."[26] Origen uses the example of the Mockery and Crowning of Jesus as a supremely impressive example of meekness and endurance in the face of suffering and torment:

> Moreover, when he was being mocked and clothed in a purple robe, and the crown of thorns was put on his head and when he took the reed in his hand for a scepter, he

---

[24]Cyril of Jerusalem, "Catechesis 13," in Migne, *Series Latina*, vol. 33, col. 793B: "τί γὰρ εἰκαὶ ἀκάνθινον; Ἧς βασιλεὺς ὑπὸ στρατιωτῶν ἀναγορεύεται• ἔδει καὶ Ἰησοῦν τυπικῶς ὑπὸ στρατιωτῶν στεφανωθῆναι•"
[25]Origen, *Contra Celsum*, VII. 53, trans. Henry Chadwick (Cambridge: Cambridge University Press, 1965), 439-440. For the Greek text see Origen, *Contra Celsum, Libri VIII*, ed. M. Marcovich (Leiden: Brill, 2001), 505: τὸν δὲ βίῳ μὲν ἐπιρρητοτάτῳ, θανάτῳ δὲ οἰκτίστῳ χρησάμενον θεὸν τίθεσθε.
[26]Origen, *Contra Celsum*, VII. 55, trans Henry Chadwick, 441. For the Greek text see Origen, *Contra Celsum, Libri VIII*, 506: τῇ παρὰ ταῖς μάστιξι καὶ ταῖς πολλαῖς αἰκίαις αὐτοῦ σιωπῇ παντὸς τοῦ ἐν Ἕλλησιν ἐν περιστάσεσι τυγχάνοντος φθεγαμένου μᾶλλον ἐνέφηνε καρτερίαν καὶ ὑπομονήν•.

showed the highest meekness. For he said nothing either ignoble or angry to those who ventured to do such terrible things to him.[27]

The episode of the mock crowning, for Origen, is one of utmost torment and humility. And because this treatment was so horrible, Jesus' silence is even more admirable. This idea of the meek, unassuming Christ who shows endurance through his calm and humble demeanor was a popular and hugely inspiring idea. It was emphasized especially in conjunction with discussion of Jesus' Mockery and Crowning, a moment which was, for early commentators, both deeply humiliating and yet obviously representative of the underlying strength of Jesus' manner.

Like Origen, John Chrysostom writes over a century later on Christ's humility in the same way. Chrysostom's homily on Matthew 27:27–29 tells people to use the example of Christ's demeanor during his Mockery and abuse as a way of shaping their behavior in their own lives. Christians, like Christ himself, he urges, should endure abuse with silence and meekness; and greet distress and anger with forgiveness.[28] For the early commentators, Jesus' silence and humility is worthy of imitation. It is an example for all Christians of how they should behave when confronted with abuse. The Jesus of the Vatican Passion Sarcophagus reflects this very demeanor—the triumph of life over death and of non-violence over violence.

The Jesus on the Vatican Sarcophagus therefore expresses several fundamental aspects of the early Christian ideologies which surround the Crown of Thorns. First, it represents their understanding of Jesus' true victory over death—the triumph of Christ and his worthy reward. Just as importantly, it also depicts the humble and tolerant Jesus who endures his Passion in silence, accepting the crown of the solider, knowing that it is a rightful wreath of victory. The Christian victory had to be one which was manifestly different from (and superior to) the normal definition of victory of the classical world. It is the triumph of the spirit rather than the body, and the victory of non-violence over oppression.

The Triumphal Wreath sarcophagus should be seen in this context as an overwhelming depiction of victory. Jesus' triumphant victory over death is depicted on such sarcophagi through the imagery of the wreath and through the depiction of the Roman military. Wreaths were inherited by Christian society as symbols with which to represent victory

---

[27]Ibid.: Ἀλλὰ καὶ ἐμπαιζόμενος καὶ ἐνδυόμενος τὴν κοκκίνην χλαμύδα καὶ τὸν ἀκάνθινον στέφανον τῇ κεφαλῇ περιτιθέμενος καὶ τὸν κάλαμον λαμβάνων ἐπὶ τῆς χειρὸς ἀντὶ σκήπτρου ἄκρᾳ πρᾳότητι ἐχρήσατο, μηδὲν μηδ' ἀγενὲς μηδ' ἀγανακτητικὸν εἰπὼν πρὸς τοὺς τοσαῦτα κατ' αὐτοῦ τολμήσαντας.

[28]Chrysostom, "Homily 87," in Migne *Series Graeca*, vol. 50, col. 661–666.

over death and were directly associated with Christ. The military imagery, especially the central *tropaeum*, and conquered soldiers, emphasize that Christ's victory over death was like a Roman military victory: strong, uncompromising and glorious.

Alongside the depiction of the silent, but implacable, triumph, there is another type of Triumphal Wreath in contemporary art. This second category replaces the Passion scenes with an uninterrupted line of apostles. In the so-called Triumph Sarcophagus of a Married Pair c. 350–400, in the Musée départemental Arles antique, for instance, twelve apostles face towards the central triumphal wreath, which lacks the chi-rho. Most of the apostles hold scrolls in their hand and gesture towards the wreath. The hand of God descends with a wreath over each of the apostles' heads, adorning them with the same victory that the standard-cross bears. The presence of the apostles and the wreaths over their heads indicates a further level of understanding of the role of the wreaths in Romano-Christian art; as one of reward for the faithful. This Triumphal Wreath type with the Apostles is part of a progression of the scene of Christ's victory.

The Enthroned Christ

Powerful though it was, however, the depiction of Jesus' Triumphal Wreath could not remain static. Eventually, the Enthroned Christ on sarcophagi begins to replace the Triumphal Wreath in the fifth century. In the course of the fifth century, the iconography shifts the focus of the theme of victory into the heavenly sphere, with the inclusion of wreaths, martyrs, and a divine, heavenly conqueror.

The Enthroned Christ appears on Romano-Christian sarcophagi by the mid-fourth century and becomes more popular by the fifth century, according to the conventionally applied dating protocol of the sarcophagi of this period. In the mid-fourth century, the Triumphal Wreath of the Passion sarcophagi are replaced with the image of Christ enthroned. It retains the scenes from Christ's Passion, the trials of the apostles, and Old Testament stories.

By the fifth century, the scene is drastically stripped, however. Gone are the columns separating the characters, gone are the Passion and Old Testament scenes. Christ remains enthroned in the center, still performing heavenly duties, and is surrounded by both familiar apostles and several new characters. In the Certosa Sarcophagus of the fifth century, found in the Ferrara Cathedral, Christ is seated on a more defined throne. It is high backed, armless, cushioned, and straight-legged, with a footstool. Christ is beardless with flowing hair. He holds a book in his left hand and makes a gesture of blessing with his right. Many describe this scene as an extension of the Christ-as-philosopher or teacher scene, where Jesus is found seated, teaching his disciples.[29] Unlike the typical philosopher/teacher scene, however, these fifth-century sarcophagi display Christ facing frontally, fully dressed and beardless while his retinue stands before him. Typical philosopher scenes, on the other hand, will show the philosopher bare-chested, in profile, and always with a full beard. The philosopher's retinue will also be seated before or in front of him, listening intently, instead of standing and moving towards the center, as they do in the sarcophagi with Christ enthroned.[30]

Inevitably, there are variations around this depiction. The Certosa Sarcophagus in the Ferrara Cathedral for instance, shows an elevated, enthroned Christ flanked by two cross-bearing men, who are generally presumed to be Peter and Paul. Two attendants stand with arms raised in praise. At either end, two more men rush towards Christ with knees bent, togas flapping, and wreaths balanced in their veiled hands.

Similarly, the Twelve Apostles Sarcophagus from the fifth century, now housed in the Basilica of Sant'Apollinare in Classe, Ravena, depicts on its front an Enthroned Christ with six attendants (Figure 5). The man to the right of the enthroned Christ, generally interpreted as Paul, receives a scroll of the Law with veiled hands from a beardless Christ, who also holds an open book. The man to the left of Christ bears a cross and possibly a key on veiled hands. Christ is seated on a high-backed, cushioned throne, facing completely frontally and holding a book in his left hand. As in the Certosa

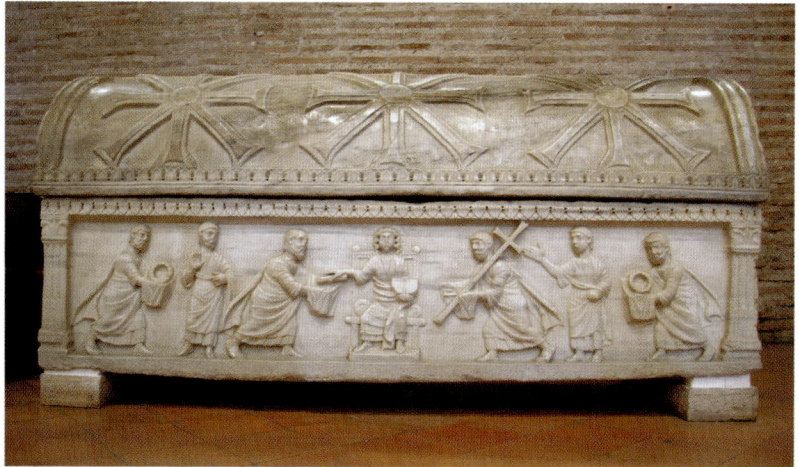

Figure 5 *Twelve Apostles Sarcophagus, fifth century, Basilica di Sant'Apollinare in Classe, Ravenna.*

---

[29]Geir Hellemo, *Adventus Domini; Eschatological Thought in 4th-Century Apses and Catecheses*, trans. E. Waaler. (Leiden: Brill, 1989), 40; Jensen, *Understanding Early Christian Art,* 44.
[30]Jensen, *Understanding Early Christian Art,* 44.

Sarcophagus, two more attendants raise their hands in praise, while the last two hold their wreaths with veiled hands. Four of the attendants on the front of this sarcophagus receive a gift from Christ. All four rush forward to receive their reward. The two outermost men receive their wreaths from Christ.

But, despite these variations, the new Enthroned Christ scene carries its own consistency and significance with it. The scene, which varies from featuring two to twelve attendants and an enthroned Christ, is yet another scene of victory. It is an overtly heavenly victory emphasized by an obviously divine representation of Christ. Christ distributes heavenly reward in the form of wreaths of victory to his attendants.

Imitating the gods of Rome

Just as the Germanic successors to Rome's glories sought to find legitimacy by continually harkening back to the symbols and formulae of their supposed classical predecessors, so too did their gods. One of the central aspects of the Enthroned Christ which make it a heavenly scene, for instance, is the style of Christ's enthronement. His enthronement is a deliberate artistic imitation of the Roman iconography of the gods. Christ's throne, in the fifth-century examples such as the Certosa Sarcophagus, the Twelve Apostles Sarcophagus, and the Rinaldo Sarcophagus, all place Christ on a large throne which, as we have seen, has a high back, is armless, cushioned, and straight

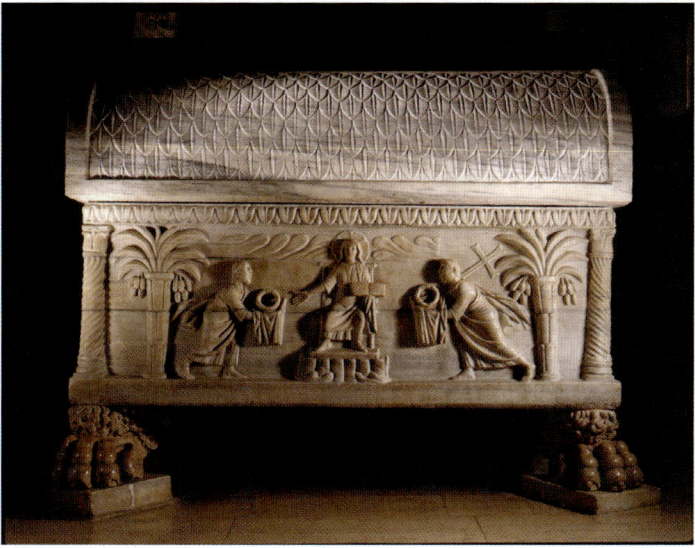

Figure 6 *Sarcophagus of Beato Rinaldo fifth century, Cathedral of Ravenna, Ravenna.*

legged (Figures 5 and 6). These thrones also have footstools for Christ, and in the case of the Rinaldo Sarcophagus (Figure 6), have the four rivers of Paradise flowing from it.

This style of ancient furniture is known as a *solium*, Latin for "throne." At its most basic, the *solium* was a chair with straight legs and a back. The legs may be rectangular or have solid sides; the back may be higher than the head of the seated person, or cut off at their shoulders; and it may or may not have armrests.

But significantly, these chairs were reserved for the gods. These types of thrones were a familiar object to the public due to their constant appearance on coins, where the gods were given a straight-legged throne with a high back.[31] Personifications of Roma, Constantinople, and Pax were also accorded this honorable seat. A typical gold aureus minted in Rome c. 284–305, for example, depicts an image of Diocletian on the obverse (Figure 7). On the reverse, Jupiter is seated on a high-backed throne with straight legs. He grasps a lightning bolt in his right hand and a vertical scepter in his left, with an eagle carrying a wreath at his feet—all of these were the attributes of Jupiter. It was the gods, therefore, who ruled from high-backed, cushioned chairs. Thus, the image of Christ seated in a *solium*, deliberately puts him in the familiar position of a ruling, heavenly god.

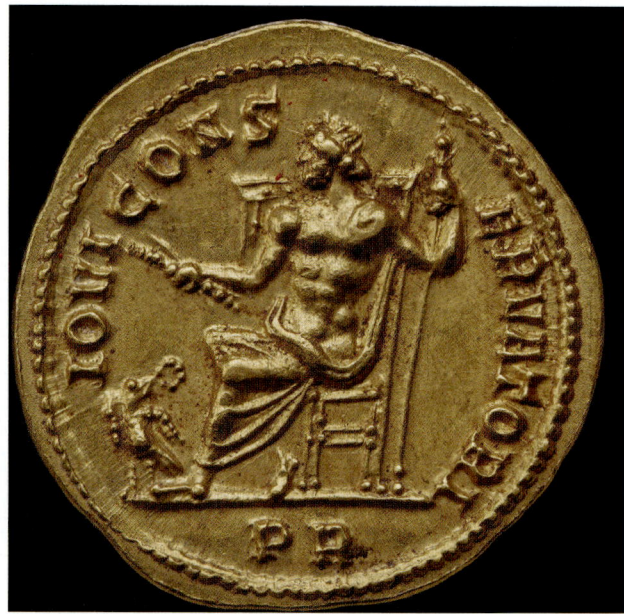

Figure 7 *Aureus of Diocletian and Jupiter Coin, Rome, c. 284–305, The British Museum, London*

---

[31]Mathews, *The Clash of Gods,* 107–108.

There is common misconception that this representation of Christ in his throne is instead an imitation of imperial imagery. It is worth emphasizing, however, that according to Roman tradition, imagery, and literature, Christ's enthronement is in almost no way imperial. The official chair of the emperor was not as extravagant as the high-backed, straight-legged, sometimes decorated throne of Christ. The emperor sat on a *sella curulis*, or the curule chair. This seat was the imperial seat of authority, from which the emperor publicly conducted the government. The curule chair was a stool which folded, had S-curved legs made of wood, and four supporting beams on the top, with leather stretched over them where a cushion could be placed.

The curule seat was the official chair of the consuls and magistrates during the Republic and remained so during the Empire.[32] Indeed, even Pilate on Romano-Christian funerary art, while he is conducting Jesus' trial, is accurately portrayed sitting on a curule chair, as he historically would have sat while overseeing trials, as governor of Judaea. Pilate's chair in both the Passion Sarcophagus (Figure 1) and the Tree Sarcophagus (Figure 2) has a plank-like seat with a cushion, is backless, and the legs curve and crisscross one another. Christ's throne is decidedly not the chair of the emperors or their governors.

Furthermore, Christ does not possess the other qualities of imperial imagery on the fifth-century sarcophagi. Christ wears no diadem, but rather is haloed. The emperor, from Constantine I onward, wore a distinguished jewel-studded crown that further identified him as emperor. The emperors would occasionally have a disk around their heads, like a halo, but it often radiated, like beams of a sun. Christ's clothes also differ significantly from the typical clothing of the emperor. The emperor would be depicted with the imperial cloak (*chlamys*), the purple boots, and the scepter. Christ, on the other hand, wears a cloak over a tunic and is barefoot. This is civilian or, or at best, magisterial dress.

Instead of being an imitation of the emperor, or even, as some argue, a challenge to the emperor, Christ here is shown as a replacement for the gods, as the one true divinity. There are obvious political, rather than aesthetic, reasons why this would be so. It would not have been wise for the Christians, who had only recently gained the patronage of the emperor, to challenge his likeness. Instead, it was more prudent to challenge the gods with their own. The audience of these images would have more readily associated Christ's position as one of divinity, since this same image was used for the Roman

---

[32]Ibid., 108.

gods.[33] Images like the Enthroned Christ on the Romano-Christian sarcophagi depict a victorious and overtly divine (and more apolitical) Christ.

The composition of Christ and his attendants in this context is thus an artistic rendering of the understanding the Romano-Christians had of heaven. As John Chrysostom explains in his homily on Matthew, "You will see the king himself, seated on the throne of that unutterable glory, together with the angels and archangels standing beside him, as well as the countless legions of the ranks of saints."[34] In doing so, Chrysostom is merely describing an image that, by the fifth century, would already have been well established in the minds of the Christians.

It is important to note that for the fifth-century observant the "ranks of the saints" would include martyrs. On both the Certosa and Twelve Apostles Sarcophagi (Figure 5), On the Twelve Apostles Sarcophagus, as will be demonstrated, the martyrs may be identified as the wreath-bearers at both ends. They receive from Christ the heavenly reward for their victory in the form of a wreath. In the next section, in the fourth and fifth centuries, the imagery of the martyrs as cross-bearers and the wreath-bearers come to the fore. The role of the cult of martyrs took on an ever-increasing importance to the imagery of the heavenly Christ, and, as imitators of Christ, their reward in the form of a heavenly wreath was a visible imitation of Jesus' own Crown of Thorns.

The wreath and the cult of martyrs

It is clear that on the Certosa, Twelve Apostles, and Rinaldo Sarcophagi (Figure 3, 4) Christ is enthroned in his heavenly position. But there remain several characters still unidentified, namely the men who race towards Christ bearing wreaths and crosses. The men who flank Christ on these sarcophagi are conventionally identified as Peter and Paul, however they are often depicted, as in the case of these sarcophagi, bearing crosses as well. By the fifth century, crosses slung over shoulders and wreaths born on veiled hands are synonymous with additional saints, as the following examples will demonstrate. To examine these characters with their crosses and wreath-crowns is to understand why and to what extent, the wreath-crown, and its associations to the Crown of Thorns, survives for several more centuries. The wreath-crown's survival hinges, as we shall see, upon the parallels between Christ and the martyrs, both artistically and literarily.

---

[33]Ibid., 100–101.
[34]John Chrysostom, "Homilies on the Gospel of Matthew, Homily Two," in Migne, *Series Graeca*, vol. 57, col. 23: ἀλλ' αὐτὸν τὸν Βασιλέα καθήμενον ἐπὶ τοῦ θρόνου τῆς ἀπορρήτου δόξης ἐκείνης, καὶ ἀγγέλους καὶ ἀρχαγγέλους παρεστῶτας αὐτῷ, καὶ τοὺς δήμους τῶν ἁγίων μετὰ τῶν ἀπείρων μυριάδων ἐκείνων.

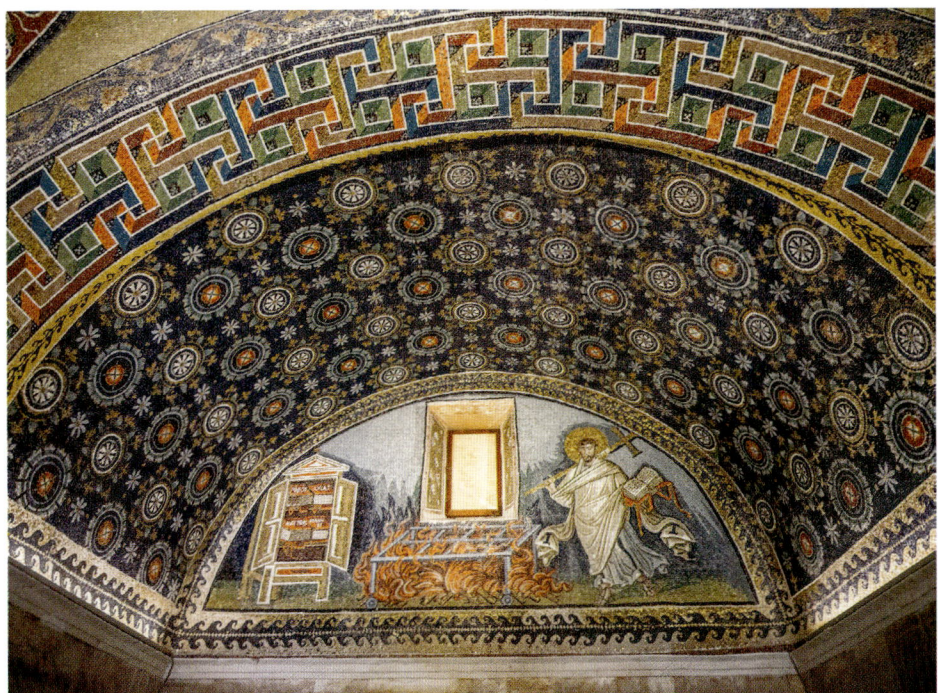

Figure 8 *Mosaic of Saint Lawrence, c. 424–425, Mausoleum of Galla Placidia, Ravenna.*

A comparative example comes from the Ravenna Mausoleum of Galla Placidia (d. 450), daughter of Theodosius I. On the south wall, directly opposite the entrance, a prominently displayed lunette contains a vivid depiction of a saint (Figure 8).[35] Against a gradated blue background, on the far left, a cupboard stands open containing four books, each labeled as one of the four Gospels: Mark, Luke, Matthew, and John. In the center under the window, a metal grill on wheels stands above a raging red fire, with wood underneath. To the right, a haloed and bearded man wears a blue tunic with a white cloak. In his left hand he holds an open book, while in his right he hoists a cross over his shoulder. He appears to be in motion, running towards the fiery grill, cloak and tunic flying around him.

The identity of the figure is disputed. It has been suggested that the man may be Christ destroying heretical books, but it is more plausible that this man is a saint.[36] Typically, he is identified as Saint Lawrence. The presence of the grill speaks to this

---

[35] Wolfgang Fritz Volbach, *Early Christian Art* (London: Thames and Hudson, 1961), 31.
[36] Deborah Deliyannis, *Ravenna in Late Antiquity* (Cambridge: Cambridge University Press, 2010), 78. See also Deborah Deliyannis, Hendrik Dey, Paolo Squatriti, *Fifty Early Medieval Things* (Cornell University Press, 2019), 78, ft. 226, for references to arguments that suggest the male figure is Christ.

interpretation, as Saint Lawrence was famously martyred by being roasted on a grill. Saint Lawrence was also popularly venerated by the Theodosian dynasty, of which Galla Placidia, the patroness of the mausoleum, was a member.[37]

Alternatively, the figure in the Mausoleum of Galla Placidia may instead depict the martyr Saint Vincent. Saint Vincent of Saragossa was possibly martyred during the fourth-century Diocletian persecutions and was, like Lawrence, a deacon who was tortured on a grill. Saint Vincent was popular throughout the Roman world, particularly in Spain, but also in Ravenna.[38] It is perhaps significant that, not only was Saint Vincent grilled, but that Prudentius' poem (d. c. 405) on Saint Vincent in his *Liber Peritephanon*, specifically mentions books which contain the teachings of the Christians. The Romans, the poem explains, desired to burn these books along with Vincent. The labelled Gospels and the book that the saint holds, may reference this part of Prudentius' poem. The poem also specifically states that Vincent ran towards his death, as the mosaic shows.[39] There is neither sufficient concrete evidence nor a label to confirm which saint is depicted here. It is enough to say that the figure in the lunette was both important to the patroness, due to its prominent position in the mausoleum, and most certainly a martyr saint, due to the presence of the grill as a tool of martyrdom. This lends support to the suggestion that the cross also identifies him as a martyr.[40]

The function of the chapel was probably both as a mausoleum and as a memorial chapel to the saint. Since memorial chapels were often used as burial sites, and vice versa, the appearance of a saint in this context is significant.[41] As we shall see, much of the iconography of the chapel is funerary, including the saint who alludes to heavenly victory and faithfulness.

The saints with their crosses continue to appear in the fifth century in the context of burial and death. The fifth century frescos in the catacombs of San Severo in Naples, for example, also depict a cross-bearing martyr. The catacombs of San Severo, who was bishop of Naples from 363 to 409, are mostly destroyed. In an ongoing project to restore the catacombs, three arcosolia, however, are clearly still in place, of which two are intelligible.[42] The arcosolium opposite the entrance depicts a man standing sideways,

---

[37]Deliyannis, *Ravenna*, 83.
[38]Gillian Mackie, "New Light on the So-Called Saint Lawrence Panel at the Mausoleum of Galla Placidia, Ravenna," *Gesta*, 29:1 (1990): 55.
[39]Ibid., 57–58.
[40]Deliyannis, *Ravenna*, 79.
[41]Ibid., 82.
[42]For information on the ongoing restoration project visit: http://www.catacombedinapoli.it/en/places/catacombs-of-san-severo-naples, Retrieved Feb. 2017.

looking out to the viewer. He wears a white tunic and gold cloak. He carries a cross over his shoulder and gestures in blessing with his right hand. Above the cross-bearing figure in a red frame the words ST PROTASIUS are still visible. Some copies that were previously sketched and preserved identify that the missing portion of the fresco also displayed the martyr Gervasius.

Saints Protasius and Gervasius became exponentially more popular after their relics were discovered in Milan by the Bishop Ambrose (d. 397), in 386—a thrilling tale which will be examined below. The cult became widespread throughout Italy and they were added to the Litany of Saints at a very early date. Churches were built in their honor at Pavia, Nola, and in Gaul at Le Mans, Rouen, and Soissons. The increased popularity of these saints in the early centuries of the Church may account for their prominent position in the catacombs by the fifth century. More importantly, this represents yet another example of a cross-bearing martyr saint who is positioned prominently in a sacred space for the dead. As with the saints on the sarcophagi and the saint who is displayed in the Mausoleum of Galla Placidia, the cross-bearing martyrs figure conspicuously in funerary art.

Why then are the figures on the sarcophagi who bear crosses closest to Christ conventionally assigned as Peter and Paul? This is probably due to their heavenly rank. The Litany of Saints is an invocation of the heavenly beings to bestow on believers mercy, deliverance from evil, salvation, and other blessings. The Litany was established in some initial form at least by the mid-third century and recited during mass. The litany starts with a call for mercy from God the Father, God the Son, and God the Holy Spirit. Since, however, the Christian faithful are unworthy to call upon God or Christ directly, it is appropriate to ask for intercession from those who reside with Christ in heaven in a hierarchical order. There are several categories in this hierarchy of which only three are of interest in the present context: angels and other heavenly creatures; apostles and evangelists; and martyrs. The Apostles, most of whom were also martyred, are invoked after the angels and heavenly beings, who reside closer to Christ. Greatest among the Apostles is Peter, then Paul, and only after these two are the rest of the Apostles called upon. After the Apostles, the remaining martyrs are invoked for intercession.

Even among the martyrs there is an order of ranking. First to be called upon is Saint Stephen, the first follower of Jesus to be martyred, and then Saint Lawrence. Eleventh and twelfth on the list are Saints Gervasius and Protasius. They are the last to be named, after whom all the remaining martyrs generally are confined to a single invocation. Saints who were particularly important to specific communities were often also named after Gervasius and Protasius. It ends with a generic invocation to all the dead holy men and women.[43] This litany demonstrates the stringent hierarchy of those who dwell in heaven. It also helps to explain why the men closest to Christ on the Twelve Apostles Sarcophagus (Figure 5), and the Rinaldo Sarcophagus (Figure 6) are probably both martyrs and Apostles.

The Apostles are included in the list as first among the saints. Their proximity to Christ reflects their heavenly rank, since these sarcophagi reflect, after all, a heavenly scene. Thus, Peter and Paul on the sarcophagi carry crosses to identify their martyrdom, and their propinquity to the enthroned heavenly Christ indicates their position as Apostles.

The remaining characters on the sarcophagi can also be identified as martyrs in this heavenly scene from the wreaths that they carry. The Church of Sant' Apollinare Nuovo in Ravenna exhibits possibly the most distinct example of martyrs bearing wreaths (Figure 9)

On the south and north walls of the nave there are two large mosaics depicting a procession of saints. On the south-side wall, a procession of twenty-six male martyrs, separated by palm trees, slowly progress east towards the enthroned Christ (Figure 9). On the north-side wall, twenty-two female martyrs, divided by date-bearing palms, are

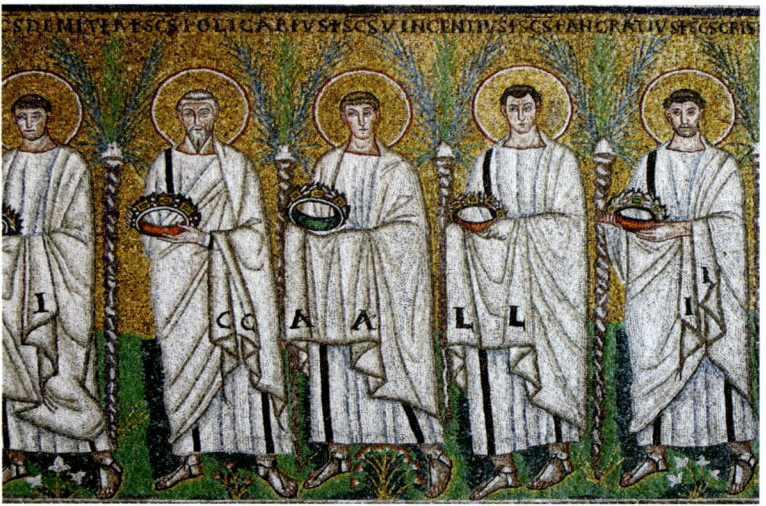

Figure 9 *Procession of Saints, c. 557–70, Basilica di Sant'Apollinare Nuovo, Ravenna.*

---

[43]The Catholic Encyclopedia, s.v. "Litany of Saints," http://www.newadvent.org/cathen/09291a.htm. Retrieved March 2015.

led by the three Magi towards the Christ child on Mary's lap at the easternmost end of the procession. All the saints, both male and female, are labeled, haloed, and carry wreaths on veiled hands. The female martyrs wear highly decorated dresses while the males dress in tunics and pallia. All of the saints on both walls are known to have been martyred, with the exception of the leading male saint, Saint Martin. The wreaths that they carry, with woven leaves and jewels at the center are attributes of their martyrdom; they are carried by the martyrs to signify their position as martyrs in heaven. Interestingly, all the male martyrs, and most of the female martyrs in the mosaics, were venerated in the litanies of the saints of Italy.[44]

The mosaics of the processing saints, however, date to the 560s. Sant'Apollinare Nuovo was redecorated when it was converted from an Arian church of Theodoric to an Orthodox church by Archbishop Agnellus.[45] Agnellus stripped the north and south walls of what was apparently a procession of Theodoric's court, and replaced it with the saints.[46]

Even earlier examples exist, however. The Catacomb of Domitilla in Rome, c. 360, contains an image of a procession of saints in the aptly named Chapel of Six Saints. Above an arcosolium, a large, toga-clad, beardless, youthful Christ sits enthroned. Six figures rush towards him on either side. To the right, three men with striped togas run towards Christ with wreaths in their hands. On the left, three veiled women also run towards Christ, apparently also bearing wreaths.

This scene of a peaceful procession converging on a deity was a common feature in the Greco-Roman world. A Mithreaum underneath the church Santa Prisca in Rome, c. 220, for example, depicts initiates in reverent procession carrying gifts to seated Mithras. It is an image of a similar vein to the only slightly later catacomb image, but the influence is unmistakable.[47] This processional, which has Greco-Roman roots, is seen in some of the earliest Romano-Christian art and exhibited continuity to not only with the sarcophagi of the fifth century, but also on the monumental art of the sixth century.

In sum, the figures on the sarcophagi of Certosa, the Twelve Apostles, and the Rinaldo can be identified as martyrs by the instruments they bear. The figures closest

---

[44]Deliyannis, *Ravenna*, 166–168.
[45]Giuseppe Bovini, *Ravenna Mosaics* (Greenwich: New York Graphic Society, 1966), 34; Volbach, *Early Christian Art,* 33; Deliyannis, *Ravenna*, 164–166.
[46]Bovini, *Ravenna Mosaics*, 35; Deliyannis, *Ravenna*, 171–172.
[47]Mathews, *The Clash of Gods,* 150–152.

to Christ in the first two examples who hold the martyrs' cross (Figure 5) are probably Peter and Paul, due to their heavenly ranking. The rest of the figures who carry wreaths, by the fifth century, were well established as imagery signifying martyrs.

It is thus important to note just how significantly the imagery of the wreath-crown has been expanded. The wreath, which dominated sarcophagi iconography, represented victory over death and alluded to the necessary suffering of Jesus to procure rightful crowning and victory in heaven. The wreath-crown, while no longer affixed to a central, militaristic standard, remains in the hands of the martyrs, who receive their wreaths in heaven.

The power and influence of the cult of martyrs as early as the fourth century reinforces the pervasive importance of the martyrs. It shows their associations with life after death as well as their defense of the subjugated believers. It further demonstrates why they figured so prominently in fifth-century sarcophagi imagery. Indeed, the closeness and parallels between the martyrs and Christ, is highly significant to the Crown of Christ.

By the fifth century, when these sarcophagi were made, the popularity of the cult of the martyrs had grown to such a degree in the Romano-Christian community, it is thus unsurprising that one would find a plethora of martyrs on the sarcophagi of the faithful.

A large portion of martyrs that were revered came from the Roman persecutions of the early Christians. The cult of the early martyrdom encompassed several key milestones—it was only after Nero's fire of 64 that persecution of Christians was undertaken by the Roman government. Christians were a widely detested group of people and thus acceptable scapegoats for the fire.[48] Under Decius, starting in 250 to 251, all Romans were required to prove their loyalty by sacrificing to the gods. Many Christians refused to do so and were martyred as a result.[49] Valerian, in 257–9, then banned Christian services and hunted down their leaders. Christians were deprived of their status and property or killed.

After Valerian, the Christians enjoyed relative peace until Diocletian, who seized power in 284. His edicts of 303 and 304 banned Christians from using the courts, Christian civil servants lost their jobs, freedmen were reduced once again to slavery, church property and scriptures were burned, and Christians were martyred more

---

[48]Tacitus, *Annals*, 15.44.
[49]Charles Freeman, *A New History of Early Christianity* (New Haven: Yale University Press, 2009), 211.

frequently.⁵⁰ Complete toleration of Christians did not become official until the edict of Galerius in 311.⁵¹

These early Christians were killed by the Roman authorities because they refused to deny their Christian faith. An affinity with martyrdom, which became, from a Roman perspective, an irksome habit of the Christian cult, was an inspiration for the growing flock of Christians. To remain resolute in one's faith, in the face of death and in denial of the Roman gods and Roman authority, was felt to be the greatest victory for the early Christians. The martyrs were revered by their communities as the most steadfast and true defenders of the faith.

These martyrs who were killed during the Roman persecutions were particularly central to the cult of saints. The cult of the saints and martyrs was of great importance already by the fourth century, both in the religious life of the lay members and life after death. A letter from Ambrose (d. 397), the Bishop of Milan, to his sister concerning the discovery of relics in Milan can singularly demonstrate the unequivocal importance of the martyrs in the fourth-century Christian communities. In his letter, Ambrose relates the story of how he found the relics of Saints Gervasius and Protasius, who, as we have seen, would feature in the fifth-century catacomb frescoes of Naples. In 386 the congregation of Ambrose wanted their newly built basilica to be consecrated in the same way that Ambrose had done for another basilica—that is, with a collection of imported relics. But instead of promising a translation of established relics from another city, Ambrose promised that if he could find relics of martyrs himself, he would consecrate the basilica with them.⁵²

Ambrose fulfilled his promise. He led his congregation to a nearby church of the martyrs Nabor and Felix, who had been translated to Milan long before. Much to the chagrin of his fellow clerics, a divinely inspired Ambrose ordered the earth at the chancel rails of the church to be dug up. As the remains of two bodies were exhumed, Ambrose brought forth some members of the congregation who were thought to be possessed by demons. When the bodies came out, the demons, speaking through one

---

⁵⁰First Edict, issued on February 23, 303. For more information on the Edicts issued under Diocletian targeting the Christians, see Geoffrey de Ste. Croix, *Christian Persecution, Martyrdom, and Orthodoxy* (Oxford: Oxford University Press, 2006), 35–55. For the legal precedence of persecuting Christians, see Croix, *Christian Persecution*, 109–128.
⁵¹Croix, *Christian Persecution*, 35–41, 108–109; Freeman, *A New History*, 312–313.
⁵²Ambrose of Milan, "Letter 77 (Maur. 22)," 1, in *Political Letters and Speeches*, trans. J. Liebeschuetz (Liverpool: Liverpool University Press, 2005), 204. For the Latin text see Otto Faller and Michaela Zelzer, *Ambrosius, Epistulae et acta; Corpus Scriptorum Ecclesiasticorum Latinorum, 82*, vol. 3 (Vienna: Austrian Academy of Sciences Press, 1968–1996), 126–127.

of the possessed women, convulsed on the ground and addressed the relics of the martyrs by name. The demon implored the skeletal remains of Saints Gervasius and Protasius to spare him from torment. Thus, through demonic recognition as well as by the intervention of some of the elderly members of the congregation who recalled reading the names Gervasius and Protasius on some nearby headstones long ago, the martyrs were perceived as real and their powers awesome.[53] The relics were later translated to the new basilica which Ambrose dedicated and where he gave several sermons, placing the new relics under the altar.

This story demonstrates the power of relics and the importance that relics of the martyrs had among members of the Christian community. The congregation not only demanded that their basilica be made special by the presence of martyrs, but when the martyrs were discovered, they were seen to have exhibited extraordinary powers that led to their further veneration.

The letter relates three distinct ways in which the relics affected the personal lives of the members of Ambrose's congregation: healing, exorcism, and defense of the faithful. The relics were dramatically able to heal the people of illness and expel demons. Ambrose wrote that "many persons have been cleansed from evil spirits, that very many, after they had merely touched the garment of the saints with their hands, have been freed from the sicknesses from which they were suffering."[54] These abilities demonstrate the martyrs' closeness to Christ and that they could perform, as relics, the same miracles Christ did, such as healing the sick and relieving the possessed of demons. Their ability to perform miracles like Christ demonstrated that the martyrs were indeed members of Christ's heavenly court. For the congregation, closeness to the martyrs meant closeness to Christ as well.

But the martyrs were more than miraculous healers and exceptional exorcists. They were also defenders of the faithful. It was believed that the martyrs, who died for their steadfastness in their faith, through their relics protect the faithful still on earth against abuse. During the time of this letter, Ambrose and his catholic congregations received

---

[53] Ambrose, "Letter 77 (Maur. 22)," 204–205. For the Latin text see Faller and Zelzer, *Ambrosius,* 127–129; Neil McLynn, *Ambrose of Milan; Church and Court in a Christian Capital* (Berkeley: University of California Press, 1994), 212. Ambrose does not specifically say that the demons named the martyrs, but McLynn points out that it is safe to assume, since later in the same letter Ambrose compares the demons of the possessed women to the demons who named Christ as Lord in the Gospels (Ambrose, "Letter 77 (Maur. 22)," 209. For the Latin text see Faller and Zelzer, *Ambrosius,* 136).

[54] Ambrose, "Letter 77 (Maur. 22)," 207. For the Latin text see Faller and Zelzer, *Ambrosius,* 131–132: *multos a daemoniis purgatos, plurimos etiam, ubi vestem sanctorum manibus contigerunt, his quibus laborabant, debilitatibus absolutos . . .*

no small level of intimidation from the Arian rulers—a rival theology and Christian sect at the time.[55]

Ambrose and his people believed that these martyrs had revealed themselves to the true faith in order to defend against the ill-will of their abusers.[56] Not only, therefore, do the martyrs provide miraculous cures for the common people, but they are their greatest and most powerful defenders against heretics.

Ambrose's letter also distinctly points to the importance of the cult of martyrs in the afterlife. Ambrose relates that it was his desire to be buried next to the martyrs upon his death.[57] Even Ambrose's brother, Satyrus, was buried next to a martyr. Ambrose's epitaph for his brother speaks to the importance of such a burial place:

> To Uranius Satyrus, his brother Ambrose
> Accorded the distinction of burial at the martyr's side.
> This the reward for his goodness, that the holy blood
> Should seep through and wash his remains, which lie beside.[58]

Satyrus' burial adjacent to a martyr hopefully provided him with a holy cleansing by the martyr's blood, thus a spiritual cleansing and an even closer position to the heavenly Christ.

Burial next to martyrs was not just for important clerics. Even before Ambrose and his congregation of Milan translated the bones of Saints Gervasius and Protasius, it is suspected that the catacombs of Rome also had designated areas as being *retro santos*, literally "behind the holy ones." Graves in the Roman catacombs would often cluster around certain burial sites, possibly in an attempt to be close to a particular martyr who had been buried in the catacombs. The martyr created a holier space by virtue of his martyrdom.[59]

The example of Ambrose's letter demonstrates the important position already held by the martyrs in the fourth-century Christian community. The martyrs' relics were healers and defenders of the faithful—close to Christ in earthly power and heavenly position. Their particular association with life after death, and as vehicles through

---

[55]Liebeschuetz, *Political Letters and Speaches,* 130–134; McLynn, *Ambrose of Milan*, 158–219.
[56]Ambrose, "Letter 77 (Maur. 22)," 207–208. For the Latin text see Faller and Zelzer, *Ambrosius*, 131–132.
[57]Ambrose, "Letter 77 (Maur. 22)," 208–209. For the Latin text see Faller and Zelzer, *Ambrosius*, 134–135.
[58]Quoted from McLynn, *Ambrose of Milan*, 78: *Uranio Satyro supremum frater honorem/ martyris ad laevam detulit Ambrosius./ Haec meriti merces ut sacri sanguinis umor/ finitimas penetrans adluat excubias.*
[59]Leonard Rutgers, *Subterranean Rome; In Search of the Roots of Christianity in the Catacombs of the Eternal City* (Leuven: Peeters, 2000), 74–76.

which Christians could become closer to Christ in heaven, makes their popularity on sarcophagi by the fifth century more explicable.

Martyrs as imitators of the passion

By the fourth century, the concept of martyrs as Christ-like was demonstrated by a relic's ability to heal the faithful and expel their demons. Martyrs were imitators of Christ. They were expected to endure suffering, humiliation, and death. Like Christ, they had to endure the hardships of abuse in order to be victorious over death, win salvation for themselves, and be an inspiration for others. The Gospels set the precedent of suffering for the sake of salvation. In Mark 8:34–35, Jesus discusses what it means to follow him:

> He called the crowd with his disciples, and said to them, 'If any want to become my followers, let them deny themselves and take up their cross and follow me. For those who want to save their life will lose it, and those who lose their life for my sake and for the sake of the gospel, will save it.[60]

"Take up your cross and follow me" itself provides an imagery of death. Not only because the early Christian audience would know that it is indeed how Christ, and some of his apostles, died, but also that the cross is itself an instrument of death. As we have seen, even in the imagery on the sarcophagi of the Enthroned Christ, the Apostles carry crosses in imitation of Christ and rich in the implications of their suffering and death as martyrs. Jesus, moreover, provides specificity. He looks to what it will mean for his followers to lose their lives for his and the Gospels' sake: it will mean salvation, and thus victory over death. Jesus directly connects the suffering of the cross, denying one's life, and ultimately losing one's life, to final victory. Jesus expects imitation.

The patristic literature of the fourth and fifth centuries, precisely the period of the sarcophagi examined here, also encouraged early Christians to imitate Jesus' behavior. Augustine (d. 430), in his Tractate 116, encourages emulating Jesus and particularly cites his behavior during the humiliation of the Mockery:

---

[60] Mk 8: 34–38.

For [the evangelist] said what the soldiers did next; he did not say, nevertheless, that Pilate had ordered it.[61] "And the soldiers," he says, "braiding a crown of thorns, put it on his head and they wrapped a purple robe around him. And they came to him and said, 'Hail, king of the Jews!' And they gave him blows. So were fulfilled that which Christ had foretold about himself; so martyrs endure and are informed of all the things that it would please persecutors to do; so, while [his] terrifying power was hidden for a brief time, patience was first recommended to be imitated; so the kingdom that was not of this world conquered the proud world not by the ferocity of fighting but by the humbleness of patiently enduring; so that grain that was to be multiplied was sown in horrendous indignity that it might sprout in wondrous glory."[62]

Humiliation through mockery and the endurance of this mockery, Augustine suggests, will ultimately be translated into glorious reward for the martyr who imitates it. Not only is Jesus' behavior to be imitated, but Augustine assures his readers that the abuse and mockery will be enacted by persecutors. Just as the soldiers' treatment of Jesus will happen to the Christians, so must the Christians be like Jesus, and receive the treatment humbly and with patience. Jesus' endurance of the Mockery led to death and then salvation; so too will the martyr's imitation lead to death and salvation.

In this context, if we return to Ambrose's letter concerning the discovery of the relics of Gervasius and Protasius, it illuminates the actual acts that the relics of martyrs could perform in imitation of Christ. At one point, when the relics were being translated to their new location in Milan's basilica, a man named Severus, who had been struck blind some time before, came to the newly exhumed relics. Ambrose relates that "as soon as he touched the fringe of a garment of the martyrs with which the sacred relics were covered, light was restored to him."[63] Ambrose compares this miracle with a similar

---

[61] Augustine seems to be trying to excuse Pilate by suggesting that he does not know whether Pilate ordered Jesus to be crowned with thorns, whether the soldiers just did it on their own initiative, or whether Pilate ordered it to further appease the Jews.

[62] Augustine, "In Joannis Evangelium, Tractatus," 116. 1, in Migne *Series Latina*, vol. 35, col. 1941: *Dixit enim quid deine fecerint milites; Pilatum tamen id jussisse non dixit. 'Et milites', inquit 'plectentes coronam de spinis imposuereunt capiti eius, et veste purpurea circumdederunt eum. Et veniebant ad eum et diceant: "Ave, rex Judoeroum." Et dabant ei alapas.' Sic implebantur quae de se praedixerat Christus: sic martyres informabantur ad omnia quae persecutores libuisset facere, perferenda; sic paulisper occultata tremenda potentia, commendabatur prius imitanda patientia; sic regnum quod de hoc mundo non erat, superbum mundum non atrocitate pugnandi, sed patiendi humilitate vincebat; sic illud granum multiplicandum seminabatur horribili contumelia, ut mirabili pullularet in gloria.*

[63] Ambrose, "Letter 77 (Maur. 22)," 210. For the Latin text see Faller and Zelzer, *Ambrosius*, 137: *Clamat quia ut contigit fimbriam de veste martyrum, qua sacrae reliquiae vestiuntur, redditum sibi lumen sit.*

miracle in the Gospel of John, where Jesus healed a man born blind.[64] Ambrose points out that just as the disbelieving Jews interrogated the blind man's parents because they did not trust in Jesus' abilities to heal him, so too did the Arians distrust the miracles of Ambrose's relics. The martyrs' relics assume some aspects of the Martyrs' experiences and behavior—not only to perform the same miracles that Jesus did, but they are also held in scorn, just as Jesus was.[65]

As mentioned, the relics of Gervasius and Protasius were initially said to have been recognized by demons that possessed members of the congregation. In the Gospels, it was also the demonic spirits who recognized Jesus' divinity. Very early in the Gospel of Mark, for example, unclean spirits who possess members of Jesus' own community cried out to him, recognizing his godliness and imploring him not to hurt them. Jesus expels the demon from the possessed man by divine command. The demon was "convulsing [the man] and crying with a loud voice, came out of him."[66] In a similar way, the woman in the presence of the relics "was seized and flung headlong towards the site of the tomb".[67] Later in his letter, Ambrose points to several examples of exorcism and demonic recognition as irrefutable evidence of the relics' legitimacy. Only true martyrs of Christ, he suggests, could both perform miracles like Christ and also be recognized by demons.[68]

The fourth-century patristics also understood that the martyrs received their wreath-reward in heaven, as reflected in the art of the sarcophagi. John Chrysostom's (d. 407) Homily on Julian the Martyr pointedly discusses the reception of the reward in heaven. He, like many authors sermonizing on the martyrs, uses the analogy of the victorious athlete to describe their struggle and eventual triumph:

> They boxed here [on earth] with the devil and proved superior, but are proclaimed winner there [in heaven]. In fact, so that you might learn that this is true and the crowns are not given them here, but all the gifts await them there, listen to Paul who says: "I've fought the good fight, I've finished the race, I've kept the faith. From now

---

[64] Jn 9:25.
[65] Ambrose, "Letter 77 (Maur. 22)," 210. For the Latin text see Faller and Zelzer, *Ambrosius*, 137.
[66] Mk 1:24-25. See also Mt. 8:28-34 and Mk 5: 1-17 for more examples of Jesus' expulsion of demons. It is a common and dramatic sign of Jesus' divinity, and so too for martyrs.
[67] Ambrose, "Letter 77 (Maur. 22)," 205. For the Latin text see Faller and Zelzer, *Ambrosius*, 205: *arriperetur una, et sterneretur prona ad locum sancti sepulcri.*
[68] Ambrose, "Letter 77 (Maur. 22)," 211. For the Latin text see Faller and Zelzer, *Ambrosius*, 138-139; for a discussion on the topic see, McLynn, *Ambrose of Milan,* 210-211.

on the crown of righteousness is stored away for me" [2 Tim 4:7–8] . . . He ran here, he's crowned there. He won here, and is proclaimed there.[69]

The martyrs were crowned only once they had proved themselves victorious.

The Enthroned Christ sarcophagi of the fifth century depicts a heavenly scene. Christ sits surrounded by apostles and attendants. Those attendants who rush forward towards the enthroned Christ receive the martyr's heavenly reward: a wreath. This reward is given only in heaven and only to those who imitate Christ in suffering and death, as well as in the ability to perform miraculous deeds. They, like Christ, are victorious over sin and death and ascend, like Christ, to heaven to win their wreath. Their power is further exhibited through their relics, which even demons, as they did with Christ himself, recognize as possessing divine powers. Christ was crowned with a wreath by the soldiers which, though ironic on the soldiers' part, indicated his victory. The martyrs receive the same sort of crown for performing the same deeds.

The triumph of humility

Victory lies at the heart of Romano-Christian funerary art. Christ's militaristic victory over his enemies, his spiritual triumph over death, the Christian victory over death through belief and perseverance, and the martyrs' victory and the rewards of their triumphs all permeate fourth- and fifth-century funerary art. This victory is primarily portrayed through wreaths. Jesus' wreath in the Gospels, though given in mockery, in the eyes of the Christian community, is a rightful decoration of victory. In the early Christian commentaries and treatises, wreaths and Jesus' wreath-crown are consistently associated with victory over death, sin, and enemies. The art of the Romano-Christians reflects this powerful early ideology.

The wreath-crown and the wreaths on the sarcophagi of the Christians depict their belief that Christ, his martyrs, and his followers, win the race against evil and, through their belief in Christ and their own suffering, they are adorned with wreaths for their victory. The Triumphal Wreath sarcophagi and the Enthroned Christ sarcophagi depict

---

[69]John Chrysostom, "Homily on Julian Martyr", 1.672, in Migne *Series Graeca*, vol. 50, col. 661-666: ἐπύκτευσαν ἐνταῦθα τῷ διαβόλῳ καὶ περιεγένοντο, ἀνακηρύττονται δὲ ἐχεῖ. Καὶ ἵνα μάθητε, ὅτι τοῦτό ἐστιν ἀληθὲς, καὶ οὐκ ἐνταῦθα αὐτοῖς οἱ στέφανοι δίδονται, ἀλλ᾽ ἐκεῖ πᾶσαι αὐτοὺς ἀναμένουσιν αἱ δωρεαὶ, ἀκούσατε τοῦ Παύλου λέγοντος, Τὸν ἀγῶνα τὸν καλὸν ἠγώνισμαι, τὸν δρόμον τετέλεκα, τὴν πίστιν τετήρηκα• λοιπὸν ἀπόκειταί μοι ὁ τῆς δικαιούνης στέφανος• ποῦ καὶ πότε; Ὃν ἀποδώσει μοι Κύριος ἐν ἐκείνῃ τῇ ἡμέρᾳ, ὁ δίκαιος κριτής. Ἐνταῦθα ἔδραμεν, ἐκεῖ στεφανοῦται• ἐνταῦθα ἐνίκησε, κἀκεῖ ἀναγορεύεται.

the development of the understanding of the wreath-crown and of wreaths in early Romano-Christian thought: Jesus' crowning was one of rightful victory and his imitators receive the same reward for similar deeds.

Indeed, it seems to be due to the parallels that were perceived between the martyrs and Christ, and the broader popularity of the cult of martyrs, that the wreath's association with victory persists as long as it does—we find it enduring well into the fourth and fifth centuries, and, in fact, even in later occasion. Christ's Crown of Thorns is widely understood within the Christian community as a wreath of victory.

The wreath itself is not the prevailing image that will crown Christ during his Mockery in later centuries, but somehow the idea of the wreath as Christ's crown of victory continues long into the fifth century. The reason for this is due to the associations of Christ's wreath of victory with the hardships experienced by his followers, and particularly by the early martyrs. The image of the wreath persists with the attributes of the martyrs, who attend Christ in heaven. Reciprocally, the iconography of the martyrs prolongs the life of the wreath and Christ's Crown of Thorns as a wreath of victory.

The wreath will recur with the same meanings in the next few centuries. The imagery of the wreath, however, will explode in popularity by the Carolingian period and the direct association with Christ's Mockery and Crowning will fade. No longer are they bestowed only on Christ or only given as heavenly reward to his martyrs. By the ninth century, the Carolingians will bestow wreaths on everyone from Christ to the saints, as well as on philosophers, psalmists, and even with demons.[70] Thus, the Crown of Thorns and Mockery will take on new significance in tandem with one another, recycling the ideas of suffering, endurance, and humility into new avenues.

The strength and resonance of the Crown of Thorns will be transferred into a new historical context and a different center of gravity for western Christianity. One which transitions away from the Classical Mediterranean world onward to a world of Germanic warlords, who had become kings and emperors.

---

[70] For example: Utrecht Psalter fol. 84v, the Canticle of Hannah, depicts a philosopher crowned with a wreath by an angel; Utrech fol. 59r shows the psalmist also being given a wreath, a depiction which is consistently repeated in the Utrecht Psalter; the Stuttgart Psalter fol. 122r shows demons rewarding the Israelites with wreaths for their evil deeds, while fol. 147v shows a demon holding a wreath flying away from Jonah, who is regurgitated by the sea monster.

3

The Crown in transition

An image divided

Though we have traversed several centuries, we still only have a single image of Jesus with his Crown of Thorns. It is a peaceful crowning by a Roman soldier. There is no Mockery. There are no thorns. We did, however, discover a reach seam in the iconography of the wreath-crown in Romano-Christian art which becomes synonymous with victory and is seen being given to Jesus, his apostles, and his martyrs. All in imitation of Jesus' initial crowning during his Passion. Over the next few centuries, the wreath is somewhat detached from this very specific association. Wreaths become a ubiquitous aspect of Christian art.

The question then remains: when and why will the Crown of Thorns appear? Surprisingly, the fully-fledged, recognizable Crown of Thorns is still a remote prospect even in the Carolingian period. In this era of Frankish nobility and emperors—the most famous of whom is none other than Charlemagne—spanning much of the eighth and ninth centuries, art and literature flourished across Europe in some of the most unique and underappreciated ways. It is during this time that we find the emergence of two lines of imagery that will eventually lead to the first appearance of the Crown, though not yet in a universally recognizable, nor widely reproduced, image.

One line is the development of the scene of the Mockery of Christ by Pilate's soldiers, though it still lacks any depiction of the Crown of Thorns itself. The other line concerns the Instruments of the Passion—or a specific collection of objects used during Jesus' trial and death. Both lines of imagery may be seen as Carolingian developments which establish notions that will lead to the Crown's depiction in centuries later.

There appears to be only one pre-Carolingian example of a recognizable scene of the Mockery, though without a Crown. It comes from the sixth-century Gospels of St. Augustine of Canterbury (Figure 10).

In this 12-frame series of images which make up part of the Passion sequence, one square depicts an abused Jesus. He stands, cross-nimbed, in the center, surrounded by

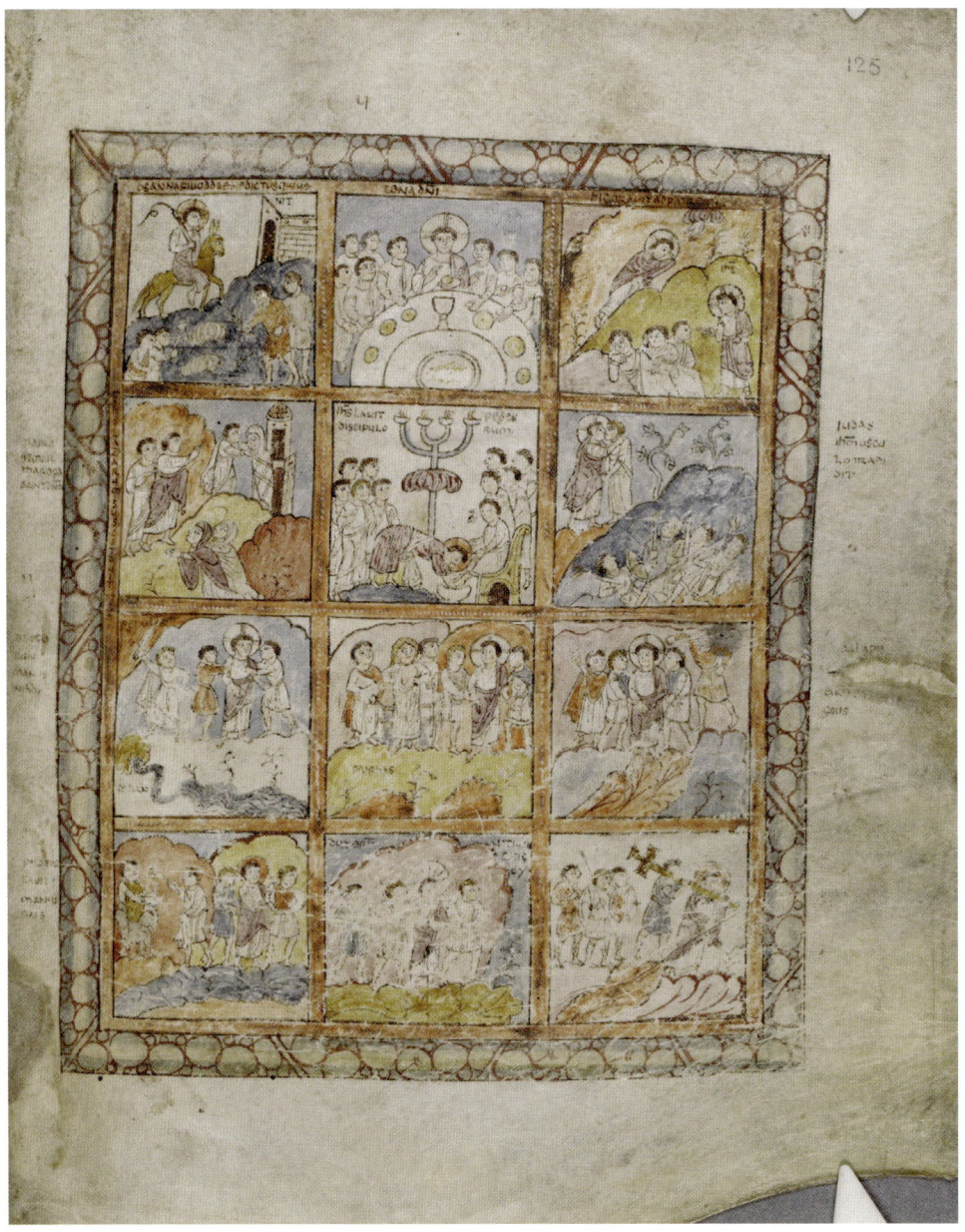

Figure 10 *Gospels of St Augustine, MS 286, fol 125r, Monte Cassino, c. 600, The Parker Library, Corpus Christi College, Cambridge.*

four men. Two men in blue cloaks hold Jesus' arms, and two others raise their hand to strike him. The upper frame bar contains an identifying marginal inscription, reading: *Hic alapis caedebant eum et pugnis*, "These [the men surrounding Jesus] struck him with blows and punches." The line is a jumbling of Mark 14:65: *et ministri alapis eum caedebant*, where Jesus is brought before the high priests, blasphemes, and is struck and mocked by the *ministri*, or servants, of the high priest.[1] The inscription adds the word *pugnis* (punches), which is not found in any of the Gospels' Mockery narratives with the *ministri*, but its inclusion emphasizes the abuse. The scene indeed reflects two men, one of whom, in a red cloak on the far left, stretches out his arm as if he will slap Jesus with the palm of his hand, while on the far right, a man in a red tunic attempts to punch Jesus with his fist. Why does this scene depict the narrative of Jesus mocked by the *ministri* instead of by Pilate's soldiers? The answer requires a short excursion into the composition of the manuscript.

The manuscript and illustrations of the St. Augustine Gospels were created in Italy.[2] The manuscript had made its way to England, probably brought by missionaries, by at least the seventh century, as attested by the seventh or eighth-century notes and corrections in the margins of the document.[3] Interestingly, these marginal additions are of an uncial form known in England during this time.[4] The marginal caption that identifies the image of the Mockery of Christ is one of these additions.

There is only one other surviving illustration that accompanies the text. It comes after the Lukan preface and chapter list and faces the start of the Gospel. It is an image of St. Luke with his evangelist symbol, seated in a chair, and surrounded by another set of scenes. The episodes that these scenes depict are exclusively found in the Gospel of Luke.[5] It has been established, however, by the presence of offsets of pigment on the folios, that there must have also been a full set of the Evangelist's portrait and another rectangular 12-frame miniature at the end of John's Gospel. It seems that there were at least two other 12-frame miniatures; one with the Gospel of John, where the imprint shows evidence of its existence, and another earlier in the manuscript. The first 12-frame

---

[1] This scene also occurs in Lk. 22: 63–65.
[2] John Lowden, "The Beginning of Biblical Illustration," in *Imaging the Early Medieval Bible*, ed. by John Williams, (University Park: Pennsylvania State University Press, 1999), 43.
[3] Francis Wormald, "The Miniatures in the Gospels of St. Augustine, Corpus Christi College, Cambridge, MS 286," in *Collected Writings; Studies in Medieval Art from the Sixth to the Twelfth Centuries*, ed. J. Alexander, et al. (New York: Oxford University Press, 1984), 13.
[4] Ibid.; Lowden, *The Beginning*, 44–45.
[5] Dorothy Verkerek "Biblical Manuscripts in Rome 400-700 and the Ashburnham Pentateuch," in *Imaging the Early Medieval Bible*, ed. John Williams (University Park: Pennsylvania State University, 1999), 100.

miniature may have depicted the birth and childhood of Christ, while the last miniature would be a continuation of the Passion cycle, including the images that the surviving middle miniature does not have, such as the Crucifixion and the Ascension.[6]

The marginal inscription accompanying the Mockery scene of the only remaining 12-frame miniature suggests that the image shows the Mockery of Christ by the *ministri*, and not by Pilate's soldiers. As noted, the collection of images in this folio is of the first part of the Passion of Christ and are not scenes exclusively taken from Luke, the Gospel with which it is in closest proximity. Rather, the images make up the cycle of the Passion, taking parts from all four Gospels. Since the images are a conflation of all four Gospel narratives, the illustrator seems to have been hard pressed for space and had to make omissions. For example, there are only eight disciples at the Last Supper and some figures are cut off at the edges of their frame. It seems then that the artist only had space to include one Mockery scene.

What the Passion imagery of the St. Augustine Gospels demonstrates is the beginning of a willingness to depict more completely the Passion of Christ and emphasize his suffering. It is perhaps the only remaining early instance of a Mockery scene depicted on its own. This innovation stands out as unique from the eighth century, and continues to influence the image in Carolingian art.

The Carolingian development of the Mockery scene

Returning to our lines of innovation in Carolingian art, the first is the appearance of the Mockery scene. Until the fifth century, there had been no recognizable Mockery scenes and, indeed, very few representations of Jesus suffering at all during his Passion. By the sixth century, however, hints of different aspects of Christ's Passion and suffering begin to emerge. While there are only a few depictions of the Mockery throughout the next few centuries, we will see that by the ninth century, the Carolingians use the imagery of the Mockery scene in their psalters to epitomize important Carolingian theological precepts about the importance of patience and humility in the face of adversity. The manner in which the Carolingians depict the Mockery scene will directly influence the later, more established imagery of the Crowning and Mockery.

Generally regarded as a well-read and well-educated group, the Carolingian clerics, and their contemporary European theologians' emphasis on extensive knowledge, on

---

[6]Wormald, "The Miniatures," 14–17.

continual learning, and on correct theology and interpretation seeped seamlessly into the illustrations of their manuscripts. It should not be surprising, given their emphasis on education, that the images of their manuscripts were largely didactic in nature.[7] The Carolingians believed that painting and art should complement the written text; serving to enhance the understanding of what is written on the page, and thus helping the reader truly comprehend the mysteries of the faith. As Theodulf of Orleans (d. 821) states in the *Libri Carolini*, images were meant to show "onlookers the true memory of historical events and to advance their minds from falseness to the fostering of truth."[8] Images could act as an aid in memory of scripture as well as a commentary on scripture, so that the reader would not forget the truth of the written word.

The didactic use of images is most obviously exemplified in the illustrations of the well-known Carolingian Stuttgart Psalter. In this Psalter, contemporary commentaries—that is, theological insights that explain the text—on the Gospels and the Psalms influence the artistic decisions made throughout the psalter. It is within the Stuttgart Psalter that the Mockery of Jesus first emerges as an illustrated commentary on Carolingian theology.

The illustration to Psalm 61 (Figure 11) of the Stuttgart Psalter depicts what is obviously the Mockery of Jesus. The reason that the image of the Mockery is placed with Psalm 61 is less obvious. To understand this image more fully, however, a brief discussion of the 'nature' of the Stuttgart Psalter will prove a worthy exercise.

The Stuttgart Psalter is a fully illustrated Psalter where almost every Psalm has at least one accompanying image. Such psalters were probably used for personal study and contemplation, particularly the highly detailed, exceedingly specific, but sometimes elusive, imagery of the Stuttgart Psalter. The psalter is attributed to the monastery

---

[7] Carolingian education programs were outlined in such mandates as the *Admonitio generalis* (798), in which Charlemagne mandated that his bishops found schools where the scripture could be properly studied and correctly copied. Similarly, in the *Epistola de litteris colendi*, he asks his monks to devote more effort to the study and teaching of literature, so that they might more seriously understand the scriptures (Frans Van Liere, "Biblical Exegesis Through the Twelfth Century," in *The Practice of the Bible in the Middle Ages*, ed. Susan Boynton and Diane Reilly (New York: Columbia University Press, 2011), 164. For the basic requirements of Carolingian clerics see: John Contreni, "Carolingian Biblical Studies," in *Carolingian Learning, Masters and Manuscripts*, ed. John Contreni (Hampshire: Variorum, 1992), 75; Celia Chazelle, "The Study of the Bible and Carolingian Culture," in *The Study of the Bible in the Carolingian Era*, ed. Celia Chazelle and Burton Van Name Edwards (Turnhout: Brepols, 2003), 3; and Marios Costambeys, et al., *The Carolingian World*, (Cambridge: Cambridge University Press, 201), 142–143.
[8] Quoted from Rosamond McKitterick, "Text and Image in the Carolingian World," in *The Frankish Kings and Culture in the Early Middle Ages*, ed. Rosamond McKitterick (Aldershot: Variorum, 1995), 298–299.

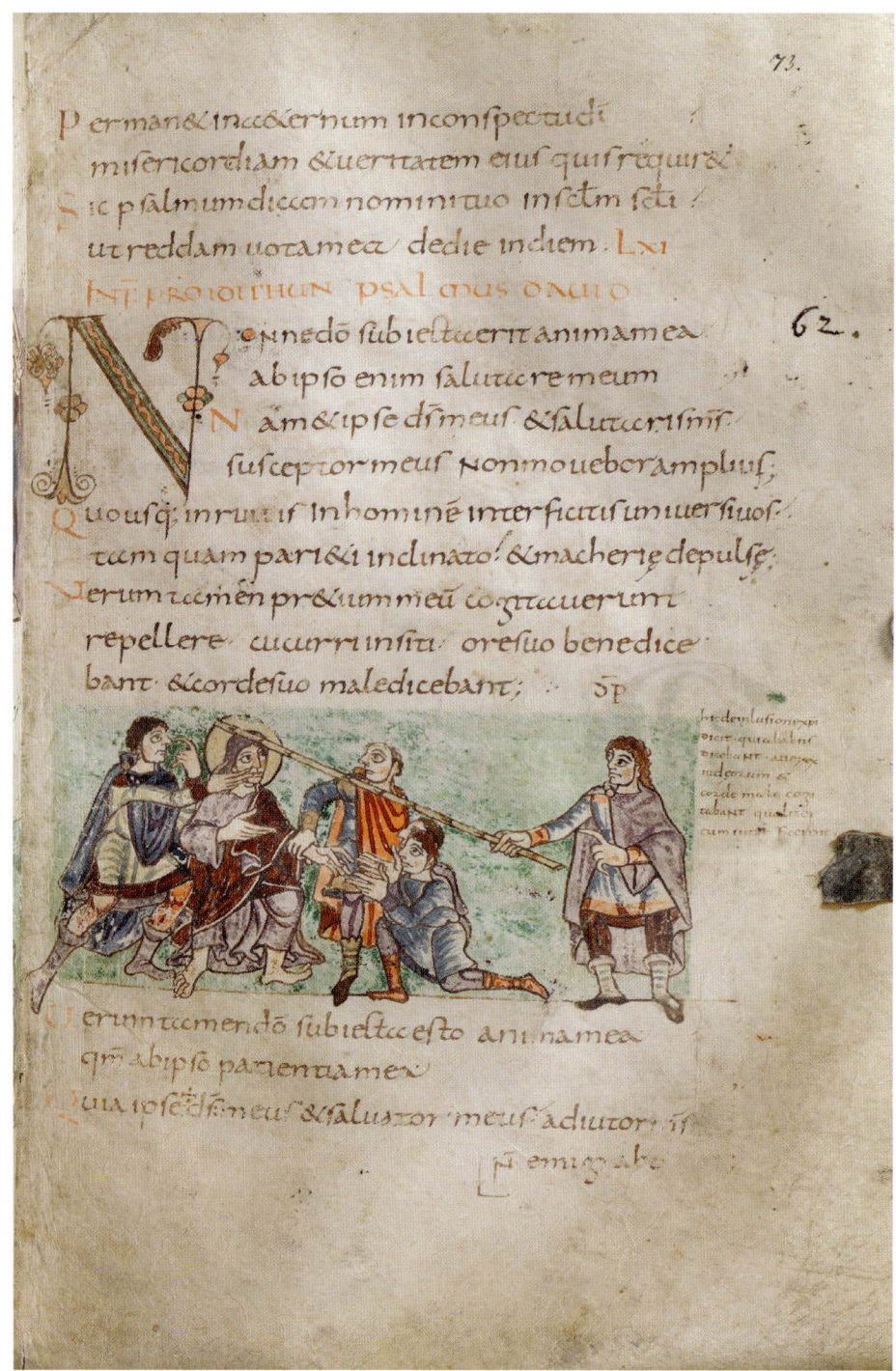

Figure 11 *Stuttgart Psalter, Cod.bibl.fol.23, fol. 73r, St. Germain-des-Pres, c. 820–830, Psalm 61*, Württembergische Landesbibliothek, Stuttgart.

of St. Germain-des-Pres in Paris and was created, based on paleographic grounds, sometime around 820–830.[9]

The illustrations themselves, which tend to be an interpretation of the verses just above or just below the illustration, fall into four categories: historical, literal, typological, and pictorial commentary. It is the typological and pictorial commentary illustrations that concern the psalms discussed here. The typological, or prophetic, images can be interpreted as prefiguring events of the New Testament, particularly events that are fulfilled in Jesus' ministry and Passion.[10] These psalms usually contain well-established typologies that are easily recognized in the images that accompany them.

Less easily recognized is the Stuttgart Psalter's unique category of pictorial commentary. These images, which make up a large portion of the Psalter's illustrations, reflect, not the words of the psalm or historical references, but are based on commentary on the psalm itself. While some of these images could also be placed under the typological category, they are more complex and elicit deeper levels of theological insights. The artist of these images draws from one or several commentaries on the psalm and creates a reflection of that commentary in the illustration.

The imagery on fol. 8r of Psalm 7 will serve as a useful example of the frequency with which pictorial commentary appears throughout the Stuttgart Psalter. The image accompanying the psalm depicts the betrayal by Judas and arrest of Jesus as well as the suicide of Judas. Jesus stands in the center, embraced and kissed by Judas. Two soldiers with spears and helmets stand to the left, one of whom grasps Jesus by his sleeve. On the right, there is a second depiction of Judas, who has hung himself. As he dies an evil spirit escapes from his open mouth. Verses 16 and 17 just above the image read: "He hath opened a pit and dug it: and he is fallen into the hole he made. His sorrow shall be turned on his own head and his iniquity shall come down upon his crown."[11] These verses could certainly be interpreted as Judas' evil deeds catching up with him in the end, but neither patristic nor Carolingian commentators of this psalm reference Judas, the betrayal, or the arrest when discussing verses 16 and 17. Rather, it is only Augustine's preface to Psalm 7 which mentions Judas. Judas is, Augustine explains, the New Testament version of Absalom, whose actions against his father is the subject of Psalm 7:

---

[9] George Henderson, "Emulation and Invention in Carolingian Art," in *Carolingian Culture: Emulation and Innovation*, ed. Rosamond McKitterick (Cambridge: Cambridge University Press, 1994), 266; Schutz, *The Carolingians in Central Europe, Their History, Arts and Architecture; A Cultural History of Central Europe, 750-900* (Leiden: Brill, 2004), 266–267.
[10] Horst, et al. *The Utrecht Psalter in Medieval Art* (Tuurdijk, Netherlands: HES, 1996), 67.
[11] Psalm 7: 16–17.

Among which interpretations, Judas, that traitor, again meets us, that Absalom should bear his image, according to that interpretation of it as a father's peace; in that his father was full of thoughts of peace towards him, although he in his guile had war in his heart.[12]

The illustrator uses Augustine's mention of Judas and places him in the psalm with verses that speak to the pitfalls of iniquity. It is a fine example of the Stuttgart Psalter's tendency to reflect the commentary on the psalms, instead of the psalm itself. Indeed, Carolingian intellectuals primarily used biblical and patristic references, like Augustine, to defend their theological arguments. The method of using tradition to defend one's theology, while not an innovation of the Carolingian scholars, nevertheless seems to have dominated their ninth-century theological works.[13] The theological arguments sometimes became the subject matter of the illustration, as notable in this psalter.[14] The Stuttgart Psalter uses the images to present the theology. The images reflect defenses, commentaries, and opinions on the psalms. This is a pronounced feature of the Stuttgart Psalter and makes it rather more challenging to read and interpret. In effect, it is a scholarly work. The reader of this psalter needed to be well-versed in patristic and contemporary Carolingian commentary to comprehend the intricacies of the illuminations of the psalms.

The scene of Christ's Mockery and abuse in the Stuttgart Psalter, which is found accompanying Psalm 61, (Figure 11) must be interpreted in a similar manner. There is no obvious connection, historically, typologically, or literally between this episode of Christ's Mockery and the text it illustrates. It is therefore safe to assume that the image reflects some commentary. To deduce the reason for the Mockery scene's placement with this psalm, we will need to analyze both the Carolingian commentaries on Psalm 61 and their extensive deliberations on Mockery of Christ.

The accompanying image to Psalm 61 (Figure 11) of the Stuttgart Psalter falls between verses 5 and 6. The image is of the Mockery of Jesus which includes a beating. As in the

---

[12] Augustine, "Enarratio in Psalmos," in Migne, *Series Latina*, vol. 36, col. 97.1: *Quibus interpretationibus rursum nobis traditor ille Iudas occurrit, ut Abessalon eius imaginem gestet, secundum quod Patris pax interpretatur; quia pacatus erga illam exstitit pater, quamvis ipse dolis suis bellum haberet in corde.*

[13] For discussions on Carolingian methodology for theological commentary see especially John Marenbon, "Carolingian Thought," in *Carolingian Culture: Emulation and Innovation*, ed. Rosemond McKitterick (Cambridge: Cambridge University Press, 1994), 179–182; Chazelle, "The Study of the Bible and Carolingian Culture," 11–12; and Contreni, "Carolingian Biblical Studies," 79–92 on both the method and the harmonization of the patristic commentaries.

[14] Kathleen Corrigan, *Visual Polemics in the Ninth Century Byzantine Psalter* (Cambridge: Cambridge University Press, 1992), 113–114.

earlier St. Augustine Gospels, Jesus stands haloed and surrounded by a crowd of abusers. In the Stuttgart Psalter, two men are on one knee before Jesus with their hands raised, palms up, towards Jesus in mock adoration. To the left a soldier in a blue chlamys cloak strikes Jesus' face with the palm of his hand while mocking him. A soldier directly on Jesus' left grasps his wrist. The third standing soldier, dressed in a purple chlamys stands farther off, beating Jesus over the head with a reed stick. This is directly comparable to the St. Augustine Gospel, in which men also hold Jesus' wrists, and one of the abusers prepares to strike Jesus with the palm of his hand. Both illustrations accentuate color, particularly Jesus' purple-red cloak, a shade which he is rarely depicted wearing in the Stuttgart Psalters.

The illustration in the Stuttgart Psalter cannot readily be identified as a Mockery scene by the surrounding psalm. The image itself, however, provides fairly conclusive evidence that the scene is the Mockery and beating of Jesus specifically by Pilate's soldiers. Certainly, the two men who kneel before Christ in mock adoration and the man who strikes Jesus with the palm of his hand could be from either the Mockery by the *ministri* episode or by Pilate's soldiers. Two additional details in the illustration, however, indicate that it is far more probable that the episode depicted takes place with the Roman soldiers.

First, the man to the right beats Jesus over the head with a reed. Second, Jesus is depicted wearing a purple-red cloak. In the Gospel texts, the Roman soldiers give Jesus a cloak of a specific color: in Matthew the cloak is scarlet (*coccineam*), while in Mark and John, the cloak is purple (*purpura*). While Jesus is seen elsewhere in the Stuttgart Psalter wearing this same purple-red color,[15] it is rare. It is especially rare in scenes of the Passion, where he is more often outfitted in bluish violet. This color choice reflects the illustrator's awareness of the importance the Carolingian commentators placed on the color of Jesus' cloak during the Mockery.

Hrabanus Maurus (d. 856), abbot of Fulda and student of Alcuin, points out in his commentary on the Gospel of Matthew, that Jesus was clothed by the soldiers specifically in a scarlet (*coccineam*) cloak instead of a purple (*purpura*) one. Purple, Hrabanus believes, was historically the color used to robe the ancient kings, and so, "The scarlet cloak was used for mocking"; that is, Jesus was further mocked by the soldiers who did not even put him in the proper color.[16] Christian of Stavelot (d. c. mid-late ninth century) in his own commentary on Matthew, similarly states that Jesus was clothed in

---

[15] Stuttgart Psalter, fol. 6v, Jesus separating the sheep from the goats; fol. 9r, Jesus preaching the beatitudes; fol. 6v, Jesus betrayed by Judas; etc.
[16] Hrabanus Maurus, "Commentariorium in Matthaeum", in Migne, *Series Latina*, vol. 107, col. 1133D; 1134 A-B: *Pro regia enim pupura chlamys illa coccinea ab illudentibus adhibita erat.*

a scarlet (*coccinea*) robe, "instead of the purple which kings were accustomed to wear."[17] Christian concedes that the purple that kings wore was similar to a red of a berry (*coccum*).[18] Christian explains that together with the crown and the reed, the soldiers dressed him with paraphernalia historically associated with kings and, so Christian says, this was in fact how a Roman soldier "was accustomed to adoring his king or his leader,"[19] Hrabanus also tackles the similarities in color between "purple" (*purpura*) and "scarlet" (*coccinea*). He compares Mark's use of the "purple" (*purpura*) to describe the color of the cloak, instead of using "scarlet" (*coccinea*), as Matthew does. He excuses Mark by indicating that the Evangelist was recalling, not specifically purple but a purple-red color that resembles a reddish-purple berry (*coccum*).[20] Typologically, Hrabanus says, the Lord was clothed in purple, like the purple-red berry, but it was foretold in Isaiah that Christ would be clothed in a distinct red (*rubrum*) and his clothes would be "like those [people] that tread in the wine press."[21] For believers, of course, the soldiers were bestowing upon Jesus, through the robe and reed, the proper sacred rites that were due to him.[22] While the commentators become somewhat entangled in color schemes and the instruments accompanying kings, it was clearly significant to them. The illustrator of the psalter noted that the choice in color of Jesus' cloak was important. He chose a distinct color, following the guidelines of the commentators, and even made sure that his color choice stood out in relation to all the other cloaks in the psalter.

The color distinction in the imagery reflects the commentaries, which demonstrates how integral they were as a major source of inspiration for this Carolingian program of illumination.

Direct commentary concerns the textual context of the psalm. The image goes with verses 5 and 6 of the psalm, which appear directly above and below the image, as is typical in the Stuttgart Psalter. The verses are as follows:

> 5. But they have thought to cast away my price; I ran in thirst: they bless with their mouth, but they curse with their heart. Selah.

> 6. But be thou, O my soul, subject to God, for from him is my patience.

---

[17]Christian of Stavelot, "Expositio in Matthaeum Evangelistam," in Migne, *Series Latina*, vol. 106, col. 1489A: *Chlamys illa coccinea, pro purpura qua reges soliti errant indui* . . .
[18]Ibid., col. 1489A.
[19]Ibid., col. 1489B: *sic erat consuetudo adorare regem, vel principes ejus*
[20]Hrabanus Maurus, "Commentariorium in Matthaeum," in Migne, *Series Latina*, vol. 107, col. 1134A-B.
[21]Ibid., col. 1134B: . . . *quasi calcantium in torculari* (Isaiah 63:2).
[22]Ibid., col. 1133D.

The marginal inscription next to the image elaborates for us. It explains that the soldiers are like the enemies in these verses of the psalm and solidly identifies the Mockery scene[23]:

hic de inlusione Christi dicit, quia labiis dicebant, ave rex iudaeorum, et corde mala cogitabant qualiter eum interficerent

"Here from the mockery of Christ it says, while from their lips they said, 'hail king of the Jews', but in their evil heart they were thinking how to kill him."

Pilate's soldiers say kind blessings with their mouths, "Hail, king of the Jews", but it is only in mockery; truly they want to kill Christ and are contemplating how they will soon achieve their heart's evil desire.

The second of the verses from the psalm quoted above asks the faithful to have patience. The Carolingian revolution and their oft-quoted predecessors emphasized in their commentary on Psalm 61 the need for patience and endurance in the face of this sort of duplicitous enemy.

Haymo of Halberstadt (d. 843) especially focuses on the kinds of suffering believers can endure with patience. Haymo sees these verses as a message to the faithful to prevail through tribulations such as persecution, injury to self, and especially deceit, that is, those who hide their imminent abuse with kind, flattering words.[24] Patience, which comes solely from God and cannot be manifested on one's own, will keep the believer strong against adversity: "Do not lose strength on account of persecutions, abuse, tribulations and the remaining bad things unjustly inflicted on you" but instead remain patient and vigilant against dishonest intentions.[25]

Cassiodorus (d. 585), who, though not a Carolingian theologian, is one of the patristic authors (like Augustine and Jerome) that the Carolingians oft quoted to form the basis of their commentaries. He interprets those who would "bless with their mouths, but curse with their hearts" as pagans and non-believers, especially those who

---

[23] It would be remiss not to note that no other psalter, either in Carolingian or the comparable Byzantine marginal psalters, which are so similar in many ways to the Stuttgart Psalter, depict the scene of the Mockery in conjunction with Psalm 61. For Byzantine marginal psalter comparisons, see Kathleen Corrigan, "Early Medieval Psalter Illustration in Byzantium and the West," in *The Utrecht Psalter in Medieval Art; Picturing the Psalms of David*, ed. Koert van der Horst, et al. (Tuurdijk, Netherlands: HES, 1996), 85–103 and Corrigan, *Visual Polemics*, 69–104, specifically pp. 97–104, which lists the psalms that correspond in both the Carolingian Psalters and the Byzantine marginal psalters.
[24] Haymo of Halberstadt, "Explainatio in Psalmos", in Migne, *Series Latina*, vol. 116, col. 400A.
[25] Ibid., col. 400A-B: *noli propter persecutiones, injurias, tribulationes et reliqua mala tibi injuste illata, deficere.*

say that they believe in Christ, but in their hearts they do not truly. Like Haymo, Cassiodorus understood that patience counters deceit, but goes further to say that "our patience is Christ the Lord."[26] Thus, if Christ is patience, then believers counter the deceit of the non-believer with Christ himself. Christ epitomizes patience and believers can therefore willingly suffer the enemy and rejoice.[27]

Bede (d. 735), though an English theologian who lived slightly earlier, his work hugely influenced his Carolingian successors. In these same verses, he sees those who bless with their mouths and curse in their heart as intending to kill those they are secretly deceiving. Those who are deceitful, he says, actively think of ways they can achieve their ill-conceived ends, but still say kind things out loud. Both patience and obedience to Christ will cause the persecuted not to retreat from adversity, but stay steadfast in strength.[28] God, says Bede, creates in the believer patience and strength. God is their helper "against attacks and persecution," guiding them to their heavenly reward for their endurance.[29] Bede likens this eventual reward to Christ's own resurrection.

Interestingly, Bede's language and the wording of this passage are very similar to the words used in the marginal caption of Psalm 61 of the Stuttgart Psalter. Bede also refers to the enemies wanting "to kill" (*interficere*) the one they persecute and "thinking" (*cogitare*) of ways in which they might do this. Bede states that the abused must also endure not just persecutions (*persequentes*), but also attacks or blows (*impugnantes*). The use of the form of *pugnare* speaks to a physical action, such as to the beating and punching of Jesus during his Mockery, not just cognitive abuse. The similarities between the language used by Bede and the marginal commentator points to the source of the margin's words and the reference for the margin's caption. While the mention of the soldiers is an addition of the caption, the idea of someone being persecuted by those who actively think of ways to kill their victim may come directly from Bede. The emphasis that Bede places on the patience, physical abuse, and ultimate resurrection, hints to the abuse Jesus endured as well.

Certain ambiguities remain. No commentator, either patristic or contemporary with the Carolingians, makes direct reference to the Mockery or general abuse of Christ

---

[26] Cassiodorus, "Expositio in Psalterium", in Migne, *Series Latina*, vol. 70, col. 430C: *Patientia quippe nostra Christus est Dominus*.
[27] Ibid.: *propter quem et adversa libenter patimur, et susceptae regulae observatione gaudemus.*
[28] Bede, "De Psalorum Libro Exegesis", in Migne, *Series Latina*, vol. 93, col. 803C.
[29] Ibid.: *'adjutor meus' contra impugnantes et persequentes, perducens me illuc, id est, in coelestem Jerusalem, unde amplius non emigrabo.*

when discussing Psalm 61 or those verses to which the image is attached. Only the marginal caption of the image in the Stuttgart Psalter does. Why then would the artist put this image of Christ's Mockery in a psalm to which no commentator makes direct reference? The answer may lie in a strikingly similar theology of the time that revolved around both Psalm 61 and the Mockery.

Alcuin (d. 804), who draws heavily from Augustine in his commentary on the Gospel of John, sees the Mockery as an example of Christ's endurance and patience. Jesus endured untold abuse during this episode, from mockery to beating, but it was his patience that made him victorious in the end. The patience of Christ, says Alcuin, ought to be imitated by his followers, especially those who would face similar abuse and mockery. Patience and humility during abuse by one's adversaries is the only way to gain victory and therefore eternal life.[30] As Jesus endured mockery and abuse, so too should his followers imitate him. For, "the kingdom, which is not of this world, overcame the proud world, not by savage battle, but by the humility of patiently enduring."[31] As Jesus did during his Passion, so his followers must endure the enemy's abuse so that they can be victorious.

This well-established idea among the Carolingians is analogous to the interpretation of Psalm 61. The adversaries who would abuse Jesus and his followers, either through physical abuse or deceit, must be countered with patience. Based on Alcuin's analysis of the Mockery, with which commentators like Hrabanus Maurus agreed,[32] the Mockery and Psalm 61 share a common theme that was probably well known. With this in mind, the author of the Stuttgart Psalter seems to connect Psalm 61's theme of patient endurance in the face of adversity with the Mockery of Jesus.

It is worth noting that Passion scenes recur in the Stuttgart Psalter alongside other psalms that refer to this same theme of patience and humility in the face of enemies. The illustration that appears on fol. 23 with psalm 35, for example, depicts Jesus before Pilate. Jesus stands in the center, looking towards a man on the right who raises his right hand in accusation. To the left sits Pilate who also points at Jesus. A soldier stands behind Pilate holding a spear. The image goes with verses 20–21: "For they spoke indeed

---

[30] Alcuin, "Commentaria in Sancti Joannis Evangelium," in Migne, *Series Latina*, vol. 100, col. 978A.
[31] Ibid.: *Sic regnum, quod de hoc mundo non erat, superbum mundum non atrocitate pugnandi, sed patiendi humilitate vincebat.*
[32] Hrabanus Maurus, "Commentariorium in Matthaeum", in Migne, *Series Latina*, vol. 107, col. 1133D–1134D. The Carolingian theology surrounding the Mockery clearly stems from the third- to fifth-century patristic analyses of the same episode, as outline above. Origen asserts that silence in the face of torment is the proper and right behavior for Jesus and his followers. John Chrysostom likewise points to Jesus' silence as humility and as an example of how one should endure abuse.

peaceably to me, and speaking in the anger of the earth they devised guile. And they opened their mouth wide against me; they said, Hooray, Hooray! Our eyes have seen it." Here again is the idea that enemies will "speak peaceably," but truly are devising treachery. The accompanying image depicts an accusation against Jesus to Pilate. Jesus' enemies have "devised guile" and carry it out in this image. Both Augustine and Cassiodorus connect these verses to Luke 23:21, where Pilate offers to release Jesus and the Jews ask for his Crucifixion. The illustrator seems to have drawn from two highly valued patristic sources for the image and appropriately chose to place Jesus before Pilate.

The Stuttgart Psalter's image of the Mockery of Christ is an illustration of patience in the face of adversaries. The Mockery of Jesus by the soldiers reflects, for the Carolingians, the pervasive idea that believers, who are abused and mocked by duplicitous enemies, should endure it with humility, like Jesus did before Pilate's soldiers. For the commentators, both Psalm 61 and the Mockery of Jesus demonstrate this idea of enduring patience.[33] By the ninth century, the Mockery was seen as the epitome of endurance and was artistically rendered in the psalm bearing the same idea.

The lone wreath

But, obviously, the Crown of Thorns is still missing from the Stuttgart Pslater's Mockery scene. The Crown, which becomes an important indicator of the scene of Christ's Mockery, appears only in the context of our second Carolingian innovation: the Instruments of the Passion. Here, interestingly, the Crown of Thorns is still depicted as a wreath.

The Instruments of the Passion, which is generally an illustration of the objects used during Jesus' trial and death, draw on three separate stories of the Passion: the Flagellation of Christ, where Jesus is flogged before being sentenced to be crucified;[34] the Mockery and Trial, during which time Jesus is questioned by Pilate and, as mentioned, is given his Crown of Thorns and several other items; and specific moments of the Crucifixion, where the lance and bitter wine were used for Jesus' continued shame and torture.[35]

---

[33]In a way, this harkens back to the idea of the endurance of the martyrs and the example it sets to all believers.
[34]Mt. 27:26; Mk 15:25; Lk. 23:16, 22; Jn 19:1.
[35]The lance was used by one of the soldiers to spear Jesus in the side, checking to make sure that Jesus was dead (Jn 19:34). The bitter wine was given to Jesus to drink while on the cross (Mt. 27:48, Mk 15:36, Jn 19:29).

The Carolingians, in their extensive exegeses and commentaries on the Gospels, invested a substantial amount of ink in discussing the tools used to torment Jesus. The instruments used in Christ's Passion, including the crown, whip, lance, and sponge are often discussed on historical, philological, and mystical levels. The Carolingian commentators looked for additional meaning in these Instruments as more than just mere literary details of Christ's Passion.

The Utrecht Psalter presents the first clear representation of the Instruments of the Passion. They appear alongside Psalm 21 (Figure 12), a psalm which is widely interpreted as prophetic of the Passion. The Utrecht Psalter was produced between 816 and c. 835

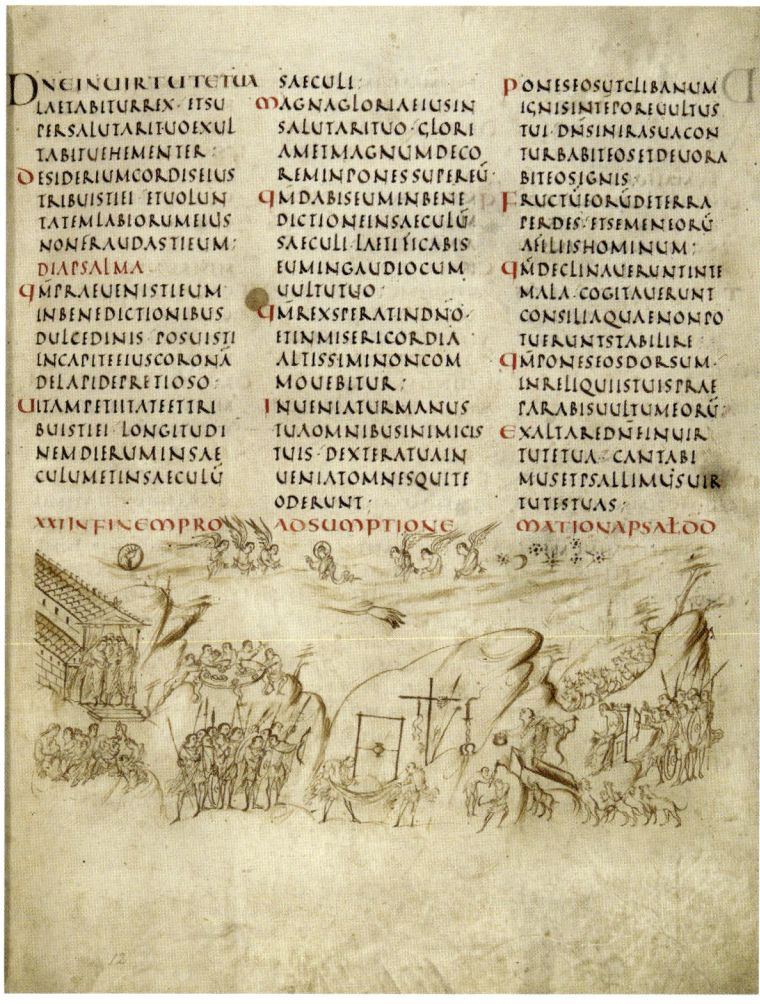

Figure 12 *Utrecht Psalter, Ms. 32, fol. 12r, c. 816–835, Reims, Utrecht University Library, Utrecht.*

in the ambience of Reims, probably at Hautvillers. It differs from the Stuttgart Psalter in that most of the illustrations are primarily literal as opposed to exegetical, and the technique used is light ink drawing—without color.[36]

There are several psalms of the Utrecht Psalter, however, that do contain typological illustrations of the verses they depict, though they are far fewer than in the Stuttgart Psalter. Psalm 21 is conveniently an example of such typological illustration (Figure 12). Verses 17–19 are those that are traditionally associated with the Passion of Christ:

17 For many dogs have encompassed me; the council of the malignant has besieged me, they have dug my hands and feet.

18 They have numbered all my bones, and they have looked and stared upon me.

19 They have parted my garments amongst them; and upon my vesture they cast lots.

The first part of verse 17 is literally illustrated by dogs which menacingly encompass the psalmist who stands in a sarcophagus. The second part of verse 17, "they have dug my hands and my feet," is both literally illustrated by men digging at the base of the sarcophagus as well as typologically by the presence of the Cross with the Instruments of the Passion (Figure 12).[37] The Instruments stand prominently near the center, under the undulating hillside between the hand of God reaching out from the heavens and the supplicating psalmist in his sarcophagus. The whip with its two fluttering tails hangs from one arm of the cross, and the wreath from the other. The spear and the sponge soaked with bitter wine on a stick are fixed in the earth next to the cross and lean listlessly away. Their reference to the Passion is unmistakable. Verse 19 also alludes to the Gospel narrative where the soldiers cast lots for Jesus' clothes. The Gospel of John directly quotes this psalm after the soldiers' discussion concerning Jesus' clothes: "[The soldiers] also took his tunic; now the tunic was seamless, woven in one piece from the top. So they said to one another, 'Let us not tear it, but cast lots for it to see who will get it.' This was to fulfill what the scripture says: 'They divided my clothes among themselves, and for my clothing they cast lots.'"[38] This is illustrated in the Utrecht Psalter as well by two men standing below a lot machine, who hold a piece of clothing between them.

---

[36] Schutz, *The Carolingians*, 269.
[37] The literal and typological illustrations for this verse may be an interpretation of the dual meaning of the Latin, *fodere*, which could mean both "to dig" and "to transfix," as to a cross (Horst, et al., *The Utrecht Psalter*, 68).
[38] Jn 19:23–24; the garment is also mentioned in Mt. 27:35; Mk 15:24; and Lk. 23:34.

The artist chose to depict the Instruments of the Passion to stand in for the Passion cycle as a whole. The Carolingians indeed looked at this entire psalm, and especially verses 17 through 19 as prophetic of the Passion, the Resurrection, and the establishment of the Church both in a literal and historical sense. Haymo of Halberstadt (d. 853) in his prologue to Psalm 21 informs his readers that not only was Christ the author of this very psalm through David, but that the psalm describes Christ's willingness to accept mortality and to suffer the Passion so that he might ultimately be resurrected, take on immortality, and establish the Church. Christ's establishment of the Church enables believers to also look forward to immortality.[39] This psalm, Haymo states, "relates human justice, neglect, and suffering, and then the glory of God the Father," which is seen through the Resurrection.[40] The psalm bemoans the human suffering of Christ, the neglected Christ who was abandoned during his suffering. All of which ends in his ultimate glorification and conquering of death.[41]

Throughout the rest of Haymo's exegesis, he alludes to several instances of Jesus' suffering in the Passion. Haymo looks to the Mockery in verse 8: "All they that saw me have laughed me to scorn: they have spoken with the lips, and wagged the head." Haymo sees here the taunting of Jesus; the jeers and provocation which were exhibited in the Mockery.[42] For several verses, Haymo looks to Jesus' time with Pilate particularly through verse 16 where "my tongue has cleaved to my jaws." Haymo interprets this verse as the moment when Jesus "fell silent, so that [he] would not respond to Pilate's interrogations."[43] Haymo also alludes to the spear that pierced Jesus' side after his death. In verse 15 the psalm reads, "I am poured out like water," which Haymo sees as an obvious prophetic indicator of the time when Jesus will be "cut open, pouring out blood from his side."[44] Haymo describes this pouring forth as a kind of cleansing, both by destruction and absolution.

Other commentators such as Walafrid Strabo (d. c. 849) also demonstrate how Psalm 21 is a typological reference to the Passion. For verse 18, "They have numbered all my bones", Strabo suggests that the author is describing the punishment of the cross,

---

[39]Haymo of Halberstadt, "Explainatio in Psalmos," in Migne *Series Latina*, vol. 116, col. 262C-D.
[40]Ibid., col. 262D: *Proponit enim hominem justum derelictum et passum, et etiam gloriam Dei Patris quam exhibet ei Christus resuscitates.*
[41]Ibid., col. 265A.
[42]Ibid., col. 264D.
[43]Ibid., col. 266A: *"Et lingua mea adhaesit faucibus meis"* . . . *conticui, ut nec Pilato interroganti responderem.*
[44]Ibid., col. 265C: *occisus sum fundendo sanguinem in latere.*

and how those who persecuted Jesus and sought to kill him and his apostles, looked on his pain with delight.[45]

The explanation of Haymo and others of Psalm 21 outlines how the psalm is perceived as both a prophecy and a literal description of Christ's Passion. They also use examples from the verses of the psalm to explain how they illustrate different episodes of the Passion. The depiction of the Instruments in the Utrecht Psalter accompanying Psalm 21 does the same, artistically. They are reflective of the intention of the psalm itself: to holistically represent Jesus' greatest moments of suffering during the Passion, especially the Flagellation, Mockery and Trial, and Crucifixion. They are artistic representations of the verses of the psalm, each typologically referencing these moments of Jesus' suffering.

The rise of the Instruments of the Passion

But still unanswered is from where the depictions of the imagery of the Instruments came. The Stuttgart Psalter illustration of the Mockery was taken at least in part from images like the one found in the St. Augustine Gospel. There is no known prototype, however, for the Utrecht theme of depicting all the Instruments together as a reference to the whole Passion. It seems to be an original creation based largely on both prior and separate representations of some of the Instruments found in Byzantine art, eighth-century Western art, and also draws on the details of the Carolingian commentaries.

The Carolingian commentators, as seen above, through formal tractates, editing, analysis, rearranging of patristic sources, and homilies, meticulously plot out the meaning of the Gospel texts. They often analyze each verse and every word of every moment of the Gospel account. For the commentators, each episode of the Gospels contains several layers of meaning. Specifically, the moments of the Passion are analyzed on historical, philological, and mystical levels.[46] The tools used during the Mockery, Flagellation, and Crucifixion were no exception. They took great pains to elicit these several layers of meaning and their emphases were exhibited in the art of the time.

We will start with the theme of the Flagellation of Christ. It is the whip, which was used to flog Jesus, that is generally depicted, but it did not appear in Western art until

---

[45] Walafrid Strabo, "Theologica," in Migne, *Series Latina*, vol. 113, col. 875A.
[46] For a separate analysis of the literal, historical, and allegorical levels of interpretation in Carolingian commentary, see Celia Chazelle, *The Crucified God in the Carolingian Era; Theology and Art of Christ's Passion* (Cambridge: Cambridge University Press, 2001), 143–146.

ninth-century Carolingian depictions. The Flagellation is, apparently, a new creation in their psalters, beginning with the Utrecht Psalter. There are also few if any precedents for representations of the whip in either the Western or the Byzantine spheres.[47] Thus, once again, the innovative addition of the Flagellation in Carolingian art probably sprung from the attention given to the episode in the contemporary commentaries.

The Utrecht Psalter depicts the Flagellation scene in the Canticle of Habbacuc, one of the odes appended to the psalms on fol. 85v. In the middle register of the illustration are scenes from the Life of Christ, which were probably prompted by verse 13: "you went forth for the salvation of thy people." The Flagellation is depicted towards the center of the image between the nativity and the Crucifixion. Jesus stands bound to a column, which is an extra-scriptural addition, and whipped.[48] Jesus is clothed in a long robe, but his face is smudged, so it is difficult to discern whether he is facing frontally. Two men stand on either side of Jesus holding two-tailed whips, extending them above their heads and beating Jesus. The two-tailed whips are identical to the whip that hangs from the cross in the illustration of the Instruments of the Passion found in Psalm 21 of the Utrecht Psalter (Figure 12). As one of the earliest Carolingian Psalters, the Utrecht's imagery of the Flagellation probably influenced a reoccurrence of the scene in the Stuttgart Psalter and several representations in ivory.[49]

The Stuttgart Psalter contains a rather provocative Flagellation scene which accompanies Psalm 35 on fol. 43v, verses 15–16: "But they rejoiced against me, and came together: scourges were gathered together upon me, and I knew not. They were separated, and repented not: they tempted me, they scoffed at me with scorn, they gnashed upon me with their teeth." Jesus is nude in the illustration, with his back to the viewer covered in bloody wounds. As in the Utrecht Psalter, Jesus is bound to a column, this time with a leafy capital. Jesus is flanked by two clothed tormentors, both of whom raise a scourge or whip above their heads and gesture mockingly at Jesus. The whips have three long tails, as opposed to the two of the Utrecht Psalter, but they are similar in design.

True to form, the Stuttgart Psalter's addition of the bleeding Jesus and the mocking tormentors, speaks to its tendency to reflect a significant level of contemporary commentary. The exegesis of the psalm is clear from the verses' mention of the gathering scourges and being scorned. The scene depicts both scoffing, from the gestures of the

---

[47]Schiller, *Iconography*, 66.
[48]The column itself will become the focus of Carolingian exegeses when discussing the Flagellation of Christ, as will be outlined below.
[49]Chazelle, *The Crucified God*, 243–244.

abusers, as well as scourges in the form of whips. These verses from Psalm 35 are well-known typologies of the Flagellation and the image itself visualizes the Carolingian fixation on the humanity of Christ—the human aspects of Jesus that made him vulnerable to bleeding and suffering.[50]

The image of the Flagellation persisted in Carolingian art, especially in ivory carvings which became a popular medium for the Crucifixion and scenes from the Passion.[51] The Louvre Ivory, probably made in Metz c. 850 (Figure 13), is covered with scenes from the Passion. It depicts an extensive Passion sequence from the Betrayal of Jesus in the Garden of Gethsemane at the bottom of the ivory to the Ascension at the top. The second register from the bottom depicts Jesus prophesying Peter's denial (complete with crowing rooster) Jesus before Pilate, and the Flagellation. In this latter image a rather large Jesus is tied again to a stylized column reminiscent of the Stuttgart's slightly simpler column. As in the Stuttgart Psalter example, Jesus stands with his back to the viewer. He is surrounded by two men who beat him. At variance with the Utrecht and Stuttgart Psalters, however, the men use large sticks rather than whips to beat Jesus.

For the Carolingian commentators, the Flagellation of Christ should speak to the faithful as an example of the liberation from sins. Jesus' flogging, says Hrabanus, liberates Christians of their sins. It also demonstrates to followers how to go through trials of their own. Their tribulations allow them to prove themselves as believers who endure the worst physical abuses.[52] As with many moments of Christ's Passion, Hrabanus explains that the flogging of Jesus was preordained: "[the flogging] was done because it was written, 'many are the whips of the sinner' (Psalm 31:10), and since he

---

[50] Lynda Coon, "Gendering Dark Age Jesus." *Gender & History* 28:1 (2016): 16–18.
[51] It is worth noting that among the many scenes of the Passion included on Carolingian ivory carvings, there is no distinguishable Mockery scene. There may be several ambiguous references to the Mockery when Christ is before Pilate, such as in the ivory book cover of the Drogo Gospels and the Louvre Carolingian ivory cover (Figure 13). In both these ivories, there is an individual who stands behind Christ as he is presented before Pilate, who may have his hand raised in mockery. But it is a dubious association and would constitute an unprecedented conflation of events. Instead, he is most likely an accuser or represents the crowd demanding Jesus' Crucifixion. In the Louvre Carolingian Ivory (Figure 13) the last scene on the bottom row at first glance is also ambiguous. Here it almost appears as though the central figure is surrounded by two other figures beating him with a stick and slapping him. On closer inspection, however, the man on the left is Jesus, carrying a scroll in his left hand with his right hand up to the ear of the central man, who wears a short tunic. The man on the right swings a sword at the central man's head. This is the scene in the garden of Gethsemane, when a disciple cuts off the ear of one of the servants of the high priest who comes to arrest Jesus, and Jesus heals his ear (Mt. 26:51; Mk 14:47; Lk. 22:50–51, only in Luke does Jesus actually heal the ear; Jn 18: 10, only in John is the disciple who cuts off the ear specifically named as Peter). Again, to place this as a Mockery or beating scene would be out of sequence with an otherwise sequential pictorial narrative.
[52] Hrabanus Maurus, "Commentariorium in Matthaeum", in Migne, *Series Latina*, vol. 107, col. 1133C.

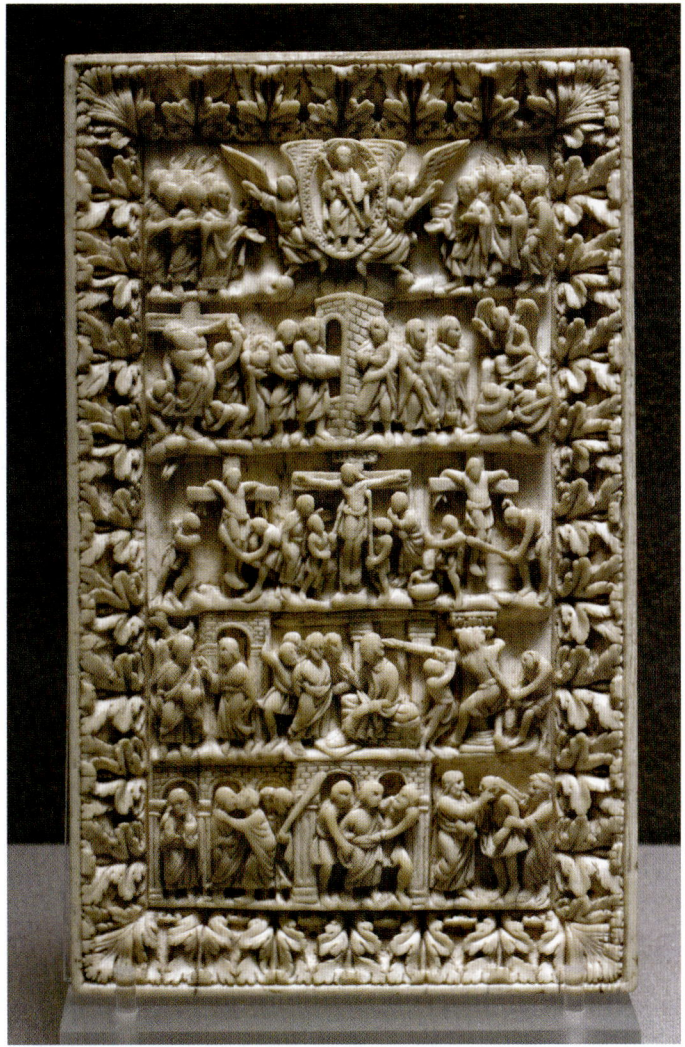

Figure 13 *Carolingian Ivory with Scenes of the Passion, Metz, c. 850, Louvre, Paris.*

was flogged, we are liberated by the beating, as scripture says. 'Nor shall the scourge come near your dwelling place' (Psalm 90:10)."[53] The Flagellation represents Christ taking on sin. The whips are the abuses that sin causes, and when Jesus is flogged, it is seen as he himself taking on humanity's sins and enduring them so that such metaphorical scourges cannot touch the believer.

---

[53] Ibid.: *Hoc autem factum est, ut quia scriptum est: "Multa flagella peccatorum'" illo flagellato nos a verberibus liberaremur, dicente Scriptura: "Flagellum non appropinquabit tabernaculo tuo."*

But Hrabanus and Christian of Stavelot also explain the Flagellation historically, which was a unique layer of interpretation particular to the Carolingian commentators.[54] They often attempted to look at the situation through the eyes of the first-century Jews and Romans, instead of solely through their own perspective. The Flagellation, says Hrabanus and Christian, happened according to Roman law: "Although Pilate was unwilling to have [Jesus] scourged, this was done because Roman law commanded it; that he who is about to be crucified, is scourged beforehand."[55] The commentators also insist that the Flagellation was ordered by Pilate as an attempt to satiate the Jews so that they would not ask for Jesus' death, which Pilate believed Jesus did not deserve. Alcuin explains that Pilate hoped the physical injuries would be enough for the Jews: "Here it is believed that Pilate had no other reason to do this except in order that [Jesus'] injuries satiate the Jews."[56] Hrabanus also indicates that Pilate, in addition to physically harming Jesus, hoped that the soldier's mockery and the shame which was inflicted upon him would "stop [the Jews] from thirsting for his death."[57]

The Flagellation is thus explained on several levels: as an act historically prescribed by Roman law, as a relatively benign act of Pilate as opposed to the vilified Jews, and as a mystical example of the believer's own liberation.

Christian delves even deeper into the Flagellation with a reference to contemporary miracles at the site of Jesus' flogging. He explains to his reader that the column upon which Jesus was tied and scourged, which appears consistently in the artistic examples, is still in Jerusalem. Frequently, women who are unable to conceive or produce milk for their babies will come to the column. After their visit they will have "blessed wombs."[58] Such details of the column and contemporary details of the holy sites of Jerusalem may, along with the extensive theology, have not only contributed to the appearance in the Carolingian psalters of the previously unprecedented scene of the

---

[54]Chazelle, *The Crucified God*, 143–145.
[55]Christian of Stavelot, "Expositio in Matthaeum Evangelistam", in Migne, *Series Latina*, vol. 106, col. 1488C: *Quod Pilatus eum flagellavit invitus, hoc fecit quia Romana lex praecipiebat, ut qui crucifigendus erat ante flagellaretur*; also Hrabanus Maurus, "Commentariorium in Matthaeum," in Migne, *Series Latina*, vol. 107, col. 1133A.
[56]Alcuin, "Commentaria in Sancti Joannis Evangelium," in Migne, *Series Latina*, vol. 100, col. 977D: *Hoc Pilatus non ob aliud fecisse credendus est, nisi ut ejus injuriis Judaei satiati . . .*
[57]Hrabanus Maurus, "Commentariorium in Matthaeum", in Migne, *Series Latina*, vol. 107, col. 1133B: *. . . ut satiati poenis et opprobriis ejus Judaei, mortem ejus ultra sitire desisterent.*
[58]Christian of Stavelot, "Expositio in Matthaeum Evangelistam," in Migne, *Series Latina*, vol. 106, col. 1488D: *Iam frequenter habent dictum beati ventres, qui non genuereunt et ubera quae non lactaverunt, et adhuc habent dicere.*

Flagellation, but also to the whip as part of the Instruments of the Passion.[59] Minute details became important, especially when they had miracles and deep, spiritual significance attached to them.

The main reason for the sudden rise in the popularity of the Flagellation is probably the connection made in the Carolingian commentaries between the suffering and the liberation from sin, and specifically with more frequent references to the Flagellation. The increased interest in the scene, with more detail and gruesomeness, also accounts for the appearance of the whip among the Instruments of the Passion.

The spear and the sponge on the stick have far older precedents in the imagery of the Crucifixion. They appear frequently with the aptly named spear bearer and sponge bearer, also known by their ecclesiastically appointed names, Longinus and Stephaton. As the iconography of the Crucifixion is a weighty subject in its own right—and already extensively and expertly addressed in the research literature—the following is limited to the salient points concerning these two figures and their instruments.

The precedent of their depiction was already set in Byzantine art by the sixth century. The Rabula Gospels miniatures, now in the Biblioteca Medicea Laurenziana,[60] contain a Crucifixion scene in which Jesus is crucified fully clothed and alive. On either side of Jesus stand two figures. Longinus, who is labeled, stands to the left, wears a short tunic and greaves, and carries a sword in his belt, indicating that he is a soldier. He spears Jesus in the side, while Stephaton, un-labeled and wearing a long tunic, holds a pail and offers Jesus a stick with a sponge soaked with bitter wine at the end of it. A similar Crucifixion scene reappears in a small cycle of the Life of Christ inside the cover of an approximately contemporary wooden reliquary box from Syria or Palestine, now in the Vatican Museum, Chapel of St. Peter Martyr. It is stylistically comparable to the Rabula Gospels. This Crucifixion scene also includes the pair Longinus and Stephaton with their instruments. One can therefore assume that the image of Longinus and Stephaton, as well as the elaborated Crucifixion scene had evolved to this form by the sixth century in the East.[61]

By the eighth century, Western art has several examples of the pair as well, including a wall painting from the mid-eighth century of the Crucifixion in the chapel of

---

[59]While the appearance of the Flagellation and the whip may have been influenced by the popularity of the column as a relic in Jerusalem, the relic of the Crown of Thorns which was also known to be in Jerusalem by the ninth century has no such influence on its depiction or development in the West. The proof and reasoning for this is addressed below.
[60]Florence, Biblioteca Medicea Laurenziana, Rabula Gospels, Cod. Plut. 1. 56, fol.13r.
[61]Schiller, *Iconography*, 91.

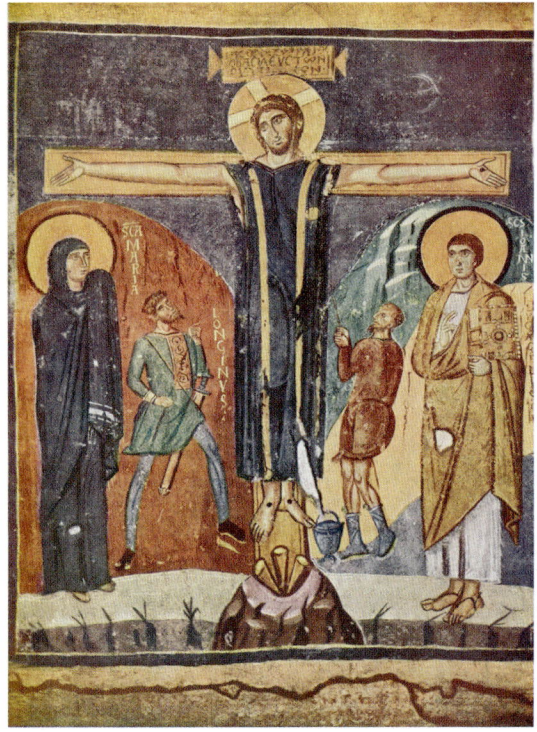

Figure 14 *Crucifixion, c. mid-eighth century, Theodotus Chapel, Santa Maria Antiqua, Rome.*

Theodotus in the Santa Maria Antiqua in Rome (Figure 14).[62] In this image Jesus, as in the Rabula Gospels and wooden reliquary, is fully clothed and alive on the cross. Longinus, labeled, is again on the left. He carries a thin spear, which he drives into Jesus' side. Stephaton stands to the right and his pail of bitter wine sits at his feet. His yellow sponge stretches up towards Jesus. The presence of Longinus and Stephaton is all the more remarkable because the image lacks many of the (conventionally more important) characters in the previous examples, such as the other Marys, the thieves crucified on either side of Jesus, or the men casting lots.

Longinus and Stephaton are indeed a major component of the Crucifixion scene as far north as Ireland by the eighth century. The Irish Evangelary from St. Gall, c. 750–60, contain a Crucifixion scene (Figure 15) that, while dissimilar from the Byzantine examples, clearly shows Jesus flanked by Longinus and Stephaton. Longinus raises his spear into Jesus' side to the right, which is a departure from Longinus' usual location on

---

[62]Ibid., p 94.

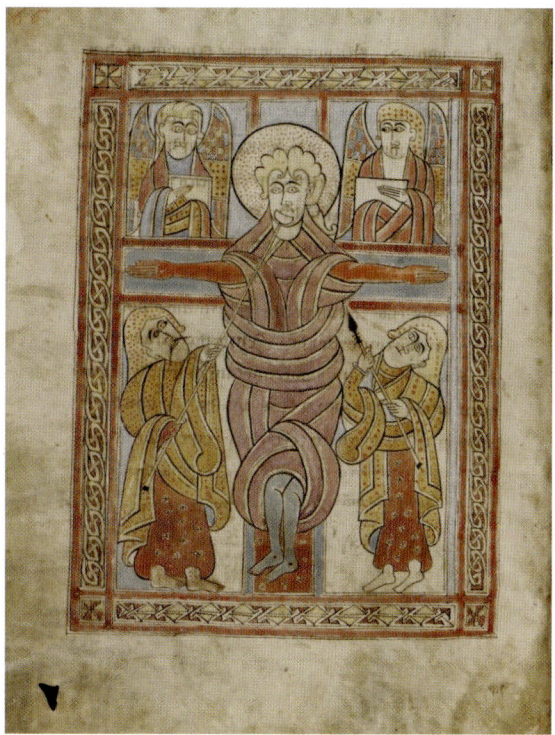

Figure 15 *Irish Evangelary, Cod. Sang. 51, p. 266, c. 750, St. Gall, Ireland, Stifsbibliothek, St. Gallen.*

the left. A stream of blood gushes into his face. Stephaton meanwhile bears a moon-shaped sponge to the left and holds it directly to Jesus' lips. The figures are more stylized, as was normal in Insular art of the time, but Jesus, along with the two angels and the two soldiers, create an obvious symmetry. Similarly, a bronze cast of the eighth century, also Insular, called the Athlone Crucifixion, now held in the National Museum of Ireland, shows a large, crucified Jesus, highly decorated with swirls in his clothes. He is surrounded above by the angels and below by Longinus again on the right and Stephaton on the left.

These examples demonstrate that the spear and sponge bearer were a surprisingly major component of Crucifixion scenes in the West, and precisely in the period preceding the Carolingian. It is significant that Western and northern Insular art of the eighth century, far from attempting to depict the full narrative of the Crucifixion, as in the Eastern examples, emphasizes the divine nature of the Crucifixion. It retains the angels, stewards of divinity; Jesus alive, which is often representative of his victory over death, rather than the death itself; and the symmetrical sponge and spear-bearer, whose purpose, as will be demonstrated presently, is to bring forth the life-saving blood from the side of Jesus. It seems that these images were the beginnings of a Crucifixion iconography that detracts from the narrative and focuses on the spiritual and theological aspects of the scene.

Since the sponge and spear bearer have been singled out as worthy to appear exclusively with Christ in Crucifixion scenes throughout the West in the eighth century, it should come as no surprise that they appear with great regularity, along with their tools, on the plethora of examples of Crucifixions in Carolingian art. There are many varieties of Carolingian Crucifixion scenes, from the detailed and political, to the stark and contemplative. A few examples will suffice to demonstrate the regular appearance of the sponge and spear bearer.

On the ivory cover of the Drogo Gospels, made in Metz c. 845–855, now held in the Bibliothéque Nationale, Paris, for example, the Crucifixion appears on the bottom panel. This extended scene depicts the two thieves with Mary and John standing on either side of the Crucified Christ. Below the cross stand the spear and sponge bearer. To the left, the spear bearer jabs Jesus in the side, while the sponge bearer, with a jar at his feet, reaches up towards Jesus with his ball-shaped sponge. The Louvre Ivory (Figure 13), c. 850, also shows an extensive Crucifixion scene. It is crowded and includes the thieves, whose legs are being broken by the soldiers. The sponge and spear bearer are close to the Cross. As in the Drogo Gospels, the sponge bearer reaches towards Jesus with a round sponge and a jar at his side. The spear bearer likewise reaches with his instrument towards Jesus' side.

The ivory book cover of the Pericopes of Henry II (Figure 16), which was carved around 840–870, before the manuscript which it accompanies, provides a similar example. Here the Crucified Jesus is surrounded by the usual figures, including Mary and John, a group of mourning women to the left, angels above the cross, Stephaton to the right offering a round sponge, his jar below him to the right, and Longinus to the left spearing Jesus' side. A female figure, next to Longinus, reaches towards the wound to collect Jesus' blood in her cup. This figure, who is generally understood to be the personification of Ecclesia, will be discussed in more detail below.

Another ivory plaque made in Reims c. 860–870, now housed in the London Victoria and Albert Museum, depicts a familiar symmetry. Jesus, apparently already dead on the cross, is flanked by an equal number of figures on either side. Above the cross, six angels crowd together to adore Jesus; Mary and John appear on either side; below the cross, eight believers emerge from their tombs at the moment of Jesus' death; and in their usual places, with their backs turned, Stephaton reaches up with yet another round-

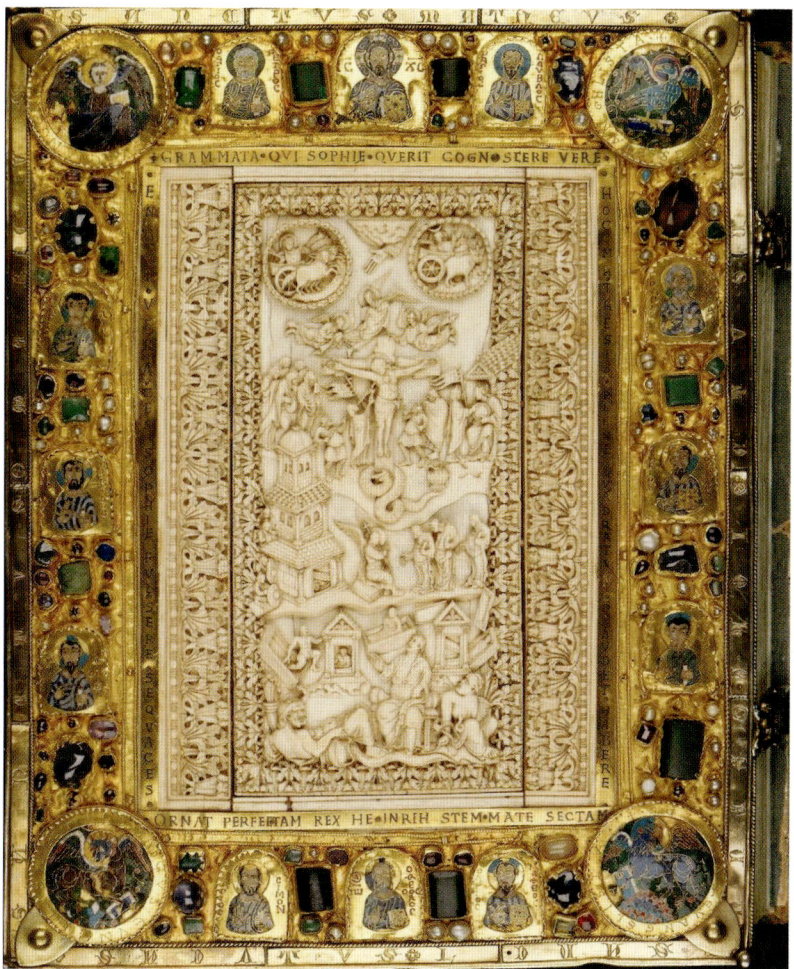

Figure 16 *Pericopes of Henry II, Court School of Charles the Bald, c. 840–870.*

shaped sponge similar to both the sponge in the Drogo Gospel and the Louvre Ivory, as well as the cover of the Pericopes of Henry II, while Longinus spears Jesus. This image, like the Insular images, is primarily focused on the divine with an eschatological slant. The multitude of angels, and the addition of the raising of the dead especially speak to this theme.

Psalm 69 of the Stuttgart Psalter predictably depicts a slightly different Crucifixion scene on fol. 80v than the above ivory examples. There is no intentional symmetry here and far fewer characters. Jesus is alive on the cross looking towards a haloed Mary mourning with a second woman. Jesus bleeds from a gaping wound from his side, supposedly made by an absent Longinus. To the right, the sponge bearer stands dressed as a soldier with a sword at his hip, holding a pail and offering Jesus a round, lumpy sponge. The circular and large shape of the sponge is once again similar in shape to the Carolingian ivory examples above. It is generally agreed that this illumination of the sponge bearer offering the vinegar to the Crucified Jesus accompanies verse 22 of this psalm: "They gave me also gall for my dish; and in my thirst they gave me vinegar to drink," which is taken as a typological reference to the soldiers offering Jesus bitter wine while on the Cross.

The long history of depicting the sponge and spear bearers, together with their tools, provided a plethora of examples for the Utrecht Psalter to imitate for its portrayal of Instruments of the Passion. Recalling that Carolingian art is didactic in nature, the prolific inclusion of the sponge and spear bearer, always with their instruments, speaks to their undeniable significance to the Carolingian audience. Indeed, the instruments of the spear and the sponge were themselves of great interest to the Carolingian commentators, which may have also influenced their extensive use in Carolingian art.

The bitter wine on the sponge given to Jesus and the spear used to lance Jesus' side are discussed on both the historical and mystical levels in the Carolingian commentaries. Christian of Stavelot asks why the soldiers would have had any wine, bitter or otherwise, to give to Jesus at all. He also questions why, indeed, the soldiers would have bothered to give Jesus anything to drink. Christian suggests that the soldiers brought the wine along since they knew the ordeals of the cross would make the criminals thirsty. But, since they were still criminals after all, the soldiers brought bitter wine in mockery of Jesus' and his fellow criminals' thirst.[63] The bitter wine is explained by Hrabanus as symbolic of death. When Jesus tastes the wine, "this indicates that he tasted the bitterness of death for us."[64]

The spear which is used to pierce the side of Jesus after his death is the tool which, most importantly and definitively, enables the establishment of the Church. Alcuin offers extensive establishment imagery in his commentary on the Gospel of John, all of which stems from the moment Jesus is stabbed in his side:

> "But when they came to Jesus and saw that he was already dead, they did not break his legs. But one of the soldiers with a spear opened his side, and immediately there came out blood and water". The Evangelist used a fine and vigilant word; he did not

---

[63]Christian of Stavelot, "Expositio in Matthaeum Evangelistam," in Migne, *Series Latina*, vol. 106, col. 1490A.
[64]Hrabanus Maurus, "Commentariorium in Matthaeum," in Migne, *Series Latina*, vol. 107, col. 1136D: *hoc indicat quod gustaverit quidem pro nobis mortis amaritudinem.*

say that his side was struck or wounded, or another word, but that it was "opened": that there is in a sense, opened the door to life, from where the sacraments of the Church flowed forth, without which is no entrance into life, which is the true life. That blood was shed for the forgiveness of sins; that water blended to greet the cup; this is better than both the bath and the drink. This was foretold when Noah was ordered to make a door in the side of the ark, in which the animals entered who did not wander to perish in the flood, which prefigured the Church (Gen. 6:16). Or for this the first woman was made from the side of the sleeping man, and is called life and the mother of lives (Gen. 2:22). Obviously it symbolized a great good . . . and this second Adam inclined his head on the cross and slept, so that thence he might shape his wife who flows forth from his side during his sleep.[65]

Like the animals who survived by entering the side of the ark, and Eve's life established from Adam's side, so too the Church comes into being from Christ's side. This imagery of establishment, together with the implication of the bitter wine as death, creates a neat symmetry. The bitter wine, or sponge which transported the wine, is death, while the spear is the life of the Church. This symmetrical commentary is seen clearly in the depictions of the Crucifixion, where the sponge and spear bearers flank the crucified Christ, simultaneously offering death and establishing life.

While the imagery of the sponge and spear bearer have a long history, the frequency of their appearance in Carolingian Crucifixion scenes and as part of the Instruments of the Passion also bore significant mystical and foundational relevance for the Carolingians. It is worth noting that eventually Longinus will indeed share his space at the side of Christ with a personification of Ecclesia, the established Church. Many Carolingian ivories, such as the previously examined ivory cover of the Pericopes of Henry II (Figure 16), succinctly demonstrate this theme. Ecclesia stands at Jesus' side, next to Longinus, and reaches up with her cup to collect the blood from the wound Longinus made. This therefore not only depicts the establishment of the Church, but

---

[65] Alcuin, "Commentaria in Sancti Joannis Evangelium", in Migne, *Series Latina*, vol. 100, col. 986 A-C: *"Ad Jesum autem cum venissent, ut viderunt eum iam mortuum, non fregerunt ejus crura. Sed unus militum lancea latus ejus aperuit, et continuo exivit sanguis et aqua." Eleganti vigilantique verbo evangelista usus est, ut non diceret: "Latus ejus" percussit, aut vulneravit, aut quid aliud; "sed aperuit": ut illic quodammodo vitae ostium panderetur, unde sacramenta Ecclesiae manaverunt, sine quibus ad vitam quae vera vita est, non intratur. Ille sanguis in remissionem fusus est peccatorum; aqua illa salutare temperavit poculum : haec et lavacrum praestat et potum. Hoc praenuntiabat quod Noe in latere arcae ostium facere jussus est, qua intrarent animalia quae non errant diluvio peritura, quibus praefigurabatur Ecclesia (Gen 6:16). Propter hoc prima mulier facta est de viri latere dormientis, et appellate est vita materque vivorum (Gen 2: 22). Magnum quippe significavit bonum . . . Et hic secundus Adam inclinato capite in cruce dormivit, ut inde formaretur ei conjux quae de latere dormientis effluxit.*

also the collection the sacrament, as Alcuin also discusses. Another parallel arises between the bitter wine of death given by the sponge bearer, and the redemptive wine collected by the Church to be given as a sacrament to the faithful.

As previously noted in the Insular crucifixions, Longinus has long been associated with the divine, foundational Crucifixion. The Carolingians bring this idea to the fore, placing Longinus as aid in Ecclesia's foundation. Alcuin's commentary is pictorially rendered in such Crucifixion images.

The Instruments of the Passion begin to show up as a group more frequently in Late Carolingian illuminations, particularly in the frontispieces to the New Testament of a complete bible.[66] The presence of the Instruments explicitly represent Jesus' suffering and the "weapons," or *arma*, which he used to conquer death. The continued visual representation of the Instruments references the commentators' increased interest in the tools used to torment Jesus, as well as the perennial theme of triumph during the Passion.[67]

The Bamberg Bible,[68] for example, made in Tours c. 834–843, is the frontispiece to the New Testament in a Carolingian pandect. The illumination of this bible frames the illustrations with a rhombus shape in the center. In the four corners the Prophets Isaiah, Jeremiah, Ezekiel, and Daniel gaze at the Lamb and the Evangelists' symbols, each of whom hold their Gospel book. The Lamb stands haloed in a clipea transected by the spear and the sponge on a stick. A chalice stands next to the Lamb as well. Interestingly, neither the whip nor the Crown of Thorns appear among the Instruments here.

The spear and sponge represent the Passion and Jesus' suffering, specifically pointing to the suffering on the cross. The spear is associated with the piercing of Christ's side, from which, according to the Gospel narrative, flowed blood and water. The chalice is paired with the spear as the "instrument" which collects the life blood that flows from the wound that the lance made, which was already depicted in Crucifixion scenes in the hands of Ecclesia. It is yet another representation of the establishment of the Church through Christ's suffering and Passion.[69] The inclusion of the Lamb as a representation of Christ along with the Instruments of the Passion by the Carolingians held apocalyptic connotations with Christ's eternal sovereignty.[70]

---

[66]Schiller, *Iconography*, 185.
[67]Ibid.: 185.
[68]Bamberg Saatsbibliothek, Bamberg Bible, Msc.Bibl.i.A.I.5, lat. Fol.339v, Tours, c. 834–843.
[69]Herbert Kessler, *The Illustrated Bibles from Tours* (Princeton: Princeton University Press, 1977), 46.
[70]Schiller, *Iconography*, 185.

Other complete bibles of the late Carolingian art also depict the Lamb accompanied by the Instruments of the Passion. The Saint Gauzelin Gospel[71] includes a rhombus held by seraphim containing the four Evangelists' creatures and the Lamb in the clipea, cross-nimbed with sponge, spear, and chalice. This image would become the so-called *Majestas Agnus*, which was strictly associated with the visions of the heavenly kingdom.[72] In these Late Carolingian representations, however, the Instruments of the Passion are more closely associated with the suffering that Jesus endured during the Passion and speak to the interest in the mystical qualities of the tools used for Jesus' torment.

Wreaths and undertaking the world's sin

As with the whip, the spear, and the sponge of bitter wine, the Crown of Thorns, not unexpectedly, held huge significance for the Carolingian authors. For both Hrabanus and Christian of Stavelot the Crown of Thorns, and especially the thorns themselves, represented the sins of humans. Not unlike the Flagellation, Christ accepted the sins (thorns) "into his own body that he might die on the cross for our sins, he who had not committed any sin."[73] When Jesus wears the Crown of Thorns, it is also interpreted as dissolving the curse bestowed upon Adam, and subsequently all humans, to toil with thorns and with sin.[74] The Crown of Thorns therefore contains several mystical layers for the commentators. Christ's "deigning to become mortal" in order to "undertake our sins" is seen through his willingness to wear the mock-crown, which itself represents sin.[75] The thorns represent both sin and the original curse upon Adam, both of which Christ abolishes through the Passion. The concept of undertaking the world's sins is placed firmly on the Crown of Thorns.

Like the spear, sponge, and whip, the Crown of Thorns appears among the Instruments of the Passion due to deep interest in its mystical and typological significance. The Carolingian authors' express focus on each tool of the Passion may have inspired the Carolingian artists to depict them more frequently in their art, finally including the first solid identification of the Crown of Thorns among the Instruments.

---

[71]Nancy, Cathedral Treasurey, St. Gauzelin Gospels, fol. 3v, Tours, c. 830.
[72]For a discussion on the development of the *Majestas Agni* see Kessler, *The Illustrated Bibles*, 44–48.
[73]Christian of Stavelot, "Expositio in Matthaeum Evangelistam," in Migne, *Series Latina*, vol. 106, col. 1489B: . . . *quae accepit ipse in corpore suo ut moreretur in cruce pro peccatis nostris, qui peccatum non fecerat ullum.*
[74]Hrabanus Maurus, "Commentariorium in Matthaeum," in Migne, *Series Latina*, vol. 107, col. 1134B.
[75]Ibid.: . . . *nostrorum susceptio peccatorum, pro qua mortalis fieri dignatus est, ostenditur.*

In the Carolingian era, several themes illustrate various concepts that will eventually manifest themselves in the depiction of the Crown of Thorns. First, the Mockery of Christ, during which time, according to the Gospel narrative, Jesus was given the Crown of Thorns, appears solely as a Mockery scene and lacks the Crown. For the Carolingians, the crowning part of the Mockery by Pilate's soldiers was secondary to their ideological concepts that surrounded the episode. The Mockery was an epitomic example of the patience and endurance required to defeat adversaries. An illustration of the Mockery is depicted in the Stuttgart Psalter with Psalm 61. The Psalm was itself seen by the Carolingian commentators as one which exemplified how to counter the duplicitous enemy who would speak kind words, but in their hearts wish to kill.

The second line illustrates Carolingian interest in the Instruments of the Passion, which conceives the first tentative appearance of the Crown of Thorns in the Utrecht Psalter. The Carolingians place the Crown of Thorns among the Instruments of the Passion, as one of a number of tools that represented Jesus' suffering. These Instruments also played a central role in the commentaries of the Gospel texts. They were scrutinized and dissected for every possible historical, typological, and mystical meaning that the Carolingian commentators could glean so that they could more fully understand the mysteries of their faith. This intense interest in the individual tools of the Passion may have led to their frequent appearance in Carolingian Crucifixion and Passion scenes and helped create the necessary foundation for the appearance of the Crown, which will later feature with more frequency.

Now the Crown and the Mockery must be reunited in one scene. The eleventh century will provide a recognizable Crown of Thorns, complete with distinguishable thorns, within its proper narrative context. The Ottonian Mockery and Crowning will utilize the theological developments of the Carolingians concerning the Mockery and Crown of Thorns and apply them to their own unique artistic interpretation of the Mockery. It is within the Ottonian and Salian depictions that the well-known imagery of the Crown of Thorns will finally be established and persist.

4

The Crown of Thorns—a humble and humiliated king

The Carolingians provided two important contributions to the concept of the Crown of Thorns. First, they created an unambiguous artistic formula for the Mockery, still bereft of the Crown, while also providing a theological and narrative context for its eventual appearance. Second, they depicted a suggestion of the form of the Crown of Thorns within the Instruments of the Passion. After seven centuries of thorough discussion, theological interpretations, and tantalizing flirtation with its depiction, the Crown of Thorns still lacks clear definition in two respects: it does not appear in its proper narrative context of the Mockery and it is not clearly a crown made of thorns. The innovations of the Ottonian artists in the mid-eleventh century resoundingly address both these issues.

The Crown of Thorns and Mockery do come together under the Ottonian dynasty, but in a very unusual setting—that of an enthronement. An appropriate backdrop for a crowning perhaps, but incredibly strange for a Mockery. Was it artistic trends or political and social undercurrents contemporaneously rippling through the Ottonian realm that allowed for this unique and innovative rendering of the Crown of Thorns? If the preceding eras are any indication, where theological trends and commentary directly influence art, the answer is likely, both.

As we shall see, the artistic adaptations of the Mockery and Crown of Thorns during the Ottonian and Salian eras, whether due to influence from politics, theology, or even patronage, are solidified—reverberating in motifs of the Mockery and Crown for centuries to come.

Establishing innovation

With barely any perceptible artistic preamble, it seems that it is only during the early-eleventh century, that the image of the crown made of thorns is finally attempted. The first example comes from the Codex Aureus (Figure 17). Its gold cover is dateable to between 985 and 990, and was commissioned under royal patronage for the Empress Theophanu and her son, the Ottonian king, Otto III. But the cover was made separately from the manuscript.[1] The date of the actual manuscript is debatable. Other than the front cover, there is no dedication, nor any sign of royal commission and thus no way of pinpointing a date for the manuscript, or its specific location of production. Generally, scholars agree that the manuscript's production falls somewhere between 1020 and 1030 and that it was made in the Benedictine abbey of Echternach.[2] This would place it somewhere between the reigns of the last of the Ottonian kings, Henry II, 1002–1024, and the first Salian king, Conrad II, 1024–1039.[3] The manuscript contains all four Gospels and was probably for liturgical use. The images are arranged just before the text of each Gospel. It is possibly the most all-encompassing life-cycle of Christ up to the beginning of the eleventh century. Each Gospel is preceded by a full four pages of illustrations, arranged in three strips on each page.[4] The image of the Crown of Thorns itself is inserted just before the Gospel of John. It is placed in chronological order, according to the Gospel narrative, beginning with the entry into Jerusalem, the betrayal, Jesus before Caiaphas, Peter's denial, and a gruesome Flagellation.

The facing page begins with the Crowning in a single panel with a gradated purple background. It depicts a dual-narrative scene. On the left side a group of men wearing bright tunics crowd around a dark-haired Jesus. They all walk forward. A man in a red

---

[1] Colum Hourihane "Echternach," in *The Grove Encyclopedia of Medieval Art and Architecture*, ed. Colum Hourihane (Oxford: Oxford University Press, 2012), 408–409.
[2] Peter Metz, *The Golden Gospels of Echternach*, trans. Ilse Schrier and Peter Gorge (New York: Frederick A. Praeger, 1957), 51–52; Schiller, *Iconography*, 69; Mayr-Harting, *Ottonian Book Illumination; An Historical Study* (London: Harvey Miller Publishers, 1999), 194.
[3] Grebe speculates, however, that the manuscript was instead made around 1045–1050 (Anja Grebe, *Codex Aureus; Das Golden Evangelienbuch von Echternach* (Darmstadt: Wissenschaftliche Buchgesellschaft, 2007), 14–15). This would place the manuscript squarely in Henry III's reign and allows Grebe to reanalyze all previous assumptions concerning the manuscript. Grebe argues that 1045 makes more sense as a date for this important manuscript because it was around 1045 that "the scriptorium received the utmost attention of the reigning Emperor Henry III" and the production of manuscripts was at its peak. Since there is little evidence provided to substantiate this, my own analysis will remain with the general consensus, which places the manuscript before 1030.
[4] Mayr-Harting *Ottonian*, 187.

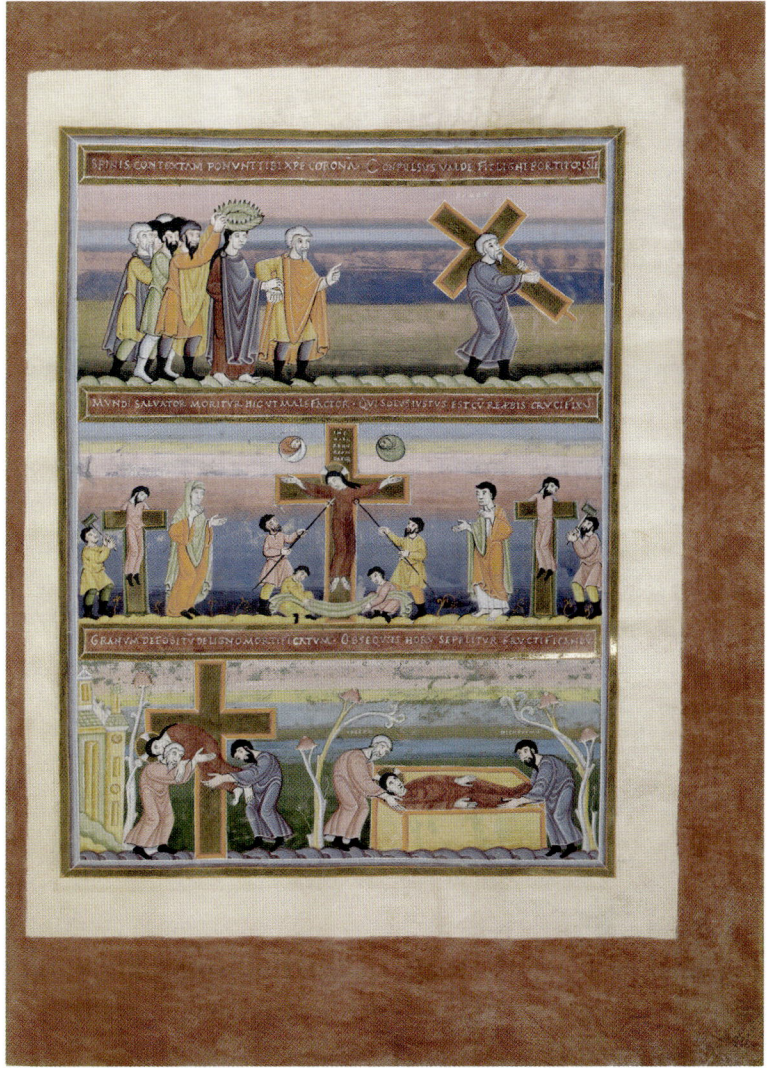

Figure 17 *Codex Aureus of Echternach, Hs156142, fol. 111v, Echternach, c. 1020–1030.*

tunic stands directly behind Jesus and with two hands holds aloft a prominent wreath-like crown over Jesus' head. The earth-toned material of the crown is twisted together, with small, sharp, triangular thorns. At last, we see an actual, woven crown inlaid with thorns. The thorns have been evenly inserted all around the top of the wreath, like jewels set in a crown. The crown is much bigger than necessary for Jesus' head. This prominence declares its importance in the image. Jesus himself wears a long purple cloak and, with both hands, he grasps the hand of the man leading the procession. The leading man ushers Jesus forward and points towards a man farther along in front of them. This cloak-less man on the right heavily bears a huge golden cross. His knees bend under the strain.

The gold-framed text above the image reads:

Spini contextam ponunt tibi XPE corona. Conpulsus valde fit ligni portitor iste.

They place the woven Crown of Thorns on your head, Christ. That man is compelled to carry the Cross.

The caption alludes to the moment when Pilate's soldiers crafted the Crown of Thorns for Jesus' Mockery.[5] It specifically states that the crown was woven (*contextam*), and the image indeed shows a crown that appears woven like a typical wreath. The inscription also explains the right side of the illumination. It refers to a later part of the Gospel narrative when Simon of Cyrene is forced to carry Jesus' cross on the way to the Crucifixion.[6] The image is therefore a conflation of two separate parts of the Gospel story: the Crowning of Jesus, and the procession to the Crucifixion. The image notably lacks any typical suggestions of a Mockery.[7] The Crown of Thorns has finally appeared, but the narrative is still incomplete.

While the Codex Aureus of Echternach provides the first rather remarkable depiction of Jesus' Crown of Thorns, the scene, as stated, lacks the full narrative. Yet at almost the same time that this distinctive Crown of Thorns appears, so too, in other works of art, does the complete narrative of Jesus' Mockery—together with the Crown of Thorns—appear in a single scene.

This comprehensive scene, which first appears also around 1020–1030, continues some trends established by previous Mockery scenes beginning with the Carolingian examples discussed above. As such, we cannot hope to fully understand this incredible circumstance of the Mockery and Crowning finally coalescing, without momentarily examining the changes and innovations of just the Mockery scene on its own—without the Crown of Thorns.

---

[5]Mt. 27: 27–31; Mk 15:16-20; Jn 19:1–3.
[6]Mt. 27:32; Mk 15:21; Lk. 23:26.
[7]It could be argued that the Mockery is implied by the Crowning. This argument, however, would be contrary to the previous artistic evidence concerning the Mockery. There is no indication that the soldiers hit, strike, spit upon, or mock-worship Jesus, as they have in other images such as the Gospels of St. Augustine of Canterbury and the Stuttgart Psalter, seen above. Thus, artistically, there is no Mockery.

An Ottonian Mockery

After the Mockery scene accompanying Psalm 61 in the Stuttgart Psalter (Figure 11), the next solidly identifiable portrayal of the Mockery of Christ emerges in the so-called Codex Egberti, made for Egbert, Archbishop of Trier from 977 to 993. This range of dates overlaps the reigns of either Otto II or Otto III, and was produced in either Trier or Reichenau.[8] The manuscript, which is a pericopes book (a sort of shortened version of the Gospels used and read during mass), contains a condensed image of the Mockery of Christ, which appears next to a reading from the Gospel of John. It depicts several groups of characters, all of whom are labeled. In this image, a cross-nimbed Jesus stands humbly with feet bare and head bowed, with the inscription *IHC XRC* above his head. He wears a blue-purple tunic under a purple cloak. Pilate, inscribed *PILATUS*, stands next to him wearing an embroidered tunic and red-orange cloak. Pilate holds Jesus' hand and ushers him towards the crowd on the right. He points towards Jesus with his other hand, looking out to the crowd.

The crowd situated on the right contains two groups. The standing group is labeled *PONTIFIC[ES]*, or "chief priests." The three men of this group stand close together looking towards Pilate and Jesus. They all wear long robes. One points his finger towards Jesus and Pilate, possibly in accusation. The last group is labeled, *MILITES*, "soldiers." These three men are dressed differently, in short tunics. All three are on one knee, bow forward, and raise their hands, palms up, out towards Jesus in mock adoration.

The image succinctly addresses several key moments from part of the rather long episode of Jesus' time with Pilate in the Gospel of John.[9] The episode begins with Pilate asking the crowd that had gathered at his headquarters who he should release for them during the Passover, as was apparently the custom. As mentioned above, the crowd responds that they want Barabbas, a convicted insurrectionist in his own right, to be released to them instead of Jesus. Pilate then has Jesus scourged (*flagellavit*), after which the soldiers (*milites*) fashion the Crown of Thorns, dress him in a purple robe, and mock him. Pilate, who is at a loss concerning Jesus, takes him out again before the crowd:

---

[8] Colum Hourihane, *Pontius Pilate, Anti-Semitism, and The Passion in Medieval Art* (Princeton: Princeton University Press, 2009), 98. The miniatures of the Codex Egberti seem to contain several artistic styles that are found in both Trier and Reichenau art, which makes placement difficult. See Gunther Franz and Franz Ronig, *Codex Egberti; Teilfaksimile-Ausgabe des Ms. 24 der Stadtbibliothek Trier*. Wiesbaden: Reichert, 1983), 40–42 for an in-depth debate about the location of production and dating.
[9] Jn 18:39–19:6.

So Jesus came out wearing the Crown of Thorns and purple robe. Pilate said to them: "Behold the man". When the chief priests (*pontifices*) and the servants (*ministri*) saw him, they shouted and said, "Crucify him, crucify him!" Pilate said to them, "Take him yourselves and crucify him; I find no case against him."[10]

The simple labeling of the characters in the Codex Egberti image indicates the three scenes chosen to represent this extensive narrative: the presentation of Jesus to the crowd by Pilate (*Pilatus*); the accusation and demand for Jesus' crucifixion by the chief priests (*pontifices*); and the Mockery by Pilate's soldiers (*milites*). Furthermore, this image illustrates the precise text from the Gospel of John which surrounds it. Directly above the image, the crowd demands the release of Barabbas, while directly below, the text conveys that the soldiers fashion the Crown of Thorns and place the purple cloak on Jesus. Despite this close relationship to the text, only the purple cloak appears. The Crown does not.

Unlike some of the other illuminations in the Codex Egberti, the image condenses significant moments of the Passion narrative, the presentation, accusation, and mockery, into a single image. By contrast, for example, the picture on the facing page, fol. 81v, fully details the Flagellation, whose accompanying text only appears just above the Mockery image. In the Flagellation image, Jesus is held roughly to a pillar by one soldier, while another beats him with sticks. The punishment is ordered by Pilate who stands gesturing towards Jesus and the soldiers. The detail of the Flagellation and other scenes probably indicates the importance that the artists and their patron Egbert gave to certain narratives over others, on which more will be said later. The Mockery, while technically included, was not deemed important enough to warrant its own scene.

The Mockery scene, once again, also lacks important textual details, such as the crown, reed, and abuse. It seems that this earliest rendering of the Mockery by Ottonian artists follows the example of the Stuttgart Psalter Mockery (Figure 11) in several ways. First, the images are incorporated in the text which they reflect, as opposed to introductory cycles of images grouped together at the beginning of the book, as they are in other contemporary codices, such as the Codex Aureus of Echternach.

Second, several characters of the Codex Egberti bear similarities to those in the Stuttgart Psalter Mockery scene, particularly the figure in the red mantle, the gesture of

---

[10] Jn 19:4–6: *Exivit ergo Iesus portans coronam spineam, et purpureum vestimentum. Et dicit eis: Ecce homo. Cum ergo vidissent eum pontifices et ministri, camabant, dicentes: Crucifige, Crucifige eum. Dicit eis Pilatus: Acipite eum vos, et crucifigite: ego enim non invenio in eo causam*

accusation, and the soldiers on bended knee (cf. Figure 11). In the Stuttgart Mockery, a man in a red mantle, like Pilate (*Pilatus*) in the Codex Egberti, leads Christ by the hand. The artistic scheme in the Stuttgart Psalter is slightly more aggressively bent, with the man grabbing Jesus by the wrist, as opposed to gently leading him by the hand as in the Codex Egberti. The gesture of pointing accusation displayed by the chief priests (*pontifices*) of the Codex Egberti is also in the Stuttgart Psalter's Mockery scene. The soldier, who beats Jesus over the head with a long reed, points with one finger raised towards Jesus. The Stuttgart Psalter elsewhere exhibits precedent for the chief priests (*pontifices*) demanding Jesus' crucifixion with this same accusatory gesture. Psalm 35 of the Stuttgart Psalter, discussed above, depicts Jesus in the center between two figures. Pilate is bearded and seated on the left and a second character points and gesticulates at Jesus in a similar fashion as the chief priests of the Codex Egberti. The illumination accompanies verses 20–21 directly above the image: "For they spoke indeed peaceably to me, and speaking in the anger of the earth they devised guile. And they opened their mouth wide against me; they said: Hooray, Hooray! Our eyes have seen it." This psalm discusses the idea of enemies of some kind exhibiting treachery and deceit against their victim. Many commentators on this psalm, such as Augustine and Cassiodorus, agree that the verses typologically refer to the episode in the Gospels when Pilate offers to release Jesus, but the crowd cries out, demanding his Crucifixion.[11] The Codex Egberti similarly depicts men who gesture in the same fashion as the Stuttgart Psalter accuser and in the same moment of the Passion. The Codex Egberti simplifies comprehension of the scene by specifying the characters' role within the Gospel of John. The Stuttgart Psalter, true to form, relies instead on the readers' knowledge of patristic exegeses to glean the typological reference.

Likewise, both sets of soldiers in the Stuttgart Mockery and the Codex Egberti are down on one knee, have short tunics, and raise their hands, palms up in adoration towards Jesus. This gesture is a well-established trend to depict adoration, as the Stuttgart Psalter can attest. In one of the images accompanying Psalm 22 in the Stuttgart Psalter, fol. 25v, Jesus is on the cross accompanied by two men. The soldier on bended knee displays the familiar gesture with his palm up towards Christ. The image is just below the first few verses of the psalm: "Oh my God, my God, why have you forsaken me? Far from my salvation are the words of my sins. O my God, I shall cry by day, and you will not hear; and by night it will not be believed as foolishness in me."[12] The

---

[11]Mt. 27: 20–23; Mk 15:3, 11–14; Lk. 23:21; Jn 19:2.
[12]Psalm 22: 2–3.

heading to the psalm reads: "The words of Christ while he suffered."[13] Depicted here, and implied by the heading, is the moment when Jesus suffers on the Cross and cries out to God just before he dies. It is possible that the men represent the characters who scoff at Jesus and his inability to save himself from his own torment. However, due to the strategic placement of the image and the well-known association of these verses with Jesus' final breath, it is probable that the men depicted are the soldiers who are the first to witness Jesus' divinity.[14] This would place the man on bended knee in a position of actual adoration, as opposed to the mock adoration seen in the Mockery of Psalm 61. It therefore looks like the imagery for the mocking soldiers in the Codex Egberti, at least, is taken from the trends established in the Stuttgart Psalter examples of adoration, whether in mockery or as genuine worship.

The innovation displayed in the Mockery of the Codex Egberti is that recognizable artistic schemes of the Gospel narrative have been redistributed to form condensed and unambiguous iterations of the narrative. The Ottonians, however, will experiment with a new and unique interpretation of the scene in an Enthroned Mockery.

Imagery united—the Enthroned Mockery

Up to the eleventh century, images of the Mockery have occurred without the Crowning, both in Carolingian and later Ottonian examples, as seen above. In parallel, there have been Crownings and Crowns from the fourth century to the eleventh century, but not within the context of the Mockery. They come together, nearly simultaneously, on two distinctly separate art forms: in the Saint Peter Gospels and on the Golden Altar of Aachen (Figures 19 and 20). Both these pieces were produced at approximately the same time.

We will start with the Saint Peter Gospels, made c. 1025–1049 in the Abbey of St. Peter at Salzburg.[15] The illumination of the Mockery combined with the Crowning

---

[13] *Verba Christi cum pateretur.*
[14] Mt. 27:54; Mk 15:39. In both these Gospels, soon after Jesus says "My God, my God, why have you forsaken me?" he dies. Upon his death, there is an eclipse and an earthquake, the tombs of the dead are opened, and the curtain of the Temple is torn in two. These supernatural occurrences prompt the soldiers, and specifically a centurion, to witness that Jesus must be the son of God.
[15] New York, Pierpont Morgan Library, Curatorial Record: 1; New York, Pierpont Morgan Library CORSAIR collection: 2. This manuscript, made in St. Peter's Abbey of Salzburg's own growing scriptorium, during the first half of the eleventh century, remained in the monastery until the Morgan Library purchased it in 1933. Thus, its provenance is more secure (Morgan Library Curatorial Record). It is presumed that the manuscript was made by the scriptorium for use in the Abbey itself to enhance the liturgical experience of the monastery.

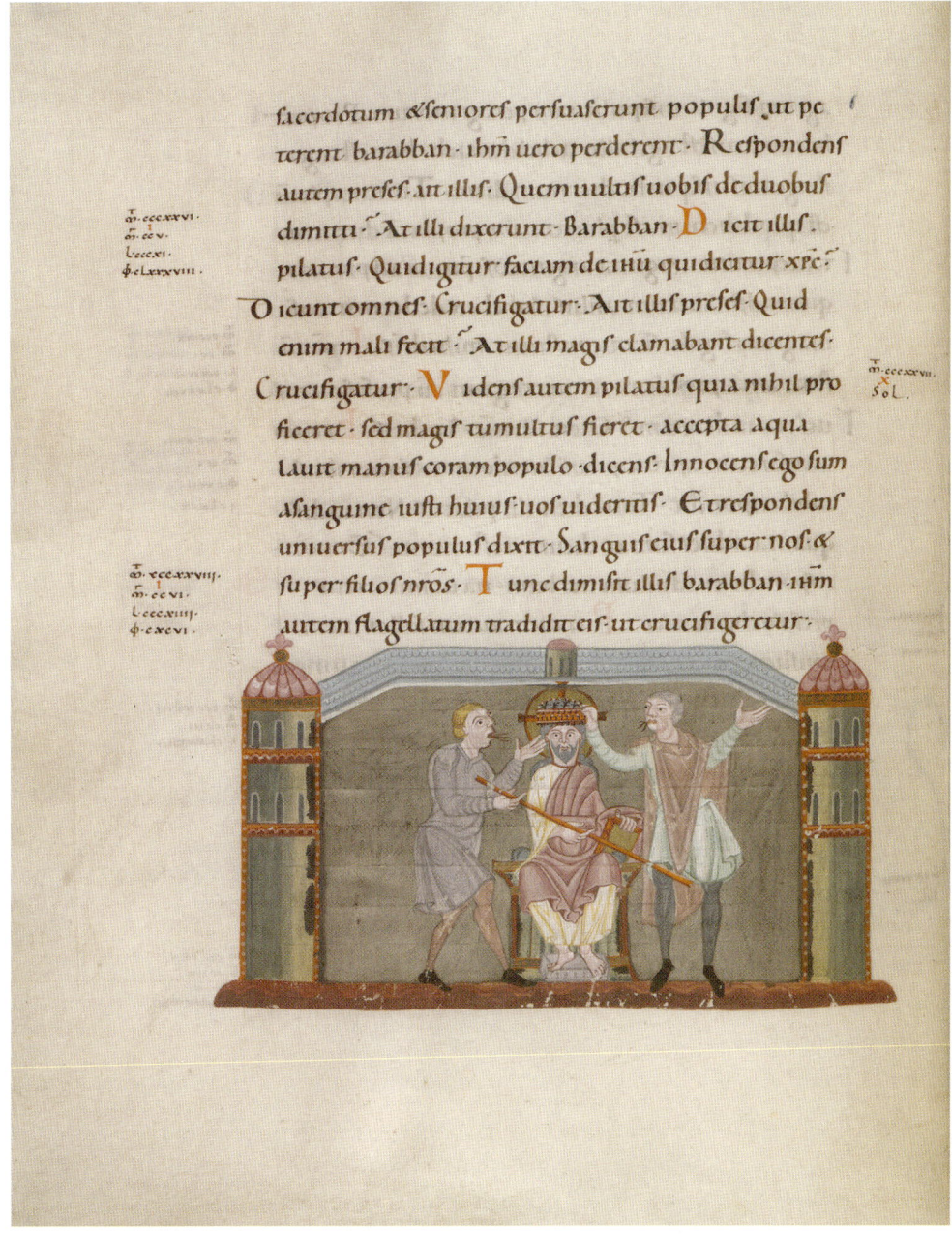

Figure 18 *Saint Peter Gospels, MS M. 781, fol. 83v, Salzburg Abbey, second quarter of the eleventh century, The Morgan Library & Museum, New York.*

occurs within the Gospel of Matthew, directly under the Gospel text of the Flagellation of Christ (Figure 18).[16] Under an architectural backdrop consisting of two green towers, pink-red domes, and golden background,[17] Jesus sits in the center of the image flanked by two men.[18] The man on the left wears a simple short tunic and hands Jesus the reed, which Jesus grasps. The same soldier gestures towards Jesus, palm facing outward, in acclamation (a similar, though slightly altered, gesture to that of the soldiers on bended knee in the Codex Egberti and Stuttgart Mockeries). The second man, presumably another soldier, stretches out his left hand in a similar manner. Both soldiers copiously expectorate on Jesus' face.

The soldier on the right places an elaborate crown on Jesus' head. This crown is uniquely and intricately decorated and deserves some explicit attention. It is dome shaped with a large solid band around the front of Jesus' head. The band is about 18mm in height, while the entire crown is 35mm. It is a vibrant orange, like the reed and border of the book which Jesus holds. The rim of the band is red and white, while the dome is spotted with red and white dots. The inside of the band is decorated with similar white spots, bordered with red. Four large thorns sprout, branch-like out of the top of the band towards the dome of the crown. There are also a series of smaller gamma-shaped black decorations that could reasonably be assumed to be thorns, set in rows all around the Crown. One set face downward from the top of the band. The second set face upward from the bottom of the band, and the third protrudes down towards Jesus' forehead from the bottom of the band. Unlike the Codex Aureus of Echternach, which is woven from a plant, this Crown is decidedly not a woven wreath, braided from some plant-like material (other than the thorns that protrude all around). The Crown is not excessively larger than Jesus' head. It is similar to the Crown of Thorns in the Codex Aureus of Echternach only in that they both have some form of small thorns affixed to the top.

Jesus, cross-nimbed, sits placidly and wears a white tunic with red-pink robe. His long hair cascades down around his shoulders to his back. He faces completely frontally, eyes looking outward towards the viewer. In his left hand he holds, propped on his knee, the orange rimmed book with a golden cover. He is seated in a cushioned, lavish

---

[16] The text is accompanied by the standard Eusebian Canons in the margins with no additional marginal inscriptions.
[17] This architectural backdrop appears frequently throughout the illuminations of the Saint Peter Gospels. While they vary in style and color, the pair of towers and roof is a static feature.
[18] The small number of characters in this image is striking. Many of the illuminations of the Saint Peter Gospels show Jesus with a larger crowd of people, which makes for busy images. The Enthroned Mockery, on the other hand, is simpler, with few characters and less movement.

chair, complete with a purple stool for his feet. It is unmistakably a throne. The throne is green, with a grey-blue cushion. The arms of the throne are a deep red-orange. The top, middle, and bottom are gold, decorated with orange lines and circles.

Several features of this excruciatingly detailed Enthroned Mockery warrant reiterated attention. Like the image of the Crowning in the Codex Aureus of Echternach, Jesus is once again given an unmistakable Crown of Thorns, though of a significantly different form. Instead of a woven wreath with thorns, the Jesus of the Saint Peter Gospels is fashioned a solid domed crown with evenly spaced, sprouting thorns. Jesus is also mocked while crowned, alluding exclusively and more fully to the episode with Pilate's soldiers in the Praetorium. It shows the spitting, striking, mocking, and bestowing of instruments by the soldiers. It is a more abusive image, like the Stuttgart Psalter's portrayal of the Mockery. Jesus, however, is not just mocked and crowned in this image, but is seated, erect, calm, and facing frontally, on what can only be a throne.

As mentioned, the Saint Peter Gospels' Enthroned Mockery is not a singular occurrence. The Golden Altar of Aachen, which currently forms the antependium of the High Altar of the Palatine Chapel in Aachen, also contains this motif (Figure 19).

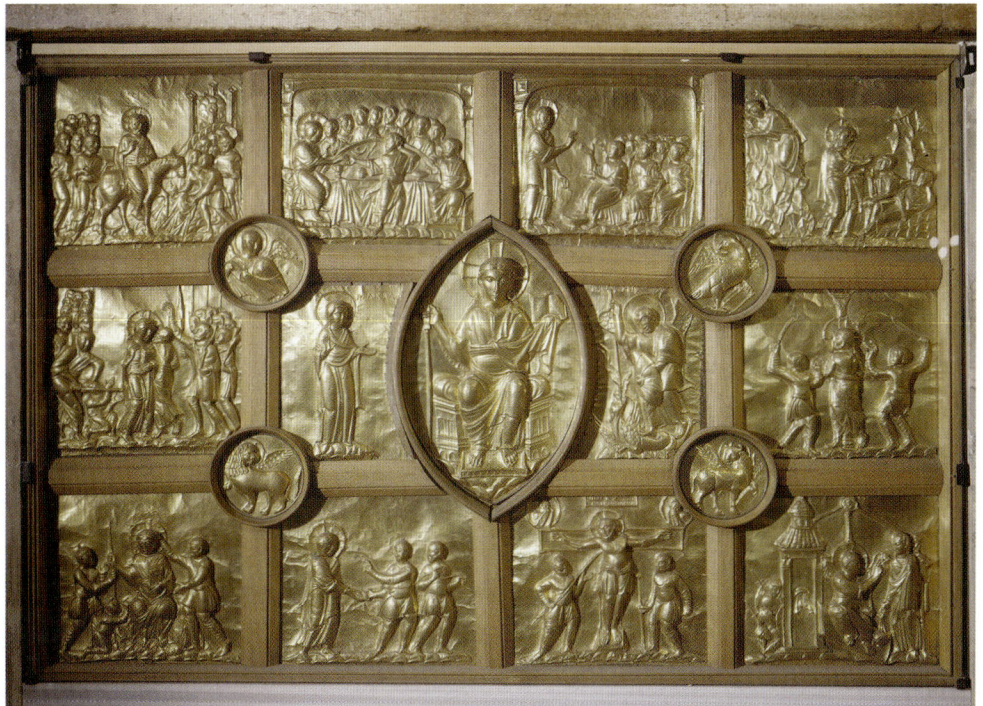

Figure 19 *The Golden Alter of Aachen, The Aachen Cathedral, Fulda, c. 1020.*

The altar is comprised of a series of golden plaques depicting scenes from the Life of Christ. The altar was donated by Henry II around 1020.[19] An Enthroned Mockery is depicted at the bottom left corner. Jesus is again enthroned, surrounded this time by three men. All three men have short tunics and wear greaves on their legs. The soldier on the left gives Jesus a scepter and raises his other hand with a gesture of adoration like the soldiers in the Saint Peter Gospels. On the opposite side, a second soldier reaches up to crown Jesus. The exact form of the Crown on this plaque is difficult to discern, but the distinctive reaching gesture of the soldier assumes there is something atop Jesus' head. The third figure kneels on the ground before the enthroned Jesus and raises his hand to point at him. This kneeling position, possibly more than anything else, is a familiar indication of the Mockery. The Stuttgart Psalter depicts two soldiers kneeling in a similar manner, while the Codex Egberti suggests the entire Mockery by condensing it into a trio of kneeling faux-adorers. The Golden Altar, however, is once again slightly different to the previous examples. The soldier kneels on both knees instead of one, and points at Jesus, instead of offering the usual open-palmed praise. On the Golden Altar Jesus, larger than the other figures, sits cross-nimbed with his head bowed and grasps a book in his left hand. He holds the scepter erect in his other hand. Many aspects of this scene are similar to the Saint Peter Gospels. They both include the scepter, book, and crown. Jesus is also both mocked and enthroned. On the Golden Altar plaque, however, there are three mockers instead of two and the manner in which Jesus holds the scepter shifts. He holds it straight and controlled, instead of having it forced into his hand as in the Saint Peter Gospels; this is an important distinction, the significance of which become apparent below.

The additions and innovations found in the Enthroned Mockery should now be clear: not only has Jesus been shifted to a central position, but the addition of the throne, the inclusion of the Crown, the reduction of the number of abusers, the soldiers' symmetrical flanking of Jesus, and their slightly altered gesture of praise all make the Enthroned Mockery a new interpretation of a well-established scene.

This Enthroned Mockery, while maintaining several trends from its predecessors, does not truly resemble them in the way that the Codex Egberti resembles the Stuttgart

---

[19]The inscription on the altar specifically states Henry's dedication. According to conventional analysis, the golden plaques of this altar may not all have been added at the same time. The Mockery, however, along with several of the Passion images and the central Christ in Majesty, was probably donated by Henry II around 1020, which would make it slightly older than the Saint Peter Gospels. See J. Gaehde, "Treasury; Aachen," in *The Dictionary of Art*, vol. 1, ed. Jane Turner (New York: Grove, 1996) 4; Eliza Garrison, *Ottonian Imperial Art and Portraiture: The Artistic Patronage of Otto III and Henry II* (Farnham, Surrey: Ashgate, 2012), 105.

Psalter. In particular, the additions of the throne, Crown, and the position of the attendants have no precedent in any known Mockery scene. It is important to acknowledge, as many do, that the image of the Enthroned Mockery on the Golden Altar of Aachen is similar to the central image of Christ in Majesty on the same altar. At the center of the altar, Christ appears contained in a mandorla, enthroned in a cushioned seat, holding an open book in the same hand as the Christ of the Enthroned Mockery, as well as a staff in his other hand. They are similarly enthroned, although the Christ in Majesty's throne is far more elaborate. They are also similarly haloed and bedecked. The Christ in Majesty is flanked by an adoring entourage consisting of Mary and the Archangel Michael, while the Jesus of the Enthroned Mockery is mock-worshiped by his own flanking soldiers. It is tempting to merely associate the two images and say that the ubiquitous image of Christ in Majesty influenced the Enthroned Mockery, both in the image on the Golden Altar and in the Saint Peter Gospels.[20] This conclusion, however, risks overlooking the highly popular, and far more analogous, images of the Coronation of the Ottonian King, which have far more convincing and contemporary similarities.[21]

The Ottonian and Salian rulers underwent at least three official coronations. They were first crowned King of Germany, then King of Italy, and eventually crowned by the Pope as Holy Roman Emperor.[22] The vast number of images of the enthroned Ottonian and Salian ruler can be a representation of one particular coronation ritual, as king or emperor, or illuminating the collective coronation and enthronement rituals at any point in his reign. Thus, when accuracy can be determined, I will adopt the appropriate title, king or emperor, depending on the historical timeframe in which the image was made or to which literary examples refer. For images that remain ambiguous or are potentially collective, I will simply label the ruler, or rulers, as king.

---

[20] For discussions on the similarities between the Christ in Majesty and the Enthroned Mockery of Christ on the Golden Altar see Schiller, *Iconography*, 70–71; Mayr-Harting, *Ottonian*, 110–111; Garrison, *Ottonian*, 106.

[21] One would be remiss not to point out the similarities between the Enthroned Mockery and the Enthroned Christ on the fifth-century sarcophagi, discussed above. While the Enthroned Christ is certainly not a scene of Mockery, the ideologies surrounding the Enthroned Christ are reflected in the contemporary understanding of Christ's Mockery by Pilate's soldiers. The scene on the sarcophagi of the fifth century was widely depicted, but it is unlikely that the scene directly influenced the image of the Enthroned Mockery. They have some similarities, such as the actual enthronement and surrounding attendants. The Enthroned Christ's throne, however, is dissimilar. He also lacks the reed and crown. It is possible that there is a direct trajectory from these sarcophagi images to the later images of the kings, and thus, eventually the Ottonian royal portraiture. If this is the case, then the fifth-century sarcophagi of the Enthroned Christ would indirectly influence the Enthroned Mockery through the images of the enthroned kings, as the following section will elucidate.

[22] The Salians from Conrad onward were also crowned King of Burgundy during their reigns.

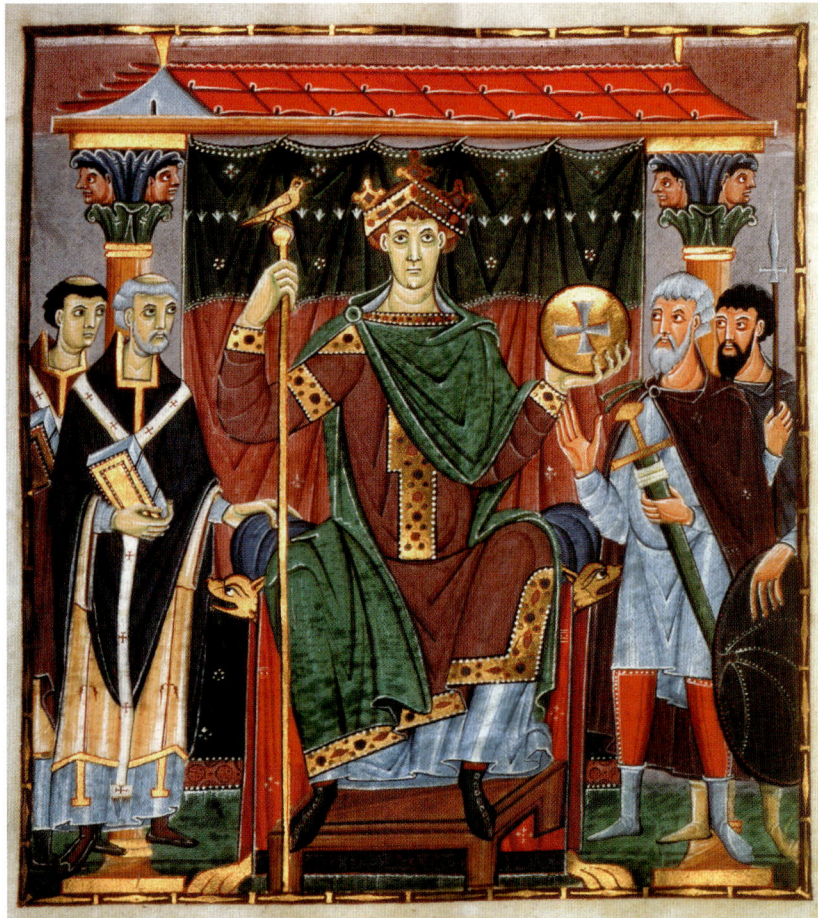

Figure 20 *Gospel Book of Otto III, Clm 4453, fol. 24, Reichenau Abbey, c. 998–1001, Bayerische Staatsbibliothek, Munich.*

A few examples from the plethora of enthronement and coronation imagery will suffice to demonstrate the trend and similarities with the Enthroned Mockery. All the following examples of the image of the enthroned king precede those of the Enthroned Mockery of the Golden Altar of Aachen and the Saint Peter Gospels, in order to establish trend and continuance.

A typical image of the coronation of the emperor appears, for example, in the Gospel Book of Otto III, c. 998–1001 (Figure 20).[23] In this image Otto III is enthroned in a high-

---

[23] Otto III was crowned King of Germany in 983, King of Italy in 996, and Emperor also in 996. Thus, this image is probably representative of all three. The emperor is not strictly being crowned in this image. I will refer to the images as "Coronations," since, as stated above, they reflect the entire coronation ritual, which will be demonstrated later in this chapter.

backed, cushioned throne, holding an orb and scepter.[24] He is crowned and surrounded by attendants. The Crown of Thorns of the Saint Peter Gospels takes on a slight yet significant similarity to the crown of Otto. Jesus' crown has thorn-like decorations that protrude regularly from the band around his head. In the same way, Otto's crown has decorations fixed atop it. Otto's crown also is decorated with small, round, white jewels, presumably pearls, just as the dome and band of Jesus' Crown are affixed with white and red circular decorations. As stated, Jesus' crown in the Saint Peter Gospels is also not distinctly woven as it is in the Codex Aureus of Echternach (Figure 17), but instead resembles the more solid form of Otto III's crown. Otto's coronation, however, is generally more elaborately decorated, from the bird atop his scepter to the surrounding architecture. The armed attendant on the right shows a clear sign of praise: hand raised and palm open towards the emperor. The soldiers in both the Saint Peter Gospels' Mockery and on the Golden Altar exhibit this same gesture.

The Coronation image of *De Bello Judaico*, c. 1000 of Otto III or Henry II is a similar image.[25] It depicts the king seated on a cushioned throne with orb and scepter, crowned with a simpler crown, and flanked by bishops and soldiers on either side. This time, both a bishop and the soldier in the background raise their hands in a gesture of praise or acclamation. The soldiers of the Enthroned Mockery of the Saint Peter Gospels mimic this same gesture, as opposed to the palm-up and bended-knee adoration of the Stuttgart and Codex Egberti examples. Otto III/Henry II's throne and the throne of the Saint Peter Gospels are similar in form, though Jesus' throne bears more elaborate decoration and color than the king's. Otto III/Henry II and the Jesus of the Golden Altar of Aachen Mockery grasp their scepters in a similar fashion. The scepter in both cases is planted on the ground and held erect and away from the body. This comparison gives the demeanor of the Jesus of the Golden Altar of Aachen an even closer connection to the ruler; the manner in which they hold their staff is imperious and, for Jesus, belies

---

[24] Bamberg, Staatsbibliothek, Josephus Flavius, *De Bello Judaico*, Msc.Class.79, fol. 1ar, Reichenau, C. 1000. These coronations of the emperors and kings are generally only half the image. The opposite page displays a procession of the approaching provinces bringing tribute to their sovereign. The present discussion, however, is limited to the portrayal of the emperor or king.

[25] The image was probably in a Gospel book in Bamberg at least since 1012. The miniature was removed in the mid-thirteenth century and placed in its current Ottonian manuscript. Interestingly, this coronation was originally meant for Otto III. Otto III's name was erased, except for the last O. Henry II's name was later inscribed, HEI(N) R(IC)HUS. Presumably, the dedication was for Otto III when it was made around 1000, but upon Otto's death in 1002, the former emperor's name was replaced with that of the new king, Henry II, who was crowned King of Germany in 1002, King of Italy in 1004, and later crowned as Emperor in 1014. The image of the coronation of the king was apparently so ubiquitous that it was quite simple to replace names to reflect changing regimes. It suggests the popularity of the image and the frequency with which they were produced.

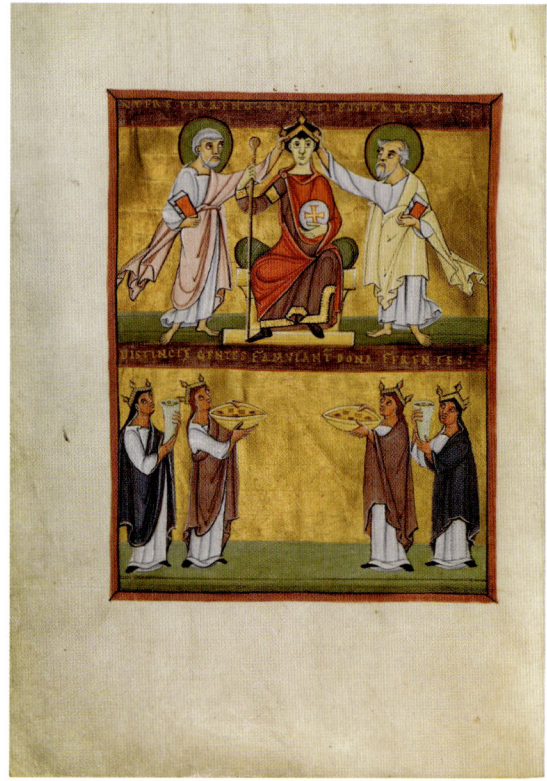

Figure 21 *Bamberg Apocalypse, Msc.Bibl.140, fol.59v, Reichenau, c. 1010, Staatsbibliothek, Bamberg.*

his assumed superior status. Likewise, the king's orb and Jesus' book are both held close to the chest.

A different example is found in the Bamberg Apocalypse c. 1010 of Henry II's Coronation (Figure 21).[26] It depicts an actual crowning, as opposed to the above, where the kings are enthroned as part of the coronation ritual, discussed below. In the Bamberg Apocalypse, Henry II is seated in a cushioned chair that lacks a back, very much like the throne of the Saint Peter Gospels. In this image, as in the preceding two, the king or

---

[26] Henry II and his wife Cunigunde donated the manuscript to the Bamberg church of St. Stephan upon its consecration in 1007. The manuscript contains the Book of Revelation as well as Gospel texts that were read during important feasts rather than for everyday liturgical use (Statsbibliothek Catalogue Msc.Bibl.140). There is some debate among scholars as to the date of this manuscript. Some, such as Mayr-Harting, emphatically argue for an earlier date of 1001–1002 (see Mayr-Harting, *Ottonian*, 215–228). Others, including the Statsbibliothek Bamberg where it is housed, places the manuscript closer to 1010, or just before. As in other manuscripts there is also some argument over the identity of the ruler in the portraiture, whether Henry II or Otto III.

emperor faces completely frontally, looking out over his subjects. In the Enthroned Mockery images Jesus also faces front, erect, and dignified. Contrasted with the bowed head and depleted Jesus of other Mockery examples, the Jesus of the Enthroned Mockery mimics the regal demeanor of the king by shifting his body to face the audience. Henry II also holds a less elaborate scepter with a simple knob atop, like the scepter in *De Bello Judaico*. He holds it erect and planted on the ground. Jesus' scepter on the Golden Altar is decorated with a similar, though smaller, knob. On either side of Henry II, Peter and Paul, both holding books, reach up to crown Henry, like the soldier does to Jesus in both the Saint Peter Gospels and the Aachen Altar. While this image was made over a decade before Henry II was crowned Emperor, the crowning by Peter, the first and model pope, may allude to a hopefully future imperial coronation. The symmetry that is created by the soldiers of the Saint Peter Gospels resembles the symmetry of Peter and Paul of the Coronation of Henry II, as well as the symmetry created by the flanking attendants in the Gospel Book of Otto III and the *De Bello Judaico*. It is a symmetry that is lacking in all the other Mockery scenes prior to the Enthroned Mockery.

The examples above show that the collective and slightly varying images of the ruler's coronation find parallels in the image of the Enthroned Mockery. The cushioned throne; the style of the crown; the manner of holding and appearance of the scepter; the exalted position of the frontally facing central figure; the particular gesture of adoration of the attendants; and the action of the attendants have an all too clear influence on the Enthroned Mockery of Christ. The material evidence draws an obvious conclusion: the Enthroned Mockery is meant to resemble the Coronation of the King.

The remaining question that has yet to be addressed concerns artistic trends of the Crown of Thorns itself. The first instance of an actual Crown of Thorns is a wreath inlaid with thorns, while the second is a band also with sharp thorns jutting out of the top. There appears to be no known source to explain why Jesus' crown is suddenly inlaid with thorns, except for the possible similarity to the king's crown, as noted above. It is possible that the Ottonian Crown of Thorns was influenced by Byzantine or Italian examples that have since been lost. Some argue that the fourth-century Vatican Passion Sarcophagus wreath-crown (Figure 1) was revived in this eleventh-century manuscript in Echternach.[27] This seems unlikely. Not only is the time and space between the two far too great for a direct influence, but there is no artistic or ideological reason for a direct influence from the fourth-century example. Rather, as suggested above, there is a parallelism between

---

[27] Some scholars, such as Ronig, look directly to the fourth-century Vatican Passion Sarcophagus as the influence for the eleventh century's Crown of Thorns, see Ronig, *Codex Egberti*, 44.

the imperial images and the mock coronation of Christ, including the shape of the crown in the Saint Peter Gospels example. From where the artists of the Codex Aureus of Echternach received their artistic inspiration must, regrettably, remain an open-ended question. I will attempt, nevertheless, to suggest a contextual answer to the question.

The Crown of Thorns, which is rendered in at least two distinct ways, finally appears as a recognizable wreath or crown made of actual thorns. The Mockery scene is also now combined with the Crown of Thorns to create an Enthroned Mockery. The Mockery scene retains several paradigms established in preceding Mockery scenes, both early Ottonian and Carolingian. The Enthroned Mockery, however, which combines the Mockery and Crowning, takes its primary influence from the contemporary portraiture of the Coronation of the Ottonian King. This Enthroned Mockery is, in fact, a unique rendition of the Mockery. Interestingly, the Enthroned Mockery will not become the prevailing depiction of the Mockery and Crowning for the remainder of the eleventh century. While many of its innovations will become standard for the Mockery for centuries to come, the throne and obvious parallels to the king in particular will disappear after the mid-eleventh century, until it is revived once again in the thirteenth century. Therefore, the Enthroned Mockery and its apparent artistic connection to the Coronation of the Ottonian king must be further investigated as a unique phenomenon of this limited period.

A humbled and humiliated king

Based on the written sources of the time, there is a complex ideological justification for the distinct parallel between the unique rendering of Jesus' Enthroned Mockery and the Coronation of the Kings. The gist of the argument is as follows: for the late Ottonian and early Salians, a significant aspect of the ideology of kingship revolved around the idea that the king, who is the perfect imitator and representative of Christ, must endure humiliation, trials, and tribulation to ultimately gain the initial throne. As we discovered in the earlier chapters, Jesus' humiliation during the Mockery led to his ultimate coronation in heaven. In the same way the Ottonian and Salian kings needed to go through periods of humility before their own earthly coronation. An understanding of this ideology will explain why imagery of Jesus' Mockery in the mid-eleventh-century parallels the coronation imagery of the king.[28]

---

[28] The following examples all concern the first coronation of the Ottonian and Salian ruler, thus they will be referred to as kings.

But to comprehend the expected transition from humiliation to exaltation for the Ottonian and Salian kings, it is important to have a sense of the extent to which the king was expected to be Christ-like. By the early eleventh century this enduring concept of "Christo-Mimesis," or the absolute imitation of Christ, was expected of all Christ's followers. But it was especially applied to the crowned kings and emperors. The Ottonian and Salian kings were considered and expected to be Christ's perfect imitator—Christ's representative on earth.[29] While this is certainly not a new idea, it is reiterated with increased frequency in the Ottonian literature, only a sampling of which will be discussed here. Thietmar's *Chronicon*, written c. 1012–1018, for example, when explaining why it is right for the king alone to distribute bishoprics, maintains that since kings:

> have been placed in this world as representatives of the highest ruler, only they rightly take precedence over all their pastors. Indeed, it would be most incongruous for the latter, whom Christ instituted for his sake as the first men of this world, to be subject to any dominion other than that exercised by rulers who, after the model of the Lord, exceed all other mortals through the glory of the benediction and crown.[30]

Two things are important in this passage. First, Thietmar states that the king is Christ's representative on earth, who, like Christ, is subject to no one. Second, kings rule after the model of Christ. Like Christ they receive the glory of the crown which allows them to rule on earth as Christ rules in heaven, that is, absolutely. The king was crowned like Christ and therefore rules like Christ.

Similarly, in Wipo's *Gesta Chuonradi*, the Deeds of Conrad II, the archbishop of Mainz tells the newly crowned Conrad II, King of Germany, that, as the one who holds the highest position on earth, he is the Vicar of Christ.[31] Additionally, he adds that "no one except the true imitator is ruler." That is, no one except the true imitator of Christ

---

[29] Eckhard Müller-Mertens, "The Ottonians as Kings and Emperors," in *The New Cambridge Medieval History*, Vol. III c. 900-1024, ed. Timothy Reuter (Cambridge: Cambridge University Press, 1999), 253; 259–260.
[30] Thietmar, "Chronicon," 1.26, in trans. David Warner, *Ottonian Germany*, 86–87. For the Latin text see *Monumenta Germaniae Historica, Scriptores, SS rer. Germ.*, vol. 9, 34: *Quin potius reges nostri et imperatores, summi rectoris vice in hac peregrineacione prepositi hoc soli ordinant meritoque pre caeteris pastoribus suis presunt, quia incongruum nimis est, ut hii, quos Christius sui memores huius terrae principes constituit sub aliquot sint dominio absque eorum, qui exempo Domini benediccionis et coronae gloria mortals cunctas precellunt.*
[31] Wipo, "Gesta Chuondradi II Imperatoris", 3, *Monumenta Germaniae Historica, Scriptores, SS rer. Germ.*, vol. 61, 22–23: *Ad summam dignitatem pervenisti, vicarius es Christi.*

could have gained the throne.³² Conrad, as vicar, now represents Christ on earth and must, like Christ, distribute justice and peace in the realm.

Occasionally, kings were admonished by their bishops for not being Christ-like enough, and they reminded the king that it was their duty as vicar to be perfect imitators of Christ—to do what Christ would do. In a letter, which can be dated to late 1008 or early 1009, Bruno of Querfurt writes to Henry II, who has already been crowned King of Germany and Italy, on the outset of his mission to the Prussians. Bruno advises the king that he ought to establish a friendship with the Polish Duke Boleslav the Brave. Instead of fighting him and making an enemy, Henry should be merciful to Boleslav and his people. Bruno implores the king to:

> Therefore act mercifully, put aside cruelty; if you want to have [Boleslav] as a knight, act with goodness, in order that he may like you. Beware, O king, if you want to do everything with power and never with mercy, which the good man loves, lest by chance Jesus, who now helps you, should be enraged by you.³³

Bruno asks the king if it might be more prudent to be less cruel and more merciful towards Boleslav. Instead of Henry persecuting him and gaining an enemy, he could gain a faithful subject. Bruno implies that if Henry acts cruelly and makes an enemy out of Boleslav, Jesus will be furious with him for his actions. Jesus, Bruno suggests, would rather see the king "fight with pagans for the sake of Christianity than to inflict violence on Christians for the sake of secular honor;"³⁴ that is, to fight to convert the pagans rather than fight over some profane squabble.

The letter demonstrates that the bishops and subjects of the king looked to his actions with the expectation that the Ottonian rulers were meant to act like Jesus. It was such a universally understood idea that when they did not, they were chastised by their clerics.

Christo-Mimesis as it applied to the Ottonian and Salian rulers meant that all aspects of the ruler's life should be in perfect imitation of Jesus. As stated, this is not an unprecedented idea. It had been expected of kings and rulers well before the Ottonians. What was new in the Ottonian and Salian era was that the idea that Christo-Mimesis

---

³²Ibid., 23: *Nemo nisi illius imitator verus est dominator*.
³³Bruno of Querfurt, "Epistola Brunona ad Henricum Regem", in H. Karwasinska, *Monumenta Poloniae Historica*, Series Nova, vol. 4, 226: *Ergo fac misericordiam, postpone crudelitatem; si vis habere fidelem, desine persequi; se vis habere militem, fac cum Bono ut deletet. Cave, o rex, si vis omnia facere cum potestate, nunquam cum Misericordia, quam amat ipse Bonus, ne forsitan irritetur qui te nunc adiuvat, Jesus*.
³⁴Ibid., 226–227: *Nonne melius pugnare cum paganis propter Christianitatem, quam Christianis vim inferre propter secularem honorem*.

did not just pertain to the way in which the kings ruled, but also how they gained their initial crown.[35] It very specifically included the imitation of Jesus' humility, trials, and hardships prior to being crowned and enthroned in heaven. Especially for Henry II, reigning from 1002–1024, and his successor Conrad II, 1024–1039, there was an expectation that for these men to prove their aptitude and worth to rule, their lives prior to their election to kingship had to have been mired by a substantial and relentless deluge of misfortune. The prospective king had to also overcome this misfortune in a Christ-like fashion: by persevering and humbling himself during times of trial. Humility in the face of tribulation was a king's greatest virtue and it was not only how he proved himself worthy of kingship, but was also a necessary progression to inaugural coronation and enthronement.

One text to conceptualize this eleventh-century ideology of Ottonian kingship, even if indirectly, is the *Life of Matilda*, wife of Henry I (919–939) and a saint. It addresses her grandson, Henry II through the deeds of his great grandmother and the rest of his Henrician ancestors. The *Vita Mathilda Posterior* (hereafter *VMP*) was dedicated to Henry II and is generally dated to 1002–1003, around the time of Henry II's ascension to the throne as King of Germany.[36] The *VMP* demonstrates how her virtuous humility and tenacious endurance leads to the highest heavenly reward of sainthood. It also functions as a commentary on Henry II's own virtues and regal legitimacy by demonstrating how the Henrician line's Christ-like humility and perseverance in the face of constant suffering was an active progression to power and kingship.[37]

To demonstrate the progression from suffering to ultimate exaltation, the *VMP* first suggests that humility makes a person virtuous and a practitioner of good deeds. Just two paragraphs in, Henry II's family is shown to be endowed with humility. Henry I, even as a young boy "directed himself to good works by following in the footsteps of

---

[35] Sean Gilsdorf, *Queenship and Sanctity; The* Lives *of Mathilda and the* Epitaph *of Adelheid* (Washington, D.C.: The Catholic University of America Press, 2004), 54.

[36] Ibid., 19–20. There are two versions of the *Life of Matilda,* neither of which the author is known. The *Vita Mathilda Antiquor* (the "Older" Life) was written by 973 or 974. The *Vita Mathilde Posterior* will therefore be the focus of this chapter, as it was written closer to the time of the images and addresses contemporaneous ideologies.

[37] Ibid., 48; The legitimacy of Henry II's claim to the throne was dubious, considering his family's notorious rebellions against the ruling kings and emperors; e.g. Otto I's brother, Duke Henry of Bavaria, revolted against Otto twice; Duke Henry's son (Henry II's father) led an uprising against Otto II in 974, which ended in the loss of Henry's Bavarian duchy; and then his father again tried to usurp the throne after Otto II's death in 983. Henry II himself only gained the kingship of Germany by seizing Otto III's body, forcing the archbishop Heribert to hand over the royal insignia—this among other, less than honorable tactics, he became king. The *VMP* attempts to allay concerns of legitimacy by demonstrating that Henry II, like his ancestors, possessed the necessary virtues and Christ-like humility to be king. See Gilsdorf, *Queenship and Sanctity*, 44–52.

humility, which steadily led him to the pinnacle of virtue."[38] Since the establishment of the Henrician line, humility was a characteristic that would undeniably predict a virtuous life. Such characteristics would prove Henry I, and by extension his descendants, to be worthy of leadership and kingship.

In addition to humility, patience was also a highly prized virtue. Henry I and Matilda's son, Duke Henry of Bavaria demonstrated "utter patience in the face of adversity ... and for this reason he was especially loved by God's holy one."[39] This idea of "patience in the face of adversity" should immediately recall the well-established theology seen in our discussion of the Carolingians. The previously examined Psalm 61, its accompanying commentaries, and the many Carolingian commentaries on the Mockery of Christ, firmly establish that Christ's endurance of the Mockery by Pilate's soldiers is the prime example of facing adversaries with patience and humility; an example that was to be imitated by Christians. The idea persists into the Ottonian era. The ability to maintain patience under duress was still a highly prized quality in the eleventh century; a quality that looked back to Jesus' own example of humble endurance in trying circumstances.

Similarly, the *VMP* reiterates this virtue by maintaining that humble acceptance of rejection leads to exaltation. Matilda reminds her inconsolable sons, Otto and Henry, of this wisdom when they mourn over their father's body. Matilda, who knows that hard times lie ahead for them because of the succession of the kingship, advises them to "not be sad when another is preferred over you; instead, always remember the words of truth contained in the Gospel: 'Everyone who exalts himself will be humbled, and whoever humbles himself will be exalted.'"[40] Prophetically, Matilda knows that her son Otto will become king and emperor and not the preferred Henry.[41] This will lead to strife

---

[38] "Vita Mathildis Reginae Posterior" 1, in Gilsdorf, *Queenship and Sanctity*, 90. For the Latin text see *Monumenta Germaniae Historica, Scriptores, SS. rer. Germ.*, vol. 66, 147: *et ab annis puerilibus intendebat bonis operibus sequens humilitatis vestigia, quibus certissime pervenitur ad culmina virtutum.*

[39] I.e. Matilda; "Vita Mathildis Reginae Posterior", 6, in Gilsdorf, *Queenship and Sanctity*, 96. For the Latin text see *Monumenta Germaniae Historica, Scriptores, SS. rer. Germ.*, vol. 66, 156: *in omni autem toleranti adversitatis ... et propter hec specialiter dilectus sancta dei.*

[40] "Vita Mathildis Reginae Posterior", 8, in Gilsdorf, *Queenship and Sanctity*, 96. For the Latin text see *Monumenta Germaniae Historica, Scriptores, SS. rer. Germ.*, vol. 66, 160: *Nec inde vester animus contristetur, quis vestrum alteri praeponatur; memoriter retinete, quod in evangelio dicitur veritatis ore: Omnis, qui se exaltat, humiliabitur, et qui se humiliate, exaltabitur* (Lk. 14:11).

[41] Ibid., 6, in Gilsdorf, *Queenship and Sanctity*, 96. For the Latin text see *Monumenta Germaniae Historica, Scriptores, SS. rer. Germ.*, vol. 66, 156. It was especially Mathilde who "desired that [Henry] should receive the kingdom after the illustrious King Henry's death" (*desideravit ipsum regno potiri post obitum incliti regis Heinrici*).

between the brothers. She advises her sons, in this case particularly Henry, not to be too troubled when thing go against him, and, as Christ commanded, to act humbly and accept diminution. Such behavior will be rewarded by exaltation.

Matilda demonstrates through her own life how steadfast endurance of injustice will lead to reward. At one point her sons forced their mother to take the veil, after falsely accusing her of hoarding wealth and emptying the royal coffers. The *VMP* enumerates her abuses and how she handles them:

> In the face of all these things, the venerable queen showed herself to be patient and vigorously steadfast in every adversity. She "set a watcher over her mouth" lest it should utter improper things, and she devoted herself to constant prayer... Instead, when beset with injuries, she became even more steadfast... she held such treatment in little regard, desiring only to be worthy in Christ's eyes; she cursed no one, but counted as a blessing every torment inflicted upon her by her hostile sons, always remembering that holy scripture teaches that we must undergo many troubles and torments in order to enter the kingdom of God.[42]

Queen Matilda accepted all the apparent torments that her sons inflicted on her as blessings. She knew that in enduring these trials by being "patient and vigorously steadfast in every adversity" she would be rewarded. In this case, the reward is heavenly, but the focus was still on undergoing hardship to gain the greatest reward. Matilda lived by example, demonstrating that, indeed, not only did her pious acceptance of humiliation and abuse lead to her eventual sainthood, but also reconciliation with her sons. As an ancestor of Henry II, Matilda's example predicates Henry's own ability to remain steadfast and patient during times of trial.

The theme of humility leading to exaltation culminates in Matilda's prophecy for the Henrician line. The *VMP* does not disguise the fact that Duke Henry of Bavaria, Otto I's brother and Henry II's great-grandfather, bore abundant suffering. So numerous in fact are his tribulations that the author of the *VMP* apologizes that "many of his sufferings are omitted here, for if they were dealt with one by one it would strike both narrators

---

[42]Ibid., 11, in Gilsdorf, *Queenship and Sanctity,* 104. For the Latin text see *Monumenta Germaniae Historica, Scriptores, SS. rer. Germ.*, vol. 66, 168: *Contra hec omnia venerabilis regina miram in cunctis exhibuit patientiam et fortem in adversis constantiam; custos oris sui, ne quid proferret incongrui, studiosa ad continue orationis usum ... immo illata sibi iniuria constantior ... leve existimans, quid ferret, tantum ne Christo vilesceret. Nulli maledixit, sed propriis deputavit meritis, quicquid angustie pertulit ab adversandtibus filiis; semper retinenes in memoria, quod in sacra didicerat scriptura, quia per multas tribulationes et angustias oportet nos introire regnum dei.*

and readers as excessive."⁴³ Matilda, who knows of her son's unremitting suffering, at the end of her life, gazes at her grandson, also a Henry, and prophesizes:

> Constant misfortunes will beset those of his successors who possess [Henry's name]. How could we describe the trials and tribulations undergone by this boy's father? Still, all that happened to him has been God's will. It is our hope that this name will remain in our family until a baby grandson springs from this young boy's seed, one who will be elevated to royal office.⁴⁴

Suffering will persist under Henry's name. His family, his descendants, including Henry II, will endure endless trials. But the Henrician line will be exalted to the highest royal office in the end. The author goes on to confirm that this prophecy came true in Henry II. Because of his family's struggle, and with the help of Matilda's prophecy, Henry II "ascended such an exalted throne."⁴⁵

Concluding with this prophecy, the Life of Matilda demonstrates the importance of the virtues of humility and patience during times of struggle. While the *VMP* does not directly showcase Henry II's own rise from humiliation to exaltation, it does so indirectly by addressing the ideology of kingship by the eleventh century. Namely that power and glory, kingship and reward are preceded by suffering and humility in the face of adversity. The *VMP* almost relentlessly reiterates that the Henrys of Matilda's family have always been, and will be, unlucky and are ceaselessly barraged with misfortune, whether of their own making or whether they were victims of abuse. The *VMP* demonstrates how the endurance of abuse, struggles, and humiliation predestined Henry II's eventual rule, and thus became the expectation of the king.⁴⁶

Thietmar's *Chronicon*, which contains his own account of King Henry and Queen Matilda's lives, agrees with several assessments put forth in the *VMP* concerning the humility and tribulations of the Henrician line. Thietmar reiterates that during the

---

⁴³Ibid., 9, in Gilsdorf, *Queenship and Sanctity*, 100. For the Latin text see *Monumenta Germaniae Historica, Scriptores, SS. rer. Germ.*, vol. 66, 161: *Hic multa de angustiis eius praetermittuntur, quia, si per singula volverentur, narrantibus simul et legentibus prolixa viderentur.*

⁴⁴Ibid., 20, in Gilsdorf, *Queenship and Sanctity*, 116. For the Latin text see *Monumenta Germaniae Historica, Scriptores, SS. rer. Germ.*, vol. 66, 185: *Postquam autem in posteros venit, numquam infortunio caruit. Quid dicimus de angustiis et tribulationibus, quas sustinuit pater ipsius? Se denim adhuc in divina dispositione est, quid huic debeat acidere. Speramus autem hoc nomen non excidere de genere nostro, priusquam aliquis parvulus nepos oriatur de eiusdem pueri seimine, qui sublimetur regali dignitate.*

⁴⁵Ibid.: *et cognosce te tante dignitatis ascendisse solium per ipsius interventum et meritum.*

⁴⁶Gilsdorf, *Queenship and Sanctity*, 54–55.

lifetimes of all the Henrys "disruption was frequent and tranquility uncertain."[47] Like the *VMP*, Thietmar notes that the cursed Henrys would suffer endlessly. Henry II would also blunder through mishaps, but with him "iniquity dried up and the vigorous bloom of the good peace burst out."[48]

Additionally, during an uprising against Henry II by Duke Boleslav and Margrave Henry around 1003, Thietmar states that "one must weather the sudden burst of injustice with the rudder of patience and, with humble supplication, await a consolation which will be truly useful."[49] Thietmar gives this advice particularly to the kings. It is they especially who must endure moments of injustice with patience and humility.

Wipo's *Gesta Chuonradi* also looks at the idea of humiliation leading to highest exultation. The *Gesta* was dedicated to Conrad II's son, Henry III, not long after he was crowned King of Italy in 1039.[50] As the title suggests, it recounts Conrad II's reign, who was the first of the Salian line. Chapter three of the *Gesta* is dedicated entirely to the first coronation of Conrad II, when he was crowned King of Germany. A large portion of this chapter is the sermon given by the archbishop of Mainz, who performed the coronation. The sermon dispenses advice to the newly crowned king as well as the reasons why he is qualified to be king; namely, Conrad's election by God and his endurance of humiliation and suffering.

The archbishop tells the king that God demands that each of his elect first be tested and tried. God is known to "scourge each one that he would receive" and it "pleases God to humiliate those whom he wishes to exalt."[51] Those whom God deems worthy, he first

---

[47] Thietmar, "Chronicon," 1.24, in trans. Warner, *Ottonian Germany*, 85. For the Latin text see *Monumenta Germaniae Historica, Scriptores, SS rer. Germ. N.S.*, vol. 9, 32: *crebra fieret commocio et quietis parva certitudo*.

[48] Ibid.: *iniquitatis exaruit et pacis bonae flos virens enituit*. Thietmar provides a fantastical excuse as to why the Henrys of the family must endure such hardships. Foolishly, Henry forces Queen Matilda to have sexual intercourse on Maundy Thursday, which is forbidden. Thietmar explains that Satan was involved in instigating the encounter and doomed the conceived child to be his. The king's mother found out about this and made sure that the pregnant queen was always surrounded by priests and when the child was born to have had him baptized immediately. Satan, furious at the ploy, swore that his companion, Discord, will plague the child and the child's offspring. The son born was Duke Henry I of Bavaria and his son would be Duke Henry the Quarrelsome, whose grandson would be Henry II.

[49] Thietmar, "Chronicon," 5.32, in trans. Warner, *Ottonain Germany*, 226–27. For the Latin text see *Monumenta Germaniae Historica, Scriptores, SS rer. Germ. N.S.*, vol. 9, 257: *subitanea vero inique mentis inflacio retrahi debet paciencie gubernaculo et per humilem prelatrorum subiectionem expectare sis bene profuturam consolacionem*.

[50] Sverre Bagge, *Kings, Politics, and the Right Order in German Historiography c. 950–1150* (Leiden: Brill, 2002), 189. Henry III was crowned King of Germany in 1028 (in Conrad's lifetime), King of Italy in 1039, and Emperor in 1046.

[51] Wipo, "Gesta Chuondradi II Imperatoris," 3, *Monumenta Germaniae Historica, Scriptores, SS rer. Germ.*, vol. 61, 22: *flagellat enim omnem, quem recipit . . . placuit ei humiliare, quem proposuit exaltare*.

afflicts with abuses; those whom God exalts, God first humiliates. The archbishop enlists the example of Old Testament heroes who also endured temptation, persecution, wrath, and exile. Conrad, like Abraham and David, is blessed to have suffered, "since he will receive his crown."[52]

The archbishop even provides a specific example from Conrad's life which points to the hardships and injuries he received. Conrad's predecessor, Henry II, expelled Conrad from his favor, which naturally would have been humiliating for Conrad and caused some level of hardship. It was in fact God who orchestrated this punishment so that Conrad could endure injury and humiliation.[53] It was also the hope, explains the archbishop, that such suffering would teach the king to pity those out of favor with himself; to forgive and recognize suffering in others.

The hardships and suffering that Conrad withstood taught him how to sustain injuries, as the Archbishop explained. In the end it was because of his endurance of these trials and humiliation that he gained the highest seat. Here in Wipo's *Gesta*, even more overtly than in the *VMP*, the idea has gained traction that the king obtained the crown through, not only a life of hardship, but also his aptitude to endure humiliation and suffering.

These ideas concerning humiliation and suffering of the king leading to power and glory are paralleled in Christ's own humiliation and suffering. The *VMP* and Wipo offer a model of gaining kingship that remarkably mimics that of Christ's eventual ascension to his throne in heaven. Christ is humiliated on earth; he endures untold trials and suffering at the hands of his enemies. But his suffering was a necessary means to a glorious end: the heavenly throne and rule over all. In the same way, the king was seen as necessarily going through periods of suffering, misfortune, and abject humiliation. The end result of suffering is the highest earthly throne and well-deserved rulership. All of this is expected as part of the Christo-Mimetic ideal.

As mentioned above, it is, of course, imperative to recall that the epitomic example of Jesus' humiliation was universally considered to be his Mockery under Pilate's soldiers.[54] Here Jesus demonstrated the greatest humility and patience so that the

---

[52]Ibid., *Beatus, qui suffert temptationem, quoniam hic accipiet [accipit] coronam.*
[53]Ibid., 21–23.
[54]This idea presumably endured unchanged in Ottonian theology as it had in Carolingian theology. The Ottonian intellectuals offered few new theological commentaries or contributions. The biblical commentaries of the Carolingians were copied and read by the Ottonian intellectuals, and they felt no need to add or tweak the Carolingian theological conclusions. Instead, the Ottonians notably focused their intellectual pursuits on historiographical and liturgical developments. See especially Claudio Leonardi, "Intellectual Life," in *The New Cambridge Medieval History, Vol. III, c. 900–1024*, ed. Timothy Reuter (Cambridge: Cambridge University Press,

mock crowning would prefigure the actual, heavenly crowning. It is a neat parallel. The king is humiliated in order to be crowned; Jesus endured the most humiliating of circumstances of a mock coronation in order to be crowned and enthroned in heaven. The king's imitation of Jesus' humiliation and endurance necessarily precedes coronation and enthronement in the highest earthly position.

This in part helps explain why the image of the Enthroned Mockery so closely resembles the coronation portrait of the king. It is the image, rather than the written sources, that draws the obvious parallel between the suffering of the king and that of Christ. By diverging from the norm of the Mockery scene and setting Jesus on a throne like Henry II or Otto's; by giving them similar instruments, symmetrical attendants, and the near exact adoration of those attendants, the artist forcefully invokes specific comparisons between Christ and the king—their expected similarities, the king's expected mimicry. The art elicits the widely accepted ideological parallels between the king and Christ. Specifically, that the king and Christ both necessarily, and humbly, endured injustice prior to their coronations.

The ideology of kingship in the tenth and early eleventh centuries explains why Jesus looks like the king in his Mockery scenes. It does not, however, answer the question of why these coronation images of the king, which allowed for the Enthroned Mockery image, would have had such a profound influence. The answer lies in the increased cultural importance of the actual ritual coronation of the king and the subsequent enthronement of the king. These factors contributed not only to portraying the Mockery as an enthronement, but also played a role in the appearance of the Crown of Thorns itself.

Coronation and enthronement of the Ottonian and Salian kings

As is widely understood, the Ottonian intellectuals contributed more to the development of literary genres such as historiography and liturgy than to any sort of theological commentaries. The lives of kings and bishops; their conflicts, uprisings, and demonstrations of piety and justice, are thoroughly detailed in many chronicles and other works. In

---

1999), 204–210; Timothy Reuter, *Germany in the Early Middle Ages, c. 800–1056* (London and New York: Longman, 1991), 146–147; and Karl Leyser, *Communication and Power in Medieval Europe; The Carolingian and Ottonian Centuries*, vol. 1 (London: Hambledon Press, 1994), 194–195.

accounts of the kings, the ritual coronation and enthronement ceremonies and all the various traditions and instruments that went into them garnered particular interest, especially their first coronation as King of Germany. The popularity of these coronations is proved by the accuracy of detail and frequency with which they are depicted in art and in turn, how the Enthroned Mockery also mimics these descriptions. A literary survey of the first coronation ceremonies of some of the Ottonian and Salian kings will illuminate the details of the artistic rendering of the coronation of the king and subsequently invoke further parallels with the Enthroned Mockery.

Beginning with an earlier work, Widukind's *Res Gestae Saxonicae*, the Deeds of the Saxons, was finished and dedicated to Matilda, Otto I's daughter, around 967–968.[55] Widukind provides important details of the coronation ritual of the Ottonian kings and emperors; rituals which would continue to be practiced in later Ottonian and the Salian coronation ceremonies.

Widukind describes how Otto I was placed on the throne in Aachen to be crowned King of Germany in 936, surrounded by "the dukes and leading counts, and a large number of other military officers" of his realm.[56] They bring Otto to the throne and swear loyalty to him, promising to support the king against all enemies of the realm.[57] The archbishop of Mainz, who had approached the enthroned king, asks all the leaders and soldiers surrounding the king that if his election by God pleases them to "show it by raising your right arms to heaven." The people do so and as one "raised their arms to heaven and cried out a great shout for the new leader to have good fortune."[58] The archbishop then equips the king with the royal insignia. After a discussion of the king's new duties, "Otto was anointed with the holy oil, and crowned with the golden diadem by Bishops Hildebert and Wigfried."[59]

Thietmar's account of Henry II's coronation as King of Germany in 1002 offers a description of similar rituals to Otto I's. When Henry was understood to be God's elect,

---

[55] Bagge, *Kings*, 23–29.

[56] Widukind, "Rerum Gestarum Saxonicarum", 2.1, in Bachrach trans., *Deeds of the Saxons* (Washington D.C.: The Catholic University of America Press, 2014), 62. For the Latin text see *Monumenta Germaniae Historica, Scriptores, SS rer. Germ.*, vol. 60, 64: *duces ac prefectorum principes cum caetera principum militum.*

[57] Widukind, "Rerum Gestarum Saxonicarum," 2.1, in trans. Bachrach, *Deeds*, 62–63. For the Latin text see *Monumenta Germaniae Historica, Scriptores, SS rer. Germ.*, vol. 60, 64.

[58] Widukind, "Rerum Gestarum Saxonicarum," 2.1, in trans. Bachrach, *Deeds*, 62–63. For the Latin text see *Monumenta Germaniae Historica, Scriptores, SS rer. Germ.*, vol. 60, 65: *si vobis ista electio placeat, dextris in caelum levatis sigSificate; Ad haec omnis populus dextras in excelsum levans cum clamore balido inprecati sunt prospera novo duci.*

[59] Widukind, "Rerum Gestarum Saxonicarum", 2.1, in trans. Bachrach, *Deeds*, 63–64. For the Latin text see *Monumenta Germaniae Historica, Scriptores, SS rer. Germ.*, vol. 60, p. 66: *Perfususque ilico oleo sancto et coronatus diademate aureo ab ipsis pontificibus Hildiberhto et Wichfrido.*

he was seated on the throne. The people and supporters with one voice declared it was Henry's right to rule and Christ would surely be his aid. They declared that "they were prepared to be supportive in all that he asked of them. They affirmed this with their right hands raised."[60]

Wipo's account of Conrad II's first coronation as King of Germany in 1024 provides more extended details of the procedure. First, Conrad proves to his peers that he is steady, worthy, and just; an ideal candidate for kingship. He is duly elected as king, as God intended.[61] After his election, he heads to Mainz with much pomp and circumstance for his anointing. Conrad arrives at Mainz where clerics and the archbishop await him. The anointing and crowning are performed, followed by a lengthy sermon by the archbishop, as discussed above. After the coronation, Conrad completes his ascension by traveling with the royal court to Aachen where he is enthroned on the "official throne of the whole kingdom, placed there by the ancient kings and by Charles [the Great]."[62] He then for the first time dispenses justice and arranges matters of state. His enthronement at Aachen surrounded by the royal court is seen as the final step to kingship. Wipo spends some time describing Conrad's itinerary about the region, his enthronement at various points, and his attention to matters of his realm. The election and affirmation by the people, the coronation, and the enthronement are all part of the process of the ritualized making of a king.

Several moments of the ritual coronation are particularly important to its artistic rendering. First, it is significant that the king is enthroned and surrounded by dukes and lay leaders, "clerics of every rank," as well as military officers, as described by Widukind.[63] In images such as the coronation scene of Otto II or Henry II in *De Bello Judaico* and the slightly earlier coronation of Otto III in his Gospel Book (Figure 20) the enthroned and bedecked emperor is surrounded by bishops to the left and soldiers to the right. This reflects, rather accurately, the literary description of the coronation, even to the extent that the men surrounding the king raise their right hands in acceptance and acclamation of his kingship. In the Enthroned Mockery images, while it is expected that soldiers

---

[60]Thietmar, "Chronicon", 5.2–3, in trans. Warner, *Ottonian Germany*, 206–207. For the Latin text see *Monumenta Germaniae Historica, Scriptores, SS rer. Germ. N.S.*, vol. 9, 223–224: *quae sibi umquam scirent esse boluntaria. Hocque dextris manibus elevatis affirmatur.*
[61]Wipo, "Gesta Chuondradi II Imperatoris", 2, *Monumenta Germaniae Historica, Scriptores, SS rer. Germ.*, vol. 61, 13–20.
[62]Wipo, "Gesta Chuondradi II Imperatoris", 6, *Monumenta Germaniae Historica, Scriptores, SS rer. Germ.*, vol. 61, 28: *ubi publicus thronus regalis ab antiquis regibus et a Carolo praecipue locates totius regni archisolium habetur.*
[63]Widukind, "Rerum Gestarum Saxonicarum", 2.1, in trans. Bachrach, *Deeds*, 61–62. For the Latin text see *Monumenta Germaniae Historica, Scriptores, SS rer. Germ.*, vol. 60, 64: *universo sacerdotali ordine.*

would surround Jesus at this moment, it is more significant that the soldiers raise their hands in the exact manner as described by Widukind and Thietmar.

This gesture of mock praise in the Enthroned Mockery is slightly altered from that of the kneeling soldiers of the Stuttgart and the Codex Egberti examples (Figure 11). Instead of the gesture of hands upturned while kneeling, the Enthroned Mockery perceptively shifts Pilate's soldiers to match the king's soldiers and bishops: they stand, arm raised in acclamation of kingship. Furthermore, Widukind notes that the actual crowning was done by two archbishops. Both the Gospel Book of Otto III as well as in *De Bello Judaico*, the enthroned king is accompanied on one side by two bishops. Maintaining the symmetry of pairs, images such as in the Bamberg Apocalypse (Figure 21), Henry II is crowned on either side by Peter and Paul, much like the literary description of the king crowned by a pair of priests. The Enthroned Mockery again, to reflect the king's coronation, diverges from the typical arrangement of the abusive soldiers crowded in an unorganized mass around Jesus. Instead, they are simply and more symmetrically on either side of Jesus in order to crown him, like the bishops in Widukind and the image in the Bamberg Apocalypse.

It is also worth noting the attention given to placing the king on a throne. Widukind and Wipo both mention the process of enthroning the king as part of the ritual coronation. For Wipo, the process of enthronement happened throughout the kingdom, in an act of displaying to the people their new king. This multiplicity of the enthronement imagery coupled with the literary evidence of ritually enthroning the king to solidify his kingship, speaks to the cultural importance of seeing the king crowned and enthroned. It also suggests another reason why Jesus is enthroned in this unique Mockery scene. If Jesus is meant to parallel the king, especially at the king's moment of coronation, then Jesus must also, like the king, be enthroned as fulfilment of the ritual.

Another part of the ritual, which is also an obvious feature of the images of the king and the Enthroned Mockery, are the instruments that accompany them. Of particular interest are the so-called Holy Lance and the Imperial Crown. In the Enthroned Mockery, Jesus is given a reed, which as noted above is like the king's scepter, known as the Holy Lance, in the coronation images. They both wear a crown, and both hold a second sacred object in their left hands. They are the instruments, both for the Ottonians and the Gospel narrative, that make a ruler. Widukind takes several opportunities to discuss the importance of these royal insignia. The first reference to them comes at King Conrad I's death bed (d. 918). He explains to his brother, Eberhard, that while he and his family have everything required of a king, an army, fortresses, weapons, and the royal insignia (*regalibus insigniis*), they lack the proper temperament for kingship.[64] Such qualifications reside in Henry I. Conrad therefore tells his brother to "take the insignia, the holy lance, the golden buckles with their cloak, the sword of the ancient kings, and crown and go to Henry."[65] These will complete Henry's worthy ascension to the highest power of the state.

When Otto I became King of Germany in 936, the meaning and intent in each of the royal insignia were explicated by the archbishop Hildebert, who bestowed them on him. As Hildebert picked up the scepter he instructs Otto that the scepter signifies his "responsibility to restrain your subjects with paternal discipline" but first offering mercy to God's subjects, who are now also Otto's subjects.[66] The crown, on the other hand, is expressly a reminder of the king's compassion. One of the king's primary duties is to be compassionate, and upholding this virtue, says Hildebert, will gain the king not only the crown on earth, but he will be crowned again in "the future with the eternal prize."[67] The reference to being crowned now and in the future is, again, not unlike the theology surrounding Jesus' Mockery. Jesus was crowned rightfully, though it was in mockery, and he will be crowned again in heaven. So too the king is crowned on earth and will be crowned for a final time in heaven.[68]

It is important to at least consider the question of how well-known the image of the king, crowned and seated on his throne, was throughout the realm. Would the people, the clerics, and artists have known this image of the king so well that they would not only depict it in their art, but recognize the artistic parallel in Jesus' Enthroned Mockery? Were the emperors and kings so commonly enthroned and his coronation so memorable that it would be the go-to image for his portraiture?

Most likely, yes. This is largely due to the fact that the Ottonian and Salian kings were itinerant.[69] With no one central location the king traveled from one bishopric or estate

---

[64]Widukind, "Rerum Gestarum Saxonicarum," 1.25, in trans. Bachrach, *Deeds*, 38. For the Latin text see *Monumenta Germaniae Historica, Scriptores, SS rer. Germ.*, vol. 60, 37–38.

[65]Widukind, "Rerum Gestarum Saxonicarum," 1.25, in trans. Bachrach, *Deeds*, 38. For the Latin text see *Monumenta Germaniae Historica, Scriptores, SS rer. Germ.*, vol. 60, p. 38: *Sumptis igitur his insigniis, lancea sacra, armillis aureis cum clamide et veterum gladio regum ac diademate, ito ad Heinricum.*

[66]Widukind, "Rerum Gestarum Saxonicarum," 2.1, in trans. Bachrach, *Deeds*, 63–64. For the Latin text see *Monumenta Germaniae Historica, Scriptores, SS rer. Germ.*, vol. 60, 66: *monitus paterna castigatione subiectos corripias.*

[67]Widukind "Rerum Gestarum Saxonicarum," 2.1, in trans. Bachrach, *Deeds*, 64. For the Latin text see *Monumenta Germaniae Historica, Scriptores, SS rer. Germ.*, vol. 60, 66: *et in futuro sempiterno premio coroneris.*

[68]The extensive interpretation of the king's accoutrement is reminiscent of the Carolingian discussion of the Instruments of the Passion above, in that they are each given implicit meaning and significance.

[69]On details concerning the movement of the emperors and kings during high feast days and the politics surrounding this itinerant travel see Gerald Beyreuther, "Die Osterfeier als Akt königlicher Repräsentanz und

to another around his realm. His visitations were accompanied with ritual crown-wearings and enthronements. During festivals and high holy days, whenever the king arrived at his new location, before judicial proceedings, matters of state, and conflict resolution began, the king participated in repeated rituals reiterating his coronation. During this ritual, elaborate ceremonies were performed in front of churches, monasteries, monks, bishops, and lay observers. He would be crowned and then participate in the sacred rites of the liturgy. The wearing of the crown and "festival coronations" reaffirmed the sanctity of the king and emperor and the fact that he had been crowned and anointed already—that he was Christ's vicar, representative, imitator, and embodiment on earth.[70]

It is most likely that when contemporary sources say that the king went forth "encrowned" it is probably referring to such solemn ceremonies.[71] Henry II, who is depicted in the Bamberg Apocalypse (Figure 21) and probably also in the *De Bello Judaico* coronation images, made a point of participating in these "solemn coronations" more often than any of his predecessors. He displayed himself crowned to more people and designated more festivals during which, liturgically, he could be crowned. This may have something to do with his particular need to affirm his rightful kingship, due to its dubious beginnings.[72] The timeline of the Enthroned Mockery images then gain more significance. Both examples show up during or soon after Henry II was seen with deliberate regularity in his crown and on a throne. The imagery of the Enthroned Mockery is also perhaps an attempt to further legitimize his kingship with a starkly obvious connection to Christ.

Once again, however, the Crown of Thorns' sudden appearance remains in question. Its appearance may have something to do, quite simply, with the increased popularity of crowns. If the above analysis is true, then anything that parallels the king to Christ is up for artistic exploitation. As explained, one of the more important royal insignia of the king was his crown. He was crowned on at least three official occasions during his reign and then countless times ritually.[73] The crown is part of what made a king, a king. Thus,

---

Herrschaftsausübung unter Heinrich II. (1002–1024)," in *Feste und Feiern im Mittelalter; Paderborner Symposion des Mediävistenbandes*, ed. Detlef Altenburg, Jörg Jarnut, and Hans-Hugo Steinhoff, 245–253 (Sigmaringen: Thorbecke, 1991).

[70]Karl Leyser, *Rule and Conflict in an Early Medieval Society; Ottonian Saxony* (Bloomington and London: Indiana University Press, 1979), 103–105; Mayr-Harting, *Church and Cosmos in Early Ottonian Germany; The View of Cologne* (Oxford: Oxford University Press, 2007), 3–4.

[71]Herwig Wolfram, *Conrad II 990-1039: Emperor of Three Kingdoms*, trans. Denise Kaiser (University Park: Pennsylvania State University Press, 2006), 154–157.

[72]Leyser, *Rule and Conflict,* 99–100.

[73]Wolfram, *Conrad II*, 154–155.

the fact that Jesus, during one of the most important narratives of the Gospel is actually given a crown is yet another opportunity to parallel the earthly king and the heavenly king. Jesus' crown is decorated with inlaid thorns that stick up from a wreath, as is shown rather prominently in the Codex Aureus of Echternach (Figure 17). While it does not exactly resemble the king's crown, it is rendered so that it looks like an obvious crown; wreath-like, but also regal. Moreover, the Saint Peter Gospels' Enthroned Mockery crown, as noted, goes so far as to resemble the kings' own crown. The popularity of the king's crown and the increased desire to parallel the king and Christ's humiliation led to the first tentative steps to rendering the Crown of Thorns.

The Mockery of Jesus does not just suddenly appear in the mid-eleventh century as an Enthroned Mockery with a recognizable Crown of Thorns, but also with Jesus enthroned while mocked, an image that has limited associations with its predecessors. This image of Jesus' Enthroned Mockery happens because of two primary developments: the new ideology of kingship plus the optics of the coronation rituals. The Ottonian and Salian emperors and kings were Christ's perfect imitators and, especially with the reigns of Henry II and Conrad II, their imitation extended to suffering existential humiliation prior to their crowning. Indeed, this particular facet of imitation is what made them worthy of kingship.

This idea seems to have led to the increased interest in Christ's prime example of enduring humility: the Mockery. But how to artistically render this parallel between the ruler and Christ? With an Enthroned Mockery. It mimics the widely known and engrained image of coronation of the king. The kings were not only emphatic about being visibly enthroned and crowned throughout their realm, but these coronations were a popular portrait for representing the sovereignty of the ruler. They were a reminder to the people, soldiers, and clerics that the king, who was once humiliated and suffered, was chosen by God as Christ's vicar and perfect imitator. The image of the Enthroned Mockery therefore came about as yet another reminder of the king's likeness to Christ. The image speaks directly to the idea that the king was humiliated like Christ, endured like Christ, was crowned like Christ, and will be crowned again in heaven like Christ. The Enthroned Mockery is optical ideology of Ottonian kingship.

As stated previously, the image of the Enthroned Mockery does not stay in this form for very long. By the end of the eleventh century and the reign of Henry III, the throne, specifically, has disappeared. Some of the innovations of the Enthroned Mockery, however, persist. First, the Crown of Thorns will immediately become a standard feature of the Mockery. Second, the symmetry of the soldiers surrounding Jesus will become more popular. And third, the episode will eventually warrant its own elaborate scene, as opposed to the conflation of several narratives into one illustration, as it was in the Codex Egberti. A brief analysis of several further examples will demonstrate the continued artistic progression of the Mockery of the eleventh century and serve to conclude this survey of the Crown of Thorns.

The Mockery solidified

The Mockery scene makes a perceptible shift in the remainder of the Salian era; curiously losing the throne, while selectively maintaining many of the Enthroned Mockery's innovations. The presence of the throne and direct parallel between the king and Christ seems to vanish with the renditions of the Mockery made under and for the second Salian king, Henry III, who succeeded Conrad in 1039 and reigned until his death in 1056. Fol. 53v of the Lectionary of Henry III, made in the Abbey of Echternach for King Henry III sometime around 1039–1043, will serve as an enlightening initiation into this progression.[74] The scene of the Mockery is part of a full-page illustration directly preceding the Gospel reading for the Wednesday Mass of Holy Week.[75] It closely follows the example of the Codex Egberti by portraying the same multiple events in the single illumination. As in the Codex Egberti, a bearded Pilate, though unlabeled, stands close to the center, holding Jesus' hand and pointing towards him. The same two groups, again unlabeled, are figured opposite Pilate and Jesus. Three men stand in long tunics with one pointing his finger towards Jesus, in a familiar gesture of accusation. The soldiers next to the standing group kneel on one knee with arms outstretched and palms up in mock adoration. All of this is in near exact imitation of the Codex Egberti.

An additional man who does not appear in the Codex Egberti stands behind Jesus, nearly out of the frame. He reaches up and places a large, woven Crown of Thorns on top of Jesus' head, who stands in serene acceptance of his condition. This Crown of Thorns has the plant-like construction of the Crown in the Codex Aureus of Echternach (Figure 17). Both depict prominent, woven crowns with inset thorns that project from

---

[74]Bremen, Staats–und Universitatisbibliothek, Lectionary of Henry III, MS. b 21, fol. 53v, Echternach, c. 1039–1043; Thomas Elsmann, "Das Evangelistar (Perikopenbuch) Kaiser Heinrich III. (msb 0021)," *Staat-und Universitätsbibliothek Bremen*, 2014. https://m.suub.uni-bremen.de/app/webroot/uploads/cms/files/Evangelistar_SuUB_Bremen.pdf, 2014, 1–2.

[75]Mayr-Harting, *Ottonian*, 199–200. In general, the illustrations of this Lectionary come before the pericope which they portray, not unlike the Carolingian examples of the Utrecht Psalter, where the illustration comes before the psalm it interprets.

all around the edges of the wreath. The Lectionary of Henry III therefore seems to borrow trends both from the Codex Egberti and the Codex Aureus of Echternach. With the addition of the Crowning, however, the Mockery narrative takes precedence over the other scenes of the illustration. The primacy of the Mockery is accentuated by the inscription, which reads: *Portas spinifera(m) derisus XPE corona(m)*; "Christ, you carry the prickly crown, having been mocked." The inscription does not derive from any particular Gospel text. Rather, it is a description emphasizing the main event of the illustration; namely the Crowning of Jesus. Thus, it is already notable that, although the throne is lacking and the scene is conflated with several other moments in the Passion narrative, the Mockery and Crowning have a preeminent position in the illustration, by virtue of the amount of space they take up and the inscriptional emphasis.

It is within the Speyer Gospels[76] that the Mockery scene demonstrates more definitive trends established by the Enthroned Mockery. The Speyer Gospels was commissioned by Henry III sometime around 1043–1046. Like the Lectionary of Henry III, it was also made in the Abbey of Echternach.[77] It was presented to Speyer Cathedral expressly for liturgical use.[78] The Mockery scene appears in the top panel in a series of three Passion images. Against a colonnaded backdrop Jesus stands in the center, rather more still than the rest of the crowd. He is flanked by two men who both grab his cloak as if dressing him in the robe, and place a wreath on his head. An equally distributed group of soldiers holding sticks jostle erratically.

The scene takes several features from the Enthroned Mockery examples. Most significant is the continuation of the presence of the Crown of Thorns, the centralized Mockery, and the symmetrically placed soldiers. This particular Crown, unlike the other examples, looks like a wrapped rope with thorny edges. The thorns are much smaller than in either the Enthroned Mockery examples or the Codex Aureus of Echternach. Jesus is in the center, flanked by two men who bestow the crown on him. The rest of the scene is filled with a crowd of soldiers who are relatively numerically balanced on either side of Jesus, which mimics the symmetry of the Enthroned Mockery. The large number of soldiers, however, is a return to the model of the Stuttgart Psalter's Mockery, as opposed to the Enthroned Mockery's two or three soldiers surrounding Jesus.

---

[76]Escorial, Real Biblioteca, Speyer Gospels (Codex Aureus Escorialensis, Gospel Book of Henry III), MS Vit. 17, fol. 83r, c. 1043–1046.
[77]Escorial, Real Biblioteca, Speyer Gospels (Codex Aureus Escorialensis, Gospel Book of Henry III), MS Vit. 17, fol. 83r, Echternach, c. 1043–1046.
[78]Mayr-Harting, *Ottonian*, 188.

As with the Enthroned Mockery of the Saint Peter Gospels, which has an entire scene to itself, the Mockery scene of the Speyer Gospels utilizes the whole strip solely for the depiction of the Mockery. It is not merely one among a number of narratives on a condensed composition, like the Codex Egberti and the Lectionary of Henry III. In addition, the inscription emphasizes the Crown of Thorns portion of the narrative: *Plectentes spineam coronam imposverunt et dixerunt: Ave Rex Iudeorum*, "Braiding a crown of thorns they put it on and said: Hail King of the Jews."[79] Out of the entire narrative of the Mockery, the inscription and the illustration focus on the moment Jesus is crowned.

The last example in the series of eleventh-century Mockery scenes comes a few decades later. The Vysehrad Codex, made in Bohemia, was dedicated to King Vratislaus II in honor of his coronation in 1085. The king kept the Codex in his residence at Vysehrad, hence the name given to the Codex.[80] The Mockery scene occurs in the top panel on the last page of a series of five full-page illuminations depicting the Passion cycle. The Passion cycle occurs directly after the readings of John 13:1–15, the Last Supper.

In the Vysehrad Codex's Mockery, Jesus once again stands in the center of the image (Figure 22). He is surrounded by a multitude of soldiery, who are equal in number on either side of Jesus, similar to the Speyer Gospels. Two soldiers flanking Jesus begin to go down on bended-knee with palms lifted upward, as in the early Stuttgart examples appropriated by the Codex Egberti and the Lectionary of Henry III (Figure 11). Now, however, they are symmetrically positioned. Several other soldiers around Jesus point with the gesture of accusation, which is a departure from the acclamation gesture of the soldiers of the Enthroned Mockery. Two soldiers standing on either side of Jesus, instead of crowning him, appear to pull his hair in a demonstration of abuse closer to that seen with the spitting soldiers of the Saint Peter Gospels and before that with the Stuttgart Psalter's soldiers. The inscription once again underscores the important features of the illustration. Here it makes explicit reference to both the abuse as well as the Crown of Thorns: *Suscipit hic alapas vestris ludibria spinas*, "Here he receives your mockeries of blows and thorns." With the previous examples, the Crown is the focus of the inscription and the scene. In the Vysehrad Codex, however, the physical abuse that Jesus receives is of equal importance.

---

[79]The inscription is based on Mk 15:17–18: *Et imponunt ei plectentes spineam coronam et coeperunt salutare eum: Ave Rex Iudaeorum*. The version above replaces *imponunt* with a similar word and simplifies the acclamation (*salutare*) of the soldiers to merely "they said" (*dixerunt*).

[80]"Vysehrad Codex," National Library of the Czech Republic.

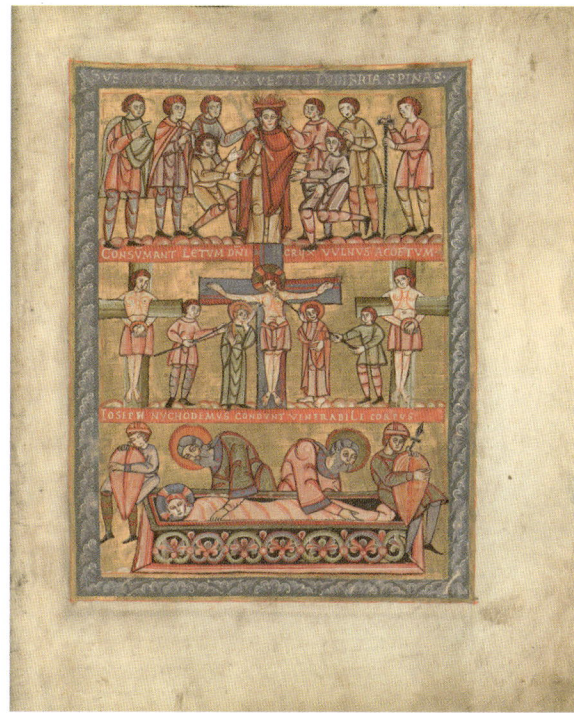

Figure 22 *Vysehrad Codex, MS. XIV A 13, fol. 42r, Bohemia, c. 1085, National and University Library of the Czech Republic, Prague.*

The central figure of Jesus, dressed in a bright red-purple cloak, once again bears a Crown of Thorns. This Crown is slightly different to the preceding two Salian examples. It is more of a solid band with no evidence of weaving. It is closer to the Crown of the Saint Peter Gospels, which in turn imitates the king's crown. The thorns here, like in the Saint Peter Gospels, protrude out of the top, instead of all around. Jesus' demeanor in this interpretation of the Mockery is also significant. He stands completely frontally holding his stick-like scepter. His other hand is outstretched in blessing, even in the midst of his torment. This is a regal Christ. He stands tall, looking out at the audience, unperturbed by the abuse going on around him. This unflappable, exalted Jesus is an imitation of the Jesus of the Enthroned Mockery, where, as discussed, he takes on a royal air in expectation of his future heavenly enthronement.

It is possible to discern from the above analysis that in the later Salian imagery, there is a shift away from some of the unique features of the Enthroned Mockery. For example, the deletion of the throne and the gesture of acclamation, confirms that the Enthroned Mockery had a very specific agenda. The deliberate comparison to the king is no longer the purpose of the Mockery scene. With that determined, it is still significant that some of the other aspects of the Enthroned Mockery become conventional, especially Jesus' still exalted position, the symmetrical soldiers, the obvious abuse, and, most importantly, the addition of the Crown of Thorns. While the artists are still experimenting with the style of the Crown of Thorns in the later part of the eleventh century, it has finally become a permanent, and indeed emphasized, fixture within the Mockery scene.

The purpose of this inquiry has been realized: the Crown of Thorns has finally found its place in the Mockery scene as a fully-fledged, recognizable crown made of actual thorns, where it will remain and flourish as an enduring tribute to Jesus' triumph over enemies, humility in the face of adversity, and supreme heavenly kingship over all.

The Crown's audience—patronage and media

The Golden Altar of Aachen, out of all the main works discussed here, was by far the most conspicuously public piece of propaganda. As discussed above, the altar, according to the inscription, was donated by Henry II as the altar piece for the Aachen Cathedral's Palace Chapel. Built by Charlemagne,[81] to whom the Ottonian kings traced their ancestry, the octagonal chapel was not only imbued with significant royal history, but was also the location for the coronation of the Ottonian kings.[82] It was in this prominent setting that Henry II displayed golden depictions of Christ soon after his imperial coronation of 1014.

The significance of this well-documented patronage and audience should not be overlooked. Brilliantly gold and probably originally bedecked with gems, the reliefs that Henry donated were primarily part of the Passion sequence, including the arrest in Gethsemane, the Flagellation, the Mockery, the Crucifixion, and the Marys at the tomb.[83] More importantly, there are not one, but two scenes of enthronement on the altar. At the center is Christ in Majesty, enthroned and surrounded by his retinue. The second is the Enthroned Mockery, as described above. Both these enthronements of Christ are similar to Henry's own coronation imagery: centralized ruler, surrounded by attendants, holding instruments. It is possible to surmise that Henry II himself dictated this imagery and displayed it so publicly in order to re-emphasize his Christ-

---

[81]The Palatine Chapel was mostly completed by 798.
[82]Walter Maas, *Der Aachener Dom* (Köln: Greven, 1984), 23–24.
[83]Garrison, *Ottonian*, 103–105.

ordained right to rule. The Enthroned Mockery, more than the Christ in Majesty, links Henry's rise from humiliation to exaltation with Christ's own example, as was necessary for the Ottonian ruler. It is a less than subtle visual: the actual crowned ruler enthroned opposite imagery of the Enthroned Christ on a sacred altar. During any one of his coronations, Henry's court, attendants, clerics and bishops, lay leaders, military officers, and the public[84] would have seen their emperor enthroned as Christ was enthroned, both making parallels to Henry's Christo-Mimetic rule, as well as his legitimacy. This enthronement tableau, of course, due to the itinerant nature of the Ottonian and Salian kingship, would not have been a one-time affair, but repeated in "festival coronations," as mentioned above, especially when the king came to the historical seat of royal power in Aachen.[85] Henry, perhaps more than other Ottonian and Salian kings and emperors, felt the need to consistently remind his people of his coronation and kingship. An altar set in a prominent place, which was already steeped in a glorious history, would have been a profound statement.

This realization and consideration of audience and patronage contributes to the argument that the Enthroned Mockery was intended to parallel the Coronation imagery of the Ottonian rulers. It is therefore worth making an excursion into the idea of patronage, media, and audience of the other major Mockery scenes in order to gain greater insight into the time, situation, and intention of these works. The Mockery scenes that survive are found, however, in only two media: monumental (the Golden Altar of Aachen) and manuscript illumination. While much of the information concerning history and intention has been lost to unrecorded time, it is possible to make several conjectures gleaned from a few known facts concerning the Codex Aureus of Echternach, the Codex Egberti, and the Saint Peter Gospels.

Even from the examination of the Mockery scenes alone, it is clear that manuscripts from the end of the tenth to the beginning of the eleventh century undergo alarmingly expedited development. The Codex Egberti and Codex Aureus of Echternach, which were both lectionaries meant to be read during worship, contain highly detailed images that reflect the surrounding gospel text. The Saint Peter Gospels, similarly a lectionary, also included extraordinary gold-coated illuminations that take up entire pages. Life

---

[84]These are a few of the groups that would have attended a coronation ritual, as expounded upon above. It is significant how a large number of leaders, both lay and church, would have witnessed such a comparison and imperial propaganda, not to mention those clergy and lay members who would look upon the altar in the church once the king was gone.
[85]Leyser, *Rule and Conflict*, 103–105; Mayr-Harting, *Church and Cosmos*, 3–4.

cycles and Passion cycles of Jesus suddenly become more comprehensive, depicting ever more details from the surrounding Gospel narrative. This is, of course, clearly demonstrated in the inclusion of the Mockery scene, which steadily progresses to incorporate both the Crown of Thorns and Mockery in one scene, as demonstrated above. This enhanced beautification of liturgical texts is notable. It begs the question of audience: who was intended to look at these images and what was the purpose of providing this audience with such beauty and detail?

To answer these questions, it is necessary to first establish exactly what artistic changes took place, specifically in liturgical manuscripts, around the eleventh century. To do so requires a survey of manuscripts over several eras, preferably from the same scriptorium, that can easily catalogue these changes. Due to the vast material available, these changes can be most easily discerned by the manuscripts made in the scriptorium of the Abbey of Echternach. The scriptorium was at its most prolific in the eighth and eleventh centuries and can elucidate obvious shifts that occurred in books exclusively meant for worship.

It is worth explaining why the other scriptoria of the primary manuscripts studied here, the Codex Egberti and the Saint Peter Gospels, are not viable candidates for comparison. The Codex Egberti's commissioner, Egbert, Archbishop of Trier from 977 to 993, is universally accepted.[86] The location of production, however, is unfortunately less firm. Stylistically, historians have argued that the art of the Codex Egberti places the production of the manuscript either in Trier or Reichenau. Since neither can be proven with any certainty, it would be inefficient to pursue the sequence of events in either.

The Saint Peter Gospels, on the other hand, was certainly made in the scriptorium of the Abbey of St. Peter at Salzburg. This is based on an eleventh-century note written on the pages of the manuscript, that included the Saint Peter Gospels on a list of privileges conferred on St. Peter's. Additionally, the manuscript did not leave the abbey until it was purchased by the Morgan Library in 1933. It was likely made by the abbey for liturgical use in the abbey. Thus, its provenance is exceptionally firm.[87] The Abbey's scriptorium, on the other hand, while it is known to have existed in the latter half of the eighth century, did not gain any prominence until at least the eleventh century. Furthermore,

---

[86] Stadtbibliothek Weberbach/Stadtarchiv, "Codex Egberti," 1–2.
[87] New York, Pierpont Morgan Library, Curatorial Record: 1; New York, Pierpont Morgan Library CORSAIR collection: 2; Friedrich Hermann, "Salzburg, St. Peter," in *Die Benediktinischen Mönchs- und nonnenklöster in Osterreich und Südtirol*, eds. Ulrich Faust and Waltraud Krassnig (St. Ottilien: EOS Verlag, 2002), 280–282.

there are only a few solidly identifiable manuscripts attributed to the St. Peter scriptorium prior to the tenth century.[88] Comparison and analysis of shifts in liturgical texts would therefore be difficult. Thus, Echternach remains as the ideal candidate for study. To appreciate the significance of this shift, an excursion into the history of the abbey's manuscript production is necessary here, and while diverting from the main theme of this study, will rejoin it in the end.

The Abbey of Echternach was founded in the early eighth century by Saint Willibrord, a native of Northumbria, who came on a mission across the channel to form a monastic community.[89] As mentioned, much of the product of its prolific scriptorium has survived, particularly from the eighth and eleventh centuries. It is possible even to select material that is specifically liturgical, that is, Gospel books or compilations from which the text for worship were read. There are several prime examples from the eighth century which can generally represent lectionary texts of the period. I will examine three texts: the Augsburg Gospels, the Trier Gospels, and the Codex Eyckensis.[90] The earliest of these, made around 704–722, soon after the foundation of the abbey, is the Augsburg Gospels. The images within the manuscript consists of a cruciform maze, which forms the words *evangeliae vertatis*, canon tables, a page of decorative tapestry, interlaced initials, and an acrostic poem. The complete canon tables consist of long, colorful, often stylized columns with single thin arches connecting them. Atop many of the capitals are decorative plants or animals, such as in the case of fol. 10r, where perched on either end of the tables are two pen-drawn birds, lightly decorated with feather crowns and long beaks.

Based on the liturgical marginal indicators throughout the text, it is likely that the Augsburg Gospels was used during worship. The acrostic found in the very end of the text on fol. 157v, provides a dedicatory inscription to the elderly Laurentius.[91] This was

---

[88] Karl Forstner, "Die Schreibschule von St. Peter," in *St. Peter in Salzburg. Das älteste Kloster im deutschen Sprachraum. 3. Landesausstellung, 15 Mai–26. Okt. 1982. Schätze europäischer Kunst und Kultur.* Red. Heinz Dopsch und Roseitha Juffinger (Salzburg: Druckhaus Nonntal, 1982), 182-83; Kurt Holter, "Hauptwerke der Buchkunst aus St. Peter in Salzburg," in *St. Peter in Salzburg. Das älteste Kloster im deutschen Sprachraum. 3. Landesausstellung, 15 Mai–26. Okt. 1982. Schätze europäischer Kunst und Kultur.* Red. Heinz Dopsch und Roseitha Juffinger (Salzburg: Druckhaus Nonntal, 1982) 154–158.
[89] Nancy Netzer, "Willibrord's Scriptorium at Echternach," in *St. Cutherbert, his Cult and his Community*, eds. Gerald Bonner, David Rollason, Clare Stancliffe (Woodbridge: Boydell Press, 1989), 203–205.
[90] Augsburg, Oettingen-Wallersteinsche Bibliothek, Augsburg Gospels, Cod. I.2.4.2; Trier, Cathedral of Trier Treasury, Trier Gospels, MS 61; Maaseik, Saint Catherine Church, Codex Eyckensis, MS 185.
[91] The first and last letters in red spell: *Laurentius vivat senio.*

likely the same Laurentius who wrote four charters bestowing properties to the abbey and scriptorium's founder, Willibrord, and who also likely accompanied Willibrord on his mission to found the abbey. Moreover, Laurentius, based on his signature found in several other manuscripts made in the eighth century at Echternach, is plausibly speculated to have run the scriptorium in the first quarter of the eighth century.[92]

The Trier Gospels, c. 720–740, likely produced just after the Augsburg Gospels, contain many of the same artistic features, though with added detail. The canon tables of the Trier Gospels are also similar to, and probably inspired by, the Augsburg Gospels. The Trier Gospels also separate the canons with columns, whose capitals are decorated with arches, flora, and fauna. The canon tables of fol. 11r, for example, contain, like the Augsburg tables, decorated columns, here resembling the texture of marble, and two ducks perched on branches on either side of the colonnade. The Trier canons, however, also contain an additional arch, with interlaced geometrical shapes, which encompasses the entire canon table. At the center of the arch a roundel depicts an illuminated apostle. On 11r, the apostle labeled as "Thomas," is haloed, holds a scroll in one hand and blesses with the other.

In addition to the canon tables, the Trier Gospels are illuminated with several images not found in the Augsburg Gospels, such as a page of the four Evangelist symbols, a tetramorph, an Incipit page with archangels, and three Evangelist portraits. The Evangelist portrait of Mark on fol. 80v depicts the Evangelist seated before a ladder-like throne with the winged figure of a lion to his left. Mark holds an open book and gestures in blessing. The portrait is intricately framed with ornamented knots.

There seem to be two primary authors of the Trier Gospels, one of whom signed his name "Thomas" after several images and preferred an Insular style script, while the other is thought to be Frankish, based on his Merovingian script.[93] Also made in the Echternach scriptorium, the Gospels were likely commissioned by Trier and undoubtedly used during worship. As in the Augsburg Gospels, the liturgical marginal notations, of which there are 120 in the Trier Gospels, indicate the beginning of each reading for a specified ceremony or festival. Interestingly, unique notations show up

---

[92] Netzer, *Cultural Interplay in the Eighth Century; The Trier Gospels and the Making of a Scriptorium at Echternach* (Cambridge: Cambridge University Press, 1994), 5.
[93] This deduction is based on both stylistic features and because "Thomas" was one of the writers and illuminators of the manuscript who was known to have been working at Echternach alongside Merovingian artists. When Willibrord founded the scriptorium, he brought with him Insular artist-scribes and forced them to work with their Merovingian counterparts, thus promoting the unique stylistic fusion exhibited in these manuscripts; Netzer, "Willibrord's Scriptorium at Echternach," 203–205.

in the Trier margins, specifying festivals and venerated saints that would have been celebrated exclusively in Trier.[94]

Lastly, the Codex Eyckensis, c. 760, now housed at Saint Catherine's church in Maaseik, was possibly brought there by traveling missionaries after it was made in Echternach. As with the prior two Gospels, it appears to have been used as a lectionary, based on the marginal liturgical inscriptions.[95] The manuscript consists of two parts: Codex A begins with a full-leaf miniature of an Evangelist portrait, which is presumed to be Matthew, placed before an incomplete, though unusually decorated, set of canon tables. Codex B begins with a complete set of canon tables, but lacks Evangelist portraits or intricate initials. Both codices were produced in Echternach. The incomplete canon tables of Codex A, like the Augsburg and Trier Gospels canons, also contain colorful, decorated columns, topped with arches and decorated throughout with plants and animals. As in the Trier canon tables, the tables of Codex A have an additional large arch over the entire canon table with a roundel of an unidentified figure, probably an apostle. The first set of arcades in fol. A.2r connecting the capitals of the canon table columns are slightly different than the previous manuscripts. They are decorated with Evangelists' symbols. Each arcade contains, from left to right: man, lion, ox, and eagle. All were colored, though much of the coloring has faded. There is a second set of arches above the Evangelists' symbol arcades, which are decorated with intricately patterned vines. The last arch is decorated with Anglo-Saxon style knot work and images of birds, similar to that found in both the Augsburg and Trier Gospels. The roundel at the center contains a front-facing, haloed figure. He wears similar clothing to the apostle in the Trier canon roundel and also gestures in blessing. This figure, though, is bearded and does not hold a scroll. The Evangelist portrait of Codex A (Figure 23), as in the Trier Gospel, sits in a stylized chair and is contained in a frame of intricate knot work. The Evangelist of the Codex A in addition to his open book, holds a pen and is seated beneath an arcade. He is not accompanied by his Evangelist symbol as in the Trier portrait, nor is his chair a laddered throne.

The second and complete set of canon tables of Codex B, fol. B.2v, are more demurely decorated. While columns are filled in with knots and color, their arcades house neither Evangelist symbols nor birds and plants. As in Codex A and the Trier Gospels, the large arch depicts a central roundel of an Evangelist. The motif is familiar, with the apostle

---

[94]Netzer, *Cultural Interplay*, 24–25.
[95]The Codex Eyckensis Online, s.v. "Details," http://depot.lias.be/delivery/DeliveryManagerServlet?change_lng=en&dps_custom_att_1=staff&dps_pid=IE5258806&mirador=true. Retrieved March 2019.

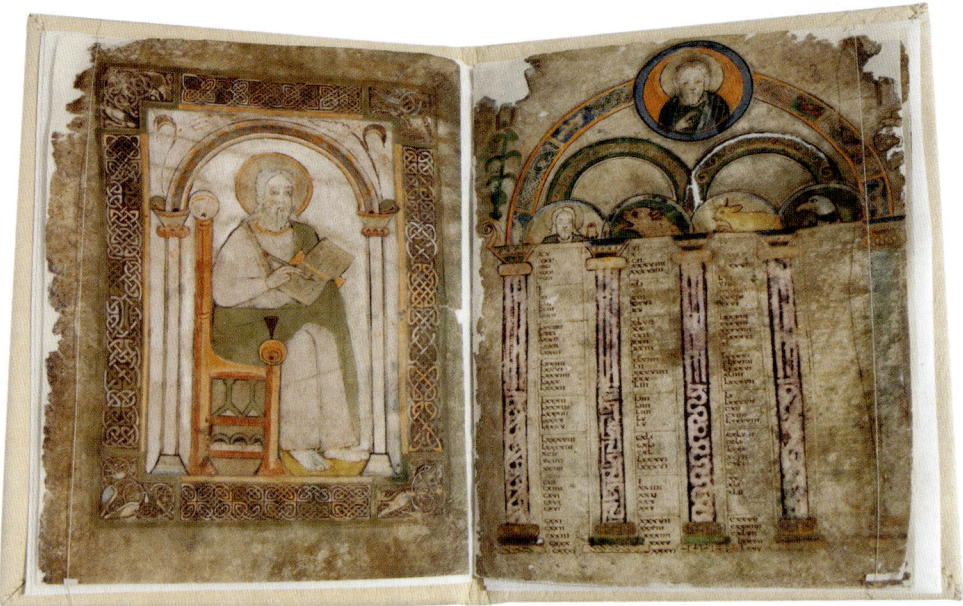

Figure 23 *Codex Eyckensis, MS 185, fol. A. 1v, Echternach, c. 760, Saint Catherine Church, Maaseik.*

similarly dressed and bearded, but unhaloed. Like the apostles of the Trier roundels, he holds something in his left hand, this time a book rather than a scroll, and also gives a gesture of blessing with his right hand. All 12 apostles feature in this complete set of canon tables. Additionally, the Evangelist symbols appear in the roundels, instead of in the arcades, as in Codex A.

It is clear, though worth reiterating, that these three liturgical gospel texts are quite similar. They were all made in Echternach in the eighth century for use during worship. They all also have similar dimensions, approximately 24 by 18 centimeters. The order of the texts is also comparable, as are the similarities between the canon tables and Evangelist portraits. The majority of these manuscripts, however, are primarily comprised of just the Gospel texts themselves with illumination limited mostly to the canon tables.

For the eleventh-century examples, the focus will revolve around material with which readers of this chapter are already acquainted, as they contain images of the Mockery or Crown of Thorns: the Codex Aureus of Echternach, the Lectionary of Henry III, and the Speyer Gospels.[96] All three were produced during a time when the

---

[96]Nuremberg, Germanisches National-Museum, Codex Aureus of Echternach, MS 156142; Bremen, Staats –und Universitatsbibliothek, Lectionary of Henry III, MS. b 21; Escorial, Real Biblioteca, Speyer Gospels (Codex Aureus Escorialensis, Gospel Book of Henry III), MS Vit. 17.

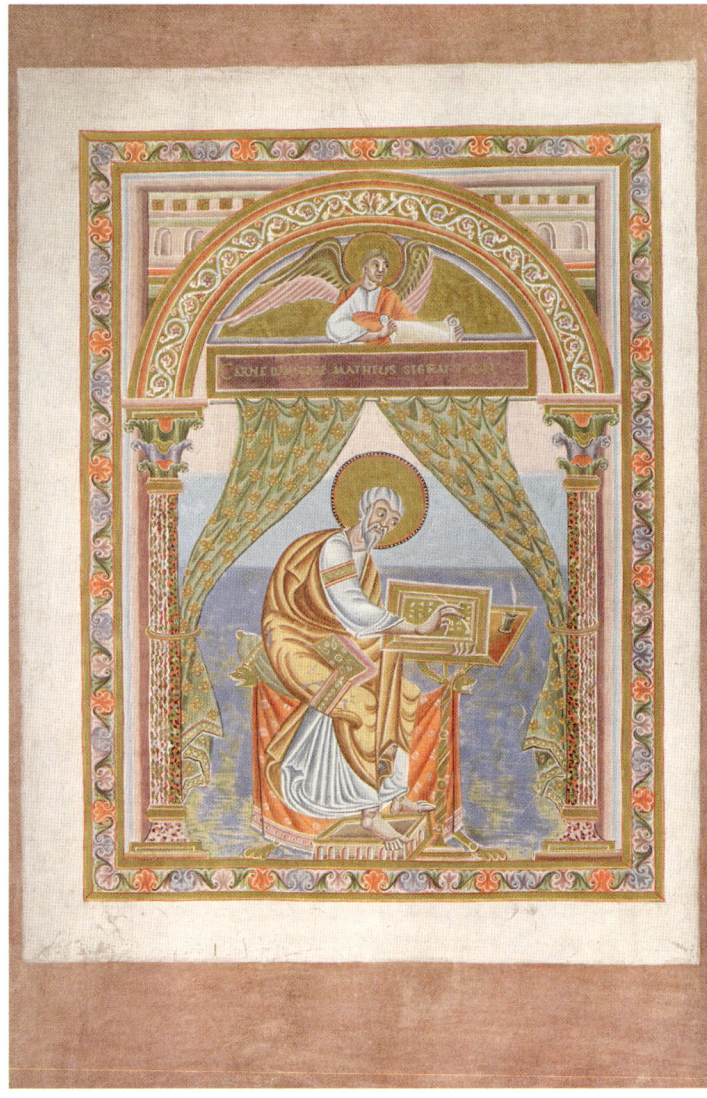

Figure 24 *Codex Aureus of Echternach, MS 156142, fol. 20v, Echternach, c. 1020–1030, Germanisches National-Museum, Nuremberg.*

Echternach scriptorium was at its most productive and enjoyed imperial patronage. Collectively they barely skim the surface of manuscripts made in Echternach during the eleventh century, but, as with the eighth-century examples, they will provide a general artistic outline of lectionaries produced in Echternach at this time.

The earliest of these, which is discussed in some detail above, is the Codex Aureus of Echternach, c. 1020–1030. It is generally accepted that the manuscript was commissioned by the Abbey of Echternach for the abbey itself, expressly for liturgical use.[97] As with the eighth-century manuscripts, the Codex Aureus of Echternach also depicts canon tables within colonnades and arches, and various animals perched on the structures, as on fol. 11v. The canon tables of Codex Aureus of Echternach, similarly to the Codex Eyckensis, Codex B canon tables, depict segmented and individually decorated columns with only two sets of arches. The Codex Aureus of Echternach, however, does not depict a roundel of apostles or Evangelist symbols. It is self-evident, even by glancing between images of the eighth-century folios and the Codex Aureus of Echternach, that the illuminations have changed drastically. The colors are still reds, greens, and yellows, but are vibrant, filled in with gold, blues, and intricate decorations. The Codex Aureus of Echternach's canon tables are bold and bring the focus more on the illumination than on the canon tables. Similarly, the Evangelist portraiture, of which all four survive, contain the elements of the eighth-century versions: an Evangelist with an open book, pen in hand, seated under arched columns, and framed in intricately patterned borders. But the eleventh-century Codex Aureus of Echternach rendition of Matthew (Figure 24) has much more detail. The arch has become an almost complete structure, the curtains are opened to reveal the studious Evangelist, inspired by his creature in the arcade above him who unfurls a scroll, all encased in an image dripping with gold.

Additionally, the Codex Aureus of Echternach does not only depict canon tables and Evangelist portraits. As briefly indicated above, the Codex Aureus of Echternach, at the beginning of each Gospel, devotes two pages with three registers of gold-framed life and Passion cycle illuminations, all highly detailed and helpfully labeled. Jesus calming the sea on fol. 54r, which is merely half of one register, exemplifies the detail employed. The image depicts a small boat with oars and figurehead tossed about on a raging sea. Jesus is depicted twice, first sleeping at the left end of the boat with a frightened disciple imploring him to wake. Jesus appears again at the right end of the boat ordering the winds to cease. The winds are represented by two monstrous, red-eyed heads in the sky, ears back, spitting fury. All characters are labeled, as is the scene in the golden frame below. The imagery of the Codex Aureus of Echternach is extensive compared to the eighth-century examples, but it is not an aberration among the manuscripts of the eleventh-century Echternach scriptorium.

---

[97] Rainer Kahsnitz, "Echternach und Trier zur Entstehungszeit des Goldenen Evangelienbuches," in *Das Goldene Evangelienbuch von Echternach*, eds., Rainer Kahsnitz, Ursula Mende, Elisabeth Rücker (Frankfurt am Main: S. Fischer Verlag GmbH, 1982), 30–31.

The Lectionary of Henry III, presumably made soon after the Codex Aureus of Echternach, c. 1039–1043, was commissioned by Henry III, made in the Echternach scriptorium, then presented to Henry III and in whose possession it remained until at least 1056.[98] It does not contain the entire Gospel texts, but rather it is a periscope containing selections of the Gospels that correspond with the liturgical readings for worship. With 38 full-page miniatures and 13 half-page miniatures (the details of which rival that of Codex Aureus of Echternach) the Lectionary of Henry III further demonstrates the trend of detailing Jesus' life and Passion in liturgical texts. Unlike the Codex Aureus of Echternach though, this Lectionary places the illuminations prior to the individual Gospel texts designated for the lectionary cycle, as was true for the Mockery scene. The Lectionary of Henry III also contains a comparable image of Jesus calming the sea, though expanded to a full-page miniature (fol. 19v) placed in the middle of the Gospel text for the fourth Sunday after Epiphany. Here too, as in the Codex Aureus of Echternach, a boat detailed with oars and a figurehead bounces atop white-capped waves. The disciples in the boat prod a sleeping Jesus on the left side of the boat. On the right Jesus is similarly depicted a second time and, as in the Codex Aureus of Echternach, gestures towards, this time, a four-headed and horned demon cloud. As in the Codex Aureus of Echternach, the scene is described in the sky above, "Christ demanded that the gales and wind calm down,"[99] so that there is no question of what is occurring in this image.

The Lectionary of Henry III, as in some of the eighth-century manuscripts, also depicts Evangelist portraiture. Like the Codex Aureus of Echternach, the portrait of Matthew in the Lectionary of Henry III (fol. 4v) sits on a cushioned chair between drawn curtains. He similarly holds a pen and writes his Gospel at a desk under a similar colonnade, with his Evangelist symbol in the arcade above holding a scroll. The Lectionary of Henry III's border, however, resembles more closely the intricate geometric patterns of the Trier Gospels, though here the patterns have a three-dimensional perspective.

The last eleventh-century lectionary example, the Speyer Gospels, c. 1043–1046, of the three incorporate the most attributes of both the eighth- and eleventh-century examples. The manuscript contains 13 full-page illuminations, 43 half-page miniatures, as well as decorated canon tables. Like the Lectionary of Henry III, the images of the

---

[98]Elsmann states that the provenance of the manuscript only reemerges in the sixteenth century, Elsmann, "Das Evangelistar," 1–2.
[99]*Imerpio XRI manuescunt flamina venti.*

Speyer Gospels are interspersed among the text. The canon tables on fol. 15v while completely colored with exceptional detail, contain elements of the canon tables of the Trier Gospels and Codex Eyckensis. All three depict a roundel with an apostle, in this example of the Speyer Gospels, Bartholomew, which is indicated in the inscription. He is bearded and haloed, as in the Trier Gospels, and holds a book in his right hand. The Trier and Speyer Gospels flank its upper arch with white birds perched on it. All three also have a colonnade of five columns each connected with an arch. While Codex A of the Codex Eyckensis is still the only set of canon tables with the Evangelist symbols in the arcades, the Speyer Gospels likewise magnificently decorates the arches. The Speyer Gospels have added a decorated frame to its entire canon table, which is unique among the eighth- and eleventh-century examples. This particular canon table also depicts Atlas and other figures holding up the canon title. By employing elements from the eighth-century lectionaries, the Speyer Gospels effectively demonstrates the significant increase in detail. To demonstrate this still further, the Speyer Gospels, similar to the Codex Aureus of Echternach and the Lectionary of Henry III includes extensive life and Passion cycles. Keeping with a familiar comparison, the Speyer Gospels also depict the story of Jesus calming the sea on fol. 70r, though are perhaps even more detailed than the previous two. The inscription, as in the Codex Aureus of Echternach and the Lectionary of Henry III, gives context to the image: "the wind was against the disciples then Jesus climbed into the boat with them and the wind ceased."[100] The same small, oared, figure-headed boat is uniquely fixed with rigging. It holds panicked disciples over a sea whose waves curl and lick the boat and sky. Even more, the sea, unlike the other manuscripts, has added dolphins and fishes. The image more accurately reflects the inscription specifically, depicting, not a sleeping Jesus, but one who climbs back into the boat while gesturing up at six monstrously personified storm heads. The Speyer Gospels' Evangelist portrait of Matthew (fol. 21v) is also seated under a stylized arch, held up by columns with his Evangelist symbol holding out a scroll above him. He is similarly seated with his book on a writing desk. The curtains, however, are closed behind him and the borders that frame the image are not as intricately decorated as in the Codex Aureus of Echternach and Lectionary of Henry III, or even the Trier Gospels and Codex Eyckensis.

The Speyer Gospels was, like the Lectionary of Henry III, also commissioned by the emperor then in turn presented to the Speyer Cathedral expressly for liturgical use.[101]

---

[100] *Discipules erat ventus contrarius et ascendit IHC ad illos in nave(m) et cessavit ventus* (Mk 6:51, variant).
[101] Mayr-Harting, *Ottonian*, 188.

All three of these lectionaries are also of similar size, though significantly larger than the eighth-century lectionaries. The lectionaries of the eleventh century become, even within the short time span covered by these examples, more colorful and reflect more details of the narrative that surrounds them. Their gilded images depict extensive life cycles and the Passion of Jesus. This was certainly clear in the examination of the increased detail of the Mockery scene, but even more so once compared to earlier lectionaries.

While similarities abound, perhaps the most substantial advances made to the late tenth- and eleventh-century lectionaries have now been made clear. First, their patronage is more explicit; second, their size has increased; and third, and most significantly, the level of detail that is exhibited in the text has exponentially expanded. Importantly, the other late tenth- and eleventh-century manuscripts, the Codex Egberti and Saint Peter Gospels, reflect similar expansive illustrations, intricate decoration, and gilded borders. It begs the question: why? What may have occurred in the Echternach scriptorium, as well as the other scriptoria of the Ottonian and Salian eras, that would have caused such an increased level of detail in their manuscripts, particularly, it seems, in those used for worship? Many reasons could contribute to this, but one, perhaps, is the reforms that swept the monasteries of this era. Since the idea of "monastic reforms" were wide and variable throughout every realm of every region of every era, a necessary brief overview of the reforms of the Ottonian and Salian realms in the tenth and early eleventh centuries will help narrow the discussion.

By the end of the tenth century the religious communities of the Ottonian and Salian realms desperately needed reform. The region had endured rampant instability at the end of the ninth and tenth centuries to the point of near collapse. As a result of this protracted instability, the religious communities had been long exploited by the unchecked lay leaders and, with few protections, had also been subject to raiding and other outside threats. In addition to this, and partly due to neglect, corruption within had been allowed to fester. Simony, marriage among the clerics and increasing sexual immorality, waning levels of education, and general lack of spirituality damaged the reputation of the religious communities.[102] The political chaos that led up to the fall of the Carolingian rulers only began to stabilize with the election in the eastern region of Henry the Fowler (919–936). As stability slowly returned so too did the attention of the

---

[102]Joseph Lynch and Phillip Adamo, *The Medieval Church* (London: Routeledge, 2014), 124; Kathleen Cushing, *Reform and Papacy in the Eleventh Century; Spirituality and Social Change*, (Manchester: Manchester University Press, 2005), 30–31.

rulers towards improving the lack-luster monasteries in their realm. In order to reestablish and regain spiritual prestige, not to mention shoring up political support, reforms were instituted in the monastic communities.

At their most basic, the reforms of this era demanded that the monastic communities return to a stricter *Rule* of Benedict, which had lapsed in the intervening years since their establishment.[103] This entailed the reinstitution or revival of a more moral, dignified, and liturgical existence; a return to a strict communal life; a fervent focus on and participation in worship and liturgy; and greater attention to commemorating the dead.[104]

There were two types of reform which occurred at this time: the so-called "radical," or "Cluniac" reform and "moderate," or "Gorze" reform. Radical reform was a monastery's conscious breaking off from, or establishment outside of, the control of lay rulers. Instead, they were placed under the jurisdiction of the papacy. These communities fought for and enjoyed relative independence, as they were able to elect their own bishops and leaders, instead of being subject to the whims of their regional ruler or king. Cluny was the first, as well as the most renowned abbey to do this. Their reforms spread throughout Italy, the eastern Frankish region, and Spain. Other monasteries which also wished to reform in the way that Cluny had, asked them to send Cluniac monks to their own monastery to establish reform and train their monks to be more like those at Cluny: orderly, dignified, and liturgical. Thus, the Cluniac reforms, and severing of lay influence, spread throughout the region.[105]

The second, "moderate" or "Gorze" type of reform, named after the monastery of Gorze in the diocese of Metz from where the reforms originated, was a more general improving of religious life in cooperation with and often directly prompted by lay rulers. In this instance, the abbeys were often, though not always, more tolerant of their lay leaders interfering with or mandating reform. This type of reform was popular in the Ottonian and Salian realms from the 930s into the beginning of the eleventh century.[106] Unlike the Cluniac reforms, the Gorze reforms were undertaken without consideration of the papacy, which functioned more as a traditional center, rather than

---

[103]Reuter, *Germany*, 243.
[104]Lynch, *The Medieval Church*, 129–131; Joachim Wollasch, "Monasticism: The First Wave of Reform," in *The New Cambridge Medieval History*, Vol. III c. 900-1024, ed. Timothy Reuter (Cambridge: Cambridge University Press, 1999), 165–166; Mayr-Harting, *Ottonian*, II, 86.
[105]Lynch, *The Medieval Church*, 129–131; Wollasch, "Monasticsim," 174–180.
[106]Mayr-Harting, *Ottonian*, 83.

one that dictated laws.[107] Where kings and lords encouraged or forced monasteries to reform, they became more enhanced as spiritual and learning centers, and in turn more prestigious.[108]

During the reforms, there was a general preoccupation, above all, with liturgy. An intense focus on liturgical life in monasteries was pervasive in both types of reform during this period and it led to a common trend: the general enhancement, or refurbishing, of the worship ceremony and worship space. This is evident in two primary trends. First, enrichment of the physical worship space. The first part of the eleventh century saw major reconstruction programs for worn-out churches as well as the building of new, grand churches. The refurbishment of churches began in the areas swept up by Cluniac reforms but also stretched to places like Echternach, Trier, Salzburg, and Speyer.[109]

The second form of enhancement of worship was through the beautification of the liturgical objects. With the elaborate worship, the monks of the reformed abbeys also wanted to make their celebration of worship more glamorous and richer; to bedeck the worship space with beautiful altars, chalices, and texts. The performance of the liturgy came hand in hand with the beautification of the ceremony. More and more, manuscripts were not only copied and recopied, but artistically enhanced and improved upon.[110] This is seen most clearly in the examples of the liturgical Gospel texts made in or for reformed abbeys. The examples from Echternach demonstrate this most acutely. There seems to be a sudden shift to larger and more ostentatious decorations, increased amounts of gold and color, several full-page illuminations dedicated to the patrons of the manuscripts, and exquisite extended detail of the life and Passion of Jesus with, in many cases, unprecedented detail. The increased number of these manuscripts made by an abbey's scriptorium explicitly for use in worship was done in part to further enhance the beauty of the ceremony as a demonstration of renewal.

Indeed, the patrons of reform, especially the Ottonian and Salian kings, were adamant to see the enhancement of the worship space as evidence of their monasteries' reform. This often meant commissioning or donating large illuminated manuscripts.

---

[107]To the Ottonian and Salian realms, Rome was useful for bestowing privileges, rank, and status, but otherwise, their influence on reform or the religious communities was limited. Reuter, *Germany*, 137.
[108]The itinerant court of the Ottonian and Salian kings did not have centers for learning and scholarship as the Carolingians did, thus it naturally fell to well-patronized abbeys to fill this role; Wollasch, "Monasticism," 137; Cushing, *Reform*, 33; Reuter, *Germany*, 243.
[109]Cushing, *Reform*, 92–93; Lynch, *The Medieval Church*, 129; Reuter, *Germany*, 240, 251–252.
[110]Leyser, *Rule and Conflict*, 194–195; Mayr-Harting, *Ottonian*, 83–86.

These beautiful books would be seen by monks, worshippers, and lay leaders, boasting the spiritual renewal and prestige of the church and its community under the kings. Henry III, for example, made gifts to the reformed bishopric of Speyer, including the illuminated manuscript, the Speyer Gospels. This is a prime example of a ruler who sought reform for his spiritual centers, which included donating worship material to suit their new heightened status.[111]

It should not be surprising then, that the abbeys that received or made the manuscripts of the late tenth and early eleventh century that exemplify the artistic progression of the Crown of Thorns, were all created in reformed religious communities. Echternach, for example, was reformed soon after the Gorze reforms began at the end of the tenth century under Abbot Humbert of St. Maximin and Poppo of Stavelot at the direct request of Henry II.[112] Humbert reorganized the scriptorium and encouraged the increased production of the sumptuous manuscripts both for the abbey itself, such as the Codex Aureus of Echternach, but also for patrons and other reformed abbeys.[113]

Trier, one of the two locations in which the Codex Egberti may have been produced, was reformed under Egbert, who was archbishop of Trier from 977. Instilled by his parents and ancestors, Egbert knew the importance of maintaining the primacy of a monastic community and how to do so: through reform, notable works of art, and refurbished worship space.[114] Egbert began his reforms and building projects almost immediately after becoming archbishop and by the early 980s a significant number of elaborate manuscripts created in Trier were distributed around the Ottonian empire, as part of Egbert's program and promotion of reforms.[115]

After its founding around 695 or 696 little is known about the monastic community at the Abbey of St. Peter at Salzburg until it was reformed in 987 by Abbot Tito. Abbot Tito was chosen to be the new abbot for St. Peter for the express reason that he was well-known as a reform-minded man from Gorze, which was, as stated above, where the moderate type of reform originated. Thus, Salzburg too was reformed in the same style as Trier and Echternach and emulated similar reform trends. As with Trier and Echternach, St. Peter became concerned with the design and splendor of worship,

---

[111]Cushing, *Reform*, 93.
[112]Stephen Wagner, "Establishing a Connection to Illuminated Manuscripts made at Echternach in the Eighth and Eleventh Centuries and Issues of Patronage, Monastic Reform and Splendor," *Peregrinations: Journal of Medieval Art and Architecture* 3:1 (2011): 61–62; Kahsnitz, "Echternach," 29–30.
[113]For more details on the eleventh-century scriptorium under Abbot Humbert see Kahsnitz, "Echternach," 29–38.
[114]For a superb and succinct outline of Egbert's reform driven family, see Thomas Head, "Art and Artifice in Ottonian Trier," *Gesta* 36:1, (1997): 69–70.
[115]Head, "Art and Artifice," 71–74.

which included the increased detail and beauty of the manuscripts. The scriptorium at St. Peter at Salzburg was flourishing by 1000 and was renowned for making manuscripts specifically for liturgy. The creation of the Saint Peter Gospels falls squarely in the time period of the monastic reforms. It is considered to be one of the first of the new style of beautified manuscripts coming out of St. Peter's scriptorium that is still in existence.[116]

The three primary illuminated manuscripts examined in this chapter have several things in common. First, they all display the new artistic concept of Jesus' Crown of Thorns and its royal connotations. They also all do so at a time when manuscripts, compared to earlier manuscripts, suddenly increase in size, detail, and vibrancy. They are bolder and their illuminations cover more pages and subjects than in previous centuries. All three manuscripts additionally come from the scriptoria of abbeys that, during the time of their production, underwent reform under royal-imperial patronage. One of the aspects of these empire-wide reforms was the beautification of worship space, including the liturgical implements. As all three manuscripts were expressly used during worship, they were likely made as part of that beautification process. The reforms, therefore, that demanded the communities, both religious and lay, should focus more on worship and the artistic enhancement of worship, helped produce the manuscripts that led to a recognizable Mockery and Crowning of Jesus.

The recipients of the imagery of the Mockery scene during the Ottonian and Salian age seem to have been the royal-imperial court, the religious communities, and even lay members of society. This applies to its occurrence in public monumental art like the Aachen altar as well as the more restricted manuscripts. The Golden Altar of Aachen was an ostentatious display of Henry II's connection to Christ and his divinely ordained right to rule. The manuscripts which depict the Mockery were intended to display to king and community the spiritual largesse of the abbey under its royal patron. Both types of media, fundamentally, were intended to prove something. The altar and manuscripts relay a message. In these cases, they give insight into several ideologies that were held in great regard in the Ottonian realm: legitimacy, stability, and improvement. In an era haunted by the prolonged chaos of their ancestors, the constant reminders in their worship spaces of stable, Godly kingship and solid, unrelenting spirituality were necessary visual elements of peace and power.

Before the Ottonian and Salian eras, the Mockery of Christ was separate from the Crown of Thorns. Indeed, the Crown had not yet been seen as something that could be

---

[116] Hermann, "Salzburg, St. Peter," 276–279; Holter, "Hauptwerke," 154–158.

identified as a crown made of thorns. The eleventh-century artists, due in part to the trends instituted by the reforms to create extremely detailed and increasingly complex works of art in the worship space, not only begin depicting a genuine Crown of Thorns, but also find a way to bring the Mockery and the Crown together for the first time in a most curious manner. The Enthroned Mockery illustrates a centralized, enthroned Jesus who is simultaneously mocked and crowned by symmetrical soldiery. The uniqueness of this image is due to the fact that it has little resemblance to its predecessors; neither in the elements of the Mockery, nor in the crown. Instead, it follows the model of the image of the coronation of the Ottonian kings, which depicts the king and emperor, similarly enthroned, crowned, and attended.

The probable cause for the Mockery scene to briefly mimic the crowned Ottonian king has to do with the shift in the ideology of kingship. The Ottonian and Salian kings were expected to fulfill a Christo-memetic ideal, in that they were to embody perfect imitations of Christ. This included, especially, the imitation of Christ's humble endurance of torments on earth. To be crowned king and gain the greatest earthly throne, the king had to be subjected to humiliation and suffering, face it all with humble acceptance, and by doing so prove himself to be worthy of kingship. It was, in essence, an imitation of what Jesus endured during his Mockery by Pilate's soldiers: he endured the torture of the soldiers to gain the throne in heaven; the king endures similarly harrowing situations to gain the throne on earth. The 'humiliation to exaltation' ideal is represented in the Enthroned Mockery motif. In this image, Jesus parallels the crowned king to demonstrate the king's fulfillment of his imitation of Christ-like humiliation, patience, and endurance, leading ultimately to enthronement.

The imagery of the Mockery does not, however, retain this optical representation of kingship. Towards the end of the eleventh century the Mockery scene dispenses with the throne and other coronation attributes. But many of the trends established in the Enthroned Mockery remain, particularly the inclusion of the Crown of Thorns. The Crown even becomes the focus of the late eleventh-century Mockery scenes, around which the entire image revolves. Finally, then, because of the artistic efforts of the eleventh century, the Crown of Thorns will endure as an omnipresent, recognizable fixture of Jesus' Mockery.

As is to be expected, neither the Crown of Thorns nor the Mockery will continue in perpetuity to look exactly as they do in the late eleventh century. The soldiers around Jesus will shift positions, become more aggressive, take on characteristics of contemporary enemies, and will generally become more monstrous. Jesus will be subjected to bloodier and more graphic torture; his Mockery will become a scene of horror and misery, meant to elicit profound pathos. More and more the scene will come to include all the instruments of the Mockery: the purple robe, the reed, and the crown. The Crown of Thorns will continue to make a regular appearance and become the defining feature of the Mockery. It will even come to remain on Jesus' head throughout the rest of the Passion-cycle. Its thorns will become more defined and any semblance of a leafy plant will disappear entirely. It will become an instrument of humiliating torment.

The trends established in this study, however, from fourth-century sarcophagi to the eleventh-century manuscripts, will continue to permeate through these centuries of change. For now, this study has accomplished its goal and gleaned the circumstances under which Jesus' wreath becomes a fully-fledged, recognizable Crown of Thorns.

5
The Crown revived and revered

The eleventh century laid the groundwork for the Crown of Thorns to become a fixture in Passion imagery. But there is a question that looms large over the depiction of the Crown of Thorns: what about the relic? The relic of the Crown of Thorns, or the supposedly literal Crown that Jesus wore during his mock trial, is well known and was widely venerated as a sacred Passion object. Would this remarkable relic not have had a huge influence on the depiction of the Crown of Thorns? Would not, for example, the pious Romano-Christians have venerated the object? Would the Ottonian artists not have copied its likeness for their own attempts at depicting the Crown in their illuminated manuscripts? The answer to each of these questions is a resounding no.

The relic of the Crown of Thorns, while revered in Jerusalem at least since the fifth century, garnered greater attention and popularity in the West only in the thirteenth century after it was purchased and brought to France by the French king, Louis IX.

As we have seen, the depiction of the Crown of Thorns came to fruition in the eleventh century in the form of the Enthroned Mockery, long before the arrival of the relic. But that same Enthroned Mockery disappears soon after it is depicted. Interestingly, though perhaps unsurprising, once the relic arrived in the West, its impact was substantial. It causes a resurgence of the image of the Enthroned Mockery. The relic, with the unprecedented ceremony and reverence it received from King Louis IX, revived the regal associations with the Crown of Thorns that developed singularly in the West.

The Crown of Thorns was likely venerated in Jerusalem from the fifth century at least until the end of the ninth century. The Crown is primarily mentioned by pilgrims visiting the Holy Land who list the relics that they come across while on their journey. The first explicit mention of the relic is from St. Paulinus of Nola in his letter to Marcarius around 409. In this letter, Paulinus discusses what drives people to come to Jerusalem. It is a place, he says, where people go to be in the same locations where Christ was present, especially the sites of his Passion and Resurrection. He lists objects and places in Jerusalem that evoke religious sentiment and piety. Among these artifacts and sacred spaces, such as the manger of Christ's birth, the river of his baptism, the wood of the cross, and the rock of the tomb, Paulinus includes the Crown of Thorns.[1] It is a selective list of the humbling experience of viewing sacred objects.

Cassiodorus also mentions the Crown of Thorns in his commentary on Psalm 86. Written around 570, he discusses the objects and places in Jerusalem that speak to the city's glory: "There [in Jerusalem] the Crown of Thorns is beheld, which everyone knows, was set upon the Lord our Salvation, in order that the thorns of the whole world might be gathered together and broken."[2] The Crown of Thorns is directly associated with salvation and sacrifice, and is explicitly mentioned as residing in Jerusalem along with objects like the Flagellation column, the Siloa bath, the cross, and the tomb, among others.

Around the same time as Cassiodorus, Antoninus of Piacenza, also known as the Anonymous Pilgrim of Piacenza, made a pilgrimage to Jerusalem around 570–590. He writes that when he came to the "Basilica of the Holy Sion" (which may have been located outside the Sion Gate in Jerusalem), he found a plethora of relics on display for veneration: "in that very church is the pillar upon which our Lord was scourged ... There is likewise the Crown of Thorns with which our Lord was crowned, and the spear which was thrust into his side, and many stones with which Stephen was stoned."[3] Antoninus states that there were so many relics in this particular basilica that he forgot quite a few of them.

Possibly one of the last accounts that mention the Crown of Thorns in Jerusalem is from Bernard the Wise, also known as Bernard the Monk. During his pilgrimage to Jerusalem around 870 he wrote a short guide for future pilgrims to use on their own trek to the Holy Land: "There is in addition in the city [of Jerusalem] itself another

---

[1] Paulinus of Nola, "Epistola ad Macarius," in Migne, *Series Latina*, vol. 61, col. 407B.
[2] Cassiodorus, "Expositio in Psalterium," in Migne, *Series Latina*, vol. 70, col. 621D: *Ibi spinea corona cernitur, quam ideo salutari Domino constat impositam, ut totius mundi aculei collecti frangerentur.*
[3] Antoninus Martyr, "De locis sanctis quae perambulavit Antoninus Martyr," in Stewart trans., 18–19.

church to the south of mount Sion, of which St. Simeon speaks, where the Lord washed his disciples' feet, in which hangs the Crown of Thorns of our Lord."[4] Thus, by 870 the Crown of Thorns was still in the same Sion Basilica that Antoninus of Piacenza had mentioned.

Before discussing the subsequent greater popularity of the relic, it is important to note the unreliable nature of certain claims concerning the relic in the eighth and ninth centuries, some of which derive from apocryphal legends of the late eleventh century. There is a general speculation that Charlemagne acquired several Thorn relics, which were thought to have been plucked off the actual Crown of Thorns. Eight such thorns had supposedly been given as gifts by the Empress Irene to Charlemagne sometime between 798 and 802.[5] It appears that this claim is somewhat dubious and unsubstantiated, however: the Empress Irene did indeed send legates to Charlemagne in 798 and 802, according to the *Annales Regni Francorum*, but there is no mention of gifts or thorns that accompanied them.[6]

The source for the legend of Charlemagne's eight thorns is in the *Descriptio qualiter*. This is a late eleventh-century prose document concerning mythological deeds of Charlemagne. The text relates a fictitious journey Charlemagne took to Constantinople and the Holy Land. The legend describes how God told the Byzantine Emperor to beg Charlemagne to come to the East and liberate Jerusalem from the Muslims. Charlemagne came, freed Jerusalem, and received a plethora of relics to bring back to Aachen.[7] When Charlemagne returned "on the Ides of the month of June, all the people came to Aachen to see what was brought from Jerusalem and from Constantinople with [Charlemagne]; of course from the Crown of Thorns, which our Lord Jesus Christ endured, namely eight thorns with a piece of the wood where they were fixed . . ."[8] Part of Charlemagne's

---

[4]Bernard the Monk, "Itinerarium," in Migne, *Series Latina*, vol. 121, col. 572C: *Est praeterea in ipsa civitate alia ecclesia ad meridiem in monte Sion, quae dicitur sancti Simeonis, ubi Dominus lavit pedes disciplorum suorum, in qua pendet spinea Domini corona.*
[5]Joan Cruz, *Relics; the Shroud of Turin, the True Cross, the Blood of Januarius . . . History, Mysticism and the Catholic Church* (Huntington: Our Sunday Visitor, 1984), 36.
[6]"Annales Regni Francorum", *Monumenta Germaniae Historica Scriptores, SS rer. Germ*, vol. 6, 102–104, 117.
[7]Matthew Gabriele, "Frankish Kingship, Political Exegesis and the Ghost of Charlemagne in the Diplomas of King Philip I of Francia," in *The Charlemagne Legend in Medieval Latin Texts*, eds. William Purkis and Matthew Garbriele (Cambridge: Boydell & Brewer, 2016), 13.
[8]Gerhard Rauschen, ed.,"Incipit Descriptio, qualiter Karolus magnus clavum et coronam domini a Constantinopoli Aquisgrani detulerit qualiterque Karlus calvus hec ad sanctum Dyonisium retulerit", in *Die Legende Karls des Grossen im 11 und 12 Jahrhundert*, (Leipzig: Verglan von Duncker & Humblot, 1980), 120: *in Idibus Iunii mensis omnes homines venirent Aquisgrani videre, que de Iherusalmem et de Constantinopoli secum detulerat, scilicet de spinea corona, quam dominus noster Iesus Christus sustinuit, octo videlicet spinas cum parte roboris, ubi fuerant infixe . . .*

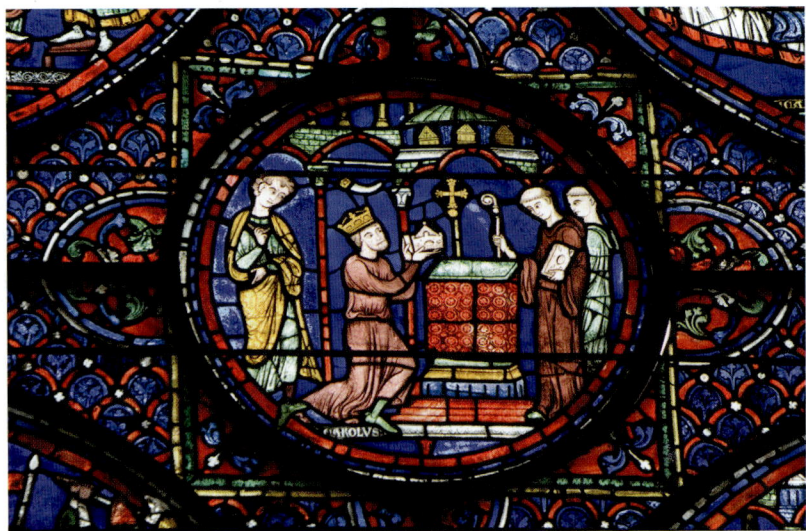

Figure 25 *Bay 7, Legends of Charlemagne, Chartres, c. 1210–1220, Chartres Cathedral, Chartres.*

reward for saving the Holy Land were the Passion relics, and pieces of the Crown of Thorns seem to have been regarded as the most significant acquisition.

The popularity of this legend is attested by several depictions of the early thirteenth century, notably in the stained glass of Chartres Cathedral, c. 1210–1220. The aptly named "Legends of Charlemagne" window, on the north-side of the ambulatory, depicts a series of images detailing the exploits of Charlemagne, both actual and legendary. In the first register on the right, Charlemagne asks the Emperor of Constantinople for relics as his only reward for his conquest of Jerusalem. The accompanying central medallion depicts Charlemagne then offering a crown-shaped reliquary to a bishop, supposedly in Aachen (Figure 25). Another rendition of the story from the *Descriptio qualiter* occurs on one of the eight reliefs on the Shrine of Charlemagne at Aachen, c. 1215. In this work, the Emperor of Constantinople presents a similar crown-shaped reliquary, presumably containing the thorns from the Crown to a kneeling Charlemagne.[9] Both works illustrate, of course, the later legend rather than any actual events.

At some point in the ninth century the Crown of Thorns may have been moved from the Sion Basilica in Jerusalem to Constantinople. It seems that it is first mentioned in its

---

[9] Elizabeth Pastan, "Charlemagne as Saint? Relics and the Choice of Window Subjects at Chartres Cathedral," in *The Legend of Charlemagne in the Middle Ages; Power, Faith, and Crusade*, eds. Matthew Gabriele and Jace Stuckey (New York: Palgrave Macmillan, 2008), 105–108.

new location in Constantinople by the so-called *Anonymus Mercati*. Originally written in Greek sometime after 1063, it lists relics and sanctuaries in Constantinople. The text may have served as a traveler's guide for Constantinople, and was translated into Latin sometime in the twelfth century.[10] The author includes a list of holy relics found in the Church of Holy Mary the Mother of Christ in Constantinople.[11] The list of Passion relics residing in the palace includes: "The bowl where Christ washed the feet of his disciples; the shroud which encircled the Lord; the Crown of Thorns; the cloak; the reed ..." and so on.[12]

Though venerated in the palace of Constantinople at least since the eleventh century, only in the thirteenth century did the Crown of Thorns attract more profound attention in the West, perhaps due in part to the increased popularity of the previously mentioned stories of Charlemagne's legendary exploits. Baldwin II, who ruled in Constantinople from 1228–61, was faced with renewed attacks in 1235 from the Bulgarians and needed money. The magistrates of the Venetian community in Constantinople agreed to give the Emperor a loan in exchange for the Crown of Thorns and other Passion relics to be placed under their care as collateral for the loan. The Crown of Thorns went to the Monastery of the Pantocrator, which was then under the jurisdiction of the Venetians. When Baldwin could not repay his loan, the Crown went to Venice. But Baldwin II managed to sell the Crown of Thorns, among other relics, to King Louis IX of France which paid off his loan to the Venetians.[13] Thus the Crown of Thorns, which had traveled from Jerusalem to Byzantium, made its way to France in the thirteenth century. Its presence in Paris brought it more attention than it ever had received in the past.

It therefore seems that the relic of the Crown of Thorns did not exert any influence on the depiction of the Crown in the West. Our first example of the wreath-crown occurs a century before there is much discussion of the relic and primarily reflects a victory narrative and dominant wreath culture of the time. It seems to also have had no bearing on the earlier Ottonian developments. Instead, the Ottonian depictions were based on regal associations.

---

[10]Ciggaar, *Western Travellers to Constantinople; The West and Byzantium, 962–1204: Cultural and Political Relations* (Leiden: E.J. Brill, 1996), 48, 148. The Greek text of the *Anonymus Mercati* does not survive.
[11]"Anonymus Mercati, Digbeianus Lat. 112," 1. 1–2, in Ciggaar, "Une description de Constantinople traduite par un pèlerin anglaise," *Revue des études byzantines*, 34 (1976): 245: *in magna palacio in templo Sanctae Mariae Dei genetricis haec sanctuaria et sacrae reliquiae.*
[12]Ibid.: *Pelvis ubi lavit Christus pedes discipulorum. Lintheum quo erat precinctus Dominus. Spinea corona, clamis, flagellum, arundo ...*
[13]Charles Freeman, *Holy Bones, Holy Dust; How Relics Shaped the History of Medieval Europe* (New Haven: Yale University Press, 2011), 127.

In the same way, Charlemagne's legendary adventures and collection of pieces of the Crown of Thorns were not popularized in the West until the end of the eleventh century, long after the Crown of Thorns appeared in Ottonian manuscripts and monumental art. The legends certainly reflect a significantly increased interest in the relic of the Crown, but the art and depictions of the Crown of Thorns were already established. Thus, as will be seen below, the relic only will only become relevant to the art of the West in the thirteenth century.

Byzantine influence—or not?

The relic itself is unrelated to the artistic developments in the West prior to the thirteenth century. But what of the Byzantine tradition, where the relic would have likely had more prominence? There are only a few ambiguous examples of both a possible Crown of Thorns as well as Mockery scenes from Byzantium before the thirteenth century. Their scarcity warrants brief examination to justify by contrast the conclusions of this study that the themes of the Crown of Thorns were largely Western.

Prior to the eighth and ninth centuries, representations in Byzantine art of the Crown of Thorns in any form are non-existent or lost. There are, however, two examples of a kind of crown or fillet that appear on Jesus' head in Crucifixion icons, possibly made in Sinai, which may date from the eighth or ninth centuries. The first is an icon residing in the St. Catherine Monastery in Sinai.[14] The extensive Crucifixion scene depicts many of the characters discussed in earlier chapters, including symmetrically placed Mary and John, soldiers playing dice, thieves, sun and moon, and angels. Jesus, who is fully clothed with eyes closed, has a string of stars, flowers, or possibly thorns wrapped around his head. If it is indeed a Crown of Thorns, this would be the first instance in which Jesus appears crowned on the Cross.[15] A second icon, also kept in St. Catherine's (Figure 26) and also possibly made near Sinai, depicts a simpler Crucifixion icon with Mary and John flanking a bleeding Jesus, whose eyes are closed, signifying his death. This Jesus also wears a band around his head strung with what appears to be small plant-like decorations. These two examples, which may be simple wreaths of victory or something more significant, seem to be rare instances. Their dates are moreover uncertain. There appears therefore to be no obvious Byzantine examples

---

[14]The Michigan-Princeton-Alexandria Expeditions to Mount Sinai, Michigan inventory no. 11.

[15]In the West, Jesus does not appear crowned with wreath or thorns on the Cross until well into the thirteenth century, with some possible outliers in the eleventh century.

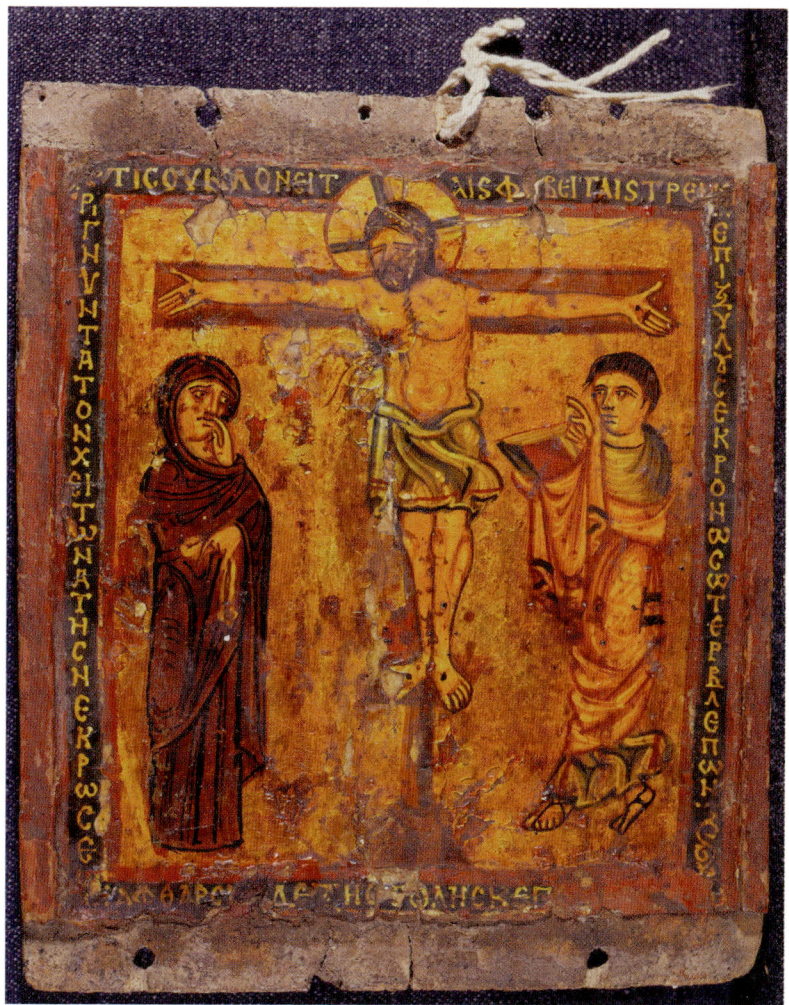

Figure 26 *Sinai collection (Princeton) image 535, Sinai, c. ninth century, St. Catherine's Monastery, Sinai.*

of the Crown of Thorns in any periods relevant to the discussions in previous chapters. The only explicit tradition of these periods is the Western.[16]

After these ambiguous Crowns, there are no Crowns and few examples of the Mockery prior to or concurrent with the Ottonian period.[17] There is one significant

---

[16] For in-depth insights into the possible twelfth-century Byzantine liturgical influence on the Adoration of the Cross and Tools of the Passion (which includes imagery of the Crown of Thorns), see Hans Belting, "An Image and Its Function in the Liturgy: The Man of Sorrows in Byzantium," *Dumbarton Oaks Papers,* 34/35 (1980): 1–16.

[17] Anne Derbes, *Picturing the Passion in Late Medieval Italy* (Cambridge: Cambridge University Press, 1996), 94–9, also concludes that there no relevant material from Byzantine art that influenced the Mockery scene in the West.

example of a series of three Mockery scenes found in a Gospel book made in Constantinople, but it is considered to be of the twelfth century at the earliest and possibly of the thirteenth century.[18] The first scene in the series on fol. 55v, is Jesus before Caiaphas, which goes along with the text of Matthew 26:62–64, when Jesus is accused and questioned by the high priests; the second is a Mockery accompanying the text from Mark 15:18 on fol. 98v, which is the Mockery by Pilate's soldiery; and the third on fol. 159r, Jesus is mocked while Peter mourns above, which accompanies Luke 22:63–65, when Jesus is mocked by the guards of the high priests. The images are of an obviously different artistic style from Western examples, but the symmetry of the soldiers, the centralized figure of Jesus, and the conflation of several scenes into a single panel are similar to the trends noted in the Ottonian and Salian examples of the Mockery. The uncertain date and similar trends, moreover, leave open the possibility of Western influence on the Byzantine work.

The physical relic of the Crown of Thorns as well as the very few ambiguous Byzantine exempla seem to have had no influence whatsoever on the depictions of the Crown in the West. The relic did, however, eventually stir in the West an explosive revival of the Enthroned Mockery.

The Sainte-Chapelle and the return of enthronement

The Crown of Thorns and the Enthroned Mockery become significantly more popular in the West during the thirteenth century due both to the arrival of the relic of the Crown of Thorns in Paris and the associations garnered between the relic and King Louis IX. The Sainte-Chapelle of Paris—the thirteenth-century monumental reliquary built to house the Crown of Thorns and Passion relics acquired by Louis IX—will help illustrate the sudden and profound importance of the relic as evidence as to why the depiction of the Enthroned Mockery is resurrected during this time.

The Enthroned Mockery made a bold, though brief appearance in the eleventh century. Its disappearance was swift, and was replaced by images that, while retaining many attributes of the Enthroned Mockery, stepped deftly away from depicting Jesus enthroned. By the mid-thirteenth century, however, the throne returns prolifically to the Mockery scene. A few examples will give a sense of the variety of locations where the image re-emerged.

---

[18] Paris, BIbl. Nat, MS, gr. 74, fol. 55v, 98v and 159r.

The Widener 9 Psalter, housed in the Free Library of Philadelphia, was made around 1270–1280.[19] It was likely composed in Amiens, based on the local saints' feast days listed in the Calendar.[20] The Psalter includes the Hours of the Virgin, the initials of which are illuminated with an extended life cycle of the Virgin.

A Mockery scene is depicted in the prefatory, just above the Flagellation on fol. 9v. It is preceded on the facing page by the betrayal and arrest in the garden and the trial before Pilate. In the Mockery scene, Jesus, larger than the other figures, is seated on a throne with his arms crossed looking out towards the viewer. The bright orange throne is simple and straight-legged. Its lack of decoration and cushion differs from the throne of, for example, the Saint Peter Gospels. Jesus is surrounded by four men. On the right, a smirking figure dressed in a short tunic, glares at Jesus while blindfolding him, instead of crowning him. A second, obscured figure stands on the right and raises his arm. On the left, a man in a long robe and domed hat kneels before Jesus, with one hand on his head, possibly in distress. A second man stands on the left, stretching out his arm as if to strike Jesus. A disemboweled Judas hangs himself on the far right.

The scene is an Enthroned Mockery. Several elements of this image, however, call into question which Mockery scene is portrayed. There is a significant lack of a Crown, which, as demonstrated earlier, became a defining feature of the Mockery scene by the end of the eleventh century. Instead, Jesus is blindfolded. He is also flanked by men who appear not to be Pilate's soldiers. This is determined by comparing the abusers of the Mockery scene to the soldiers in the facing illumination, fol. 10r. Significant differences arise. In fol. 10r, the soldiers in the garden and the soldiers who bring Jesus before Pilate are dressed in full-body mail with short tunics. The men in the Mockery scene do not appear to be of the same ilk. The lack of armor and weaponry, as well as the lack of Crown may signify that this is the Mockery by Caiaphas' *ministrati*. It is then reasonable to assume that the kneeling, hat-wearing[21] figure is Caiaphas himself.

The near contemporary Beauvais Psalter depicts a similar Mockery. The Beauvais Psalter, now in the Morgan Library in New York, was made around 1260–1270, slightly before the Widener.[22] It was written and illuminated in France, probably in Beauvais since it too lists local saints in the calendar and the litany. The images of the life cycle of

---

[19] Philadelphia, Free Library, Widener Psalter, MS.lat. Widener 9.
[20] For example: Saint Firminus, the first bishop of Amiens; Saint Honoratus, a sixth-century bishop of Amiens; and Saint Fuscian, an Amiens third-century martyr; Noel, "Psalters," in *Leaves of Gold; Manuscript Illuminations from Philadelphia Collections*, edited by James Tanis (Philadelphia: Philadelphia Museum of Art, 2001), 54–55.
[21] The domed hat is a typical feature for Jewish characters in Christian art by the thirteenth century.
[22] New York, Morgan Library Beauvais Psalter, MS M. 101.

Christ appear just before the psalms in a series of full-page illuminations. Each of the ten pages contains four individual subjects enclosed in mandorla-shaped medallions. In the Mockery scene (fol. 20v) Jesus, larger than the accompanying figures, is seated on a throne that is mostly concealed by his body. The throne appears to be simple and backless. His arms are folded over his chest and he has been given a blindfold that ties at the side of his head. His face is completely covered by the soldier on the left, slapping him open palmed. Jesus appears to be looking down and to the left instead of straight forward, as he is typically depicted in the Enthroned Mockeries.[23] Once again, he is not crowned.

Like the eleventh-century Enthroned Mockery, there are fewer soldiers who abuse Jesus. It is noteworthy that there is again no Crown of Thorns. Due to the blindfold and lack of Crown, it is possible that this is also the Mockery with Caiaphas instead of Pilate.

The Passion cycle portion of the prefatory of the Huth Psalter, now in the British Library, made some time c. 1280–90 either in Lincolnshire or Yorkshire, includes the same scene in a form closer to its eleventh-century predecessors.[24] The Mockery image in fol. 11r occurs alongside the Flagellation. Jesus is large and seated on a white, stylized throne. Though blindfolded, he faces the audience directly, holds a book in his left hand, and gives a gesture of blessing with his right. He is haloed and wears a crown. This is not a crown made of thorns, but instead resembles a crown one might find on a king. This type of crown is closer to that found on Jesus in the Saint Peter Gospels' Mockery, which depicts a large band with thorn-like decorations protruding out of the top. The implication of the Huth Psalter Crown seems to be that it is meant to be the Crown of Thorns and, like the Saint Peter Gospels' Crown, contains royal connotations. The figure to the left reaches up with his left hand to crown, blindfold, or pull Jesus' hair abusively. The figure on the right has blueish skin, curly hair, and spits on Jesus. This Enthroned Mockery has several elements that pertain exclusively to the Mockery with Pilate's soldiers and are suggestive of previous imagery, including the Crown, the abuse, and the spitting. It also, however, has Jesus blindfolded, which seems to be associated more with the Mockery under Caiaphas. This Enthroned Mockery, like several others during this time, may be an intentional conflation of the two Mockeries.

---

[23] For example, see Figure 24.
[24] The location is based, once again, on the convenient inclusion of local saints, particularly St. Hugh of Lincoln; London, British Library, Huth Psalter, Add. 38116.lat.

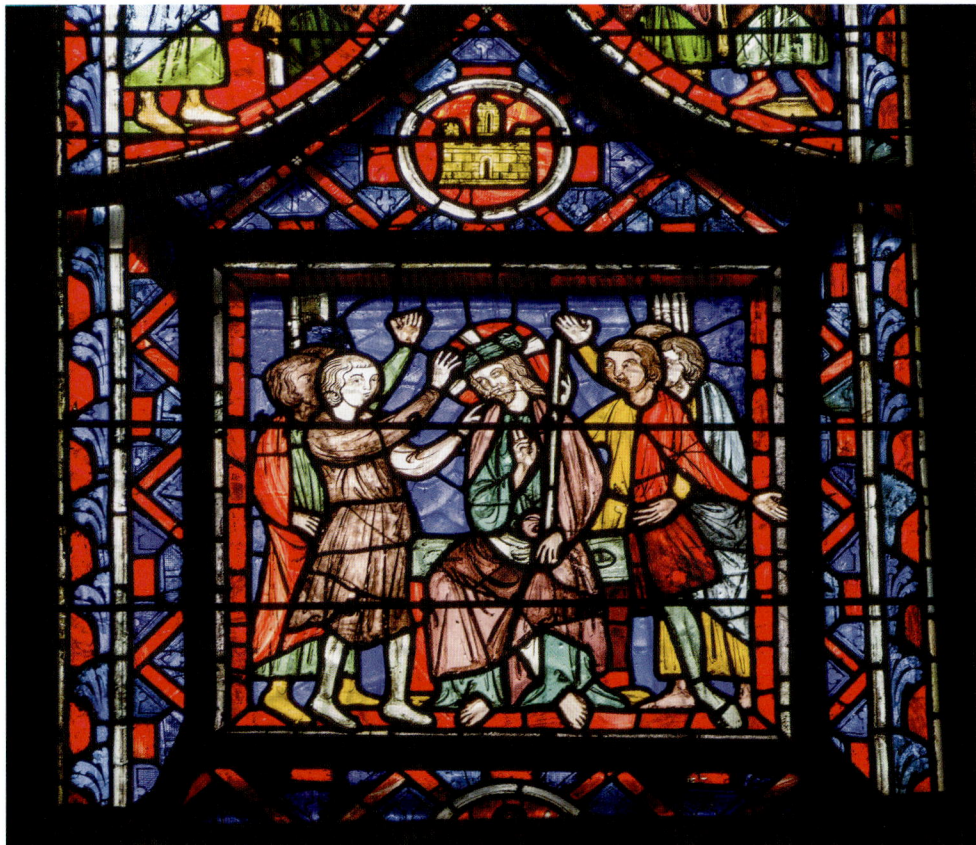

Figure 27 *Sainte-Chapelle, Paris, c. 1241–1248.*

The final example of this brief survey is found, most significantly, in the stained glass of the Sainte-Chapelle, the chapel that housed the relic of the Crown of Thorns in Paris beginning sometime around 1248. The stained glass of the central bay directly behind the *Grand-Chasse*, or the Great Reliquary—which was the large display above the altar of the Sainte-Chapelle where the relics would have resided—features a strategically, centrally placed Enthroned Mockery (Figure 27). It also bears close similarities to the eleventh-century Enthroned Mockeries. Jesus is seated on a cushioned throne with straight legs and no back, which resembles the form of the throne in the Saint Peter Gospels' Mockery scene. Jesus holds the reed in his left hand and makes a gesture of blessing with his right. He is surrounded by a large group of mockers. On the left, one mocker reaches up to crown Jesus with what appears to be a wreath made of thorns, while placing his other hand on Jesus' shoulder, possibly dressing him in the purple robe. This Crown of Thorns, with its sharp edges and woven form, resembles the Crown found, for example, in the Codex Aureus of Echternach, examined above. The figure directly to the left of Jesus appears to be handing him the reed, or perhaps striking him. The rest of the abusers raise their right hands in mock adoration, like the mockers of the Saint Peter Gospels and Golden Altar of Aachen.

With the inclusion, not only of the Crown of Thorns, but also the reed, the purple cloak, and the explicit Mockery, this scene, more than any of the others examined in this chapter, is unquestioningly the Mockery with Pilate's soldiers. It is additionally an Enthroned Mockery similar to the eleventh-century examples and therefore likely exhibits regal connotations.

The above examples of the thirteenth-century Enthroned Mockeries are a mere sampling of the dozens of Mockery scenes depicted around Europe during the mid to late thirteenth century, but some interesting developments are nevertheless clear. First and foremost, the Mockery, whether with or without the Crown, is depicted with exponential frequency. Second, the return of the Enthroned Mockery has superseded other variations of the Mockery scene, and may once again be evoking royal associations. These royal associations probably stem from the ultimate translation, and the extensive elevation of the relic of the Crown of Thorns by Louis IX through the construction of the Sainte-Chapelle. The Sainte-Chapelle was built immediately after the arrival of the relic, and specifically for the relic. The purpose of the monument, and the artistic program within, is testament to the importance of the Crown of Thorns for Louis IX.

The Crown of Thorns and the Crowning of Christ represented true and worthy kingship. The imagery of the Crown of Thorns and the Mockery reflected the likeness of the king to Christ, in humility, patience, and sovereignty. These ideas were ingrained in the ideologies of kingship and the Crown of Thorns was representative of these ideologies. For a Western ruler to therefore possess the actual, physical Crown of Thorns would, with utter finality, justify the absolute worth and rule of the king. The king was deemed worthy to not only be associated with Christ as Christ's greatest imitator, but to possess the very object that represented Christ's humiliation, sacrifice, victory, and future enthronement in heaven. The value and importance of these ideas clearly did not escape Louis IX.

As stated above, Louis IX purchased the relic of the Crown of Thorns from Baldwin II, the last Latin Emperor of Constantinople, in 1239. The relic made its way to Paris and it was received by the king, who processed with it, humbly, barefoot, and without his kingly regalia, in front of the entire city, demonstrating a humility equal to that of

Christ's. Upon arrival in 1242, the Crown was placed in Saint-Denis for safekeeping until its gigantic new chapel, the Sainte-Chapelle, was completed in 1248.[25]

There are several relevant and interesting elements of the Sainte-Chapelle's architecture and construction that should be addressed here. It was built primarily for the purpose of housing the plethora of Passion relics acquired by Louis IX. Foremost among them was the Crown of Thorns. In a way, the building was a giant reliquary. Attached to the king's palace, it also served as his personal chapel.

The Sainte-Chapelle consisted, not unusually, of two chapels: the Upper Chapel, which both exhibited the relics in the *Grand-Chasse*, and also contained an extensive stained glass program; and the Lower Chapel, which primarily served as an architectural support for the Upper Chapel. The thirteenth-century Upper Chapel had no external entrance, but instead maintained a single entrance leading from the royal chambers of the palace. A spiral staircase at the west end of the chapel led from the Upper to the Lower Chapel.[26] Based on the fact that there was no exterior entrance to the Sainte-Chapelle, it is safe to reason that the relics were not for public display. Rather they were exclusively viewed by the king, the king's court, and his guests.[27]

The artistic program of the stained glass displays themes that promote kingship, coronation, notions of God's new chosen people, and the primary duties of kings to their people—to name just a few.[28] One of these themes is of particular relevance here: coronations. Scenes of coronation are by far the most prolific of the entire stained glass program, such as the enthroned Old Testament kings in the window of the Tree of Jesse.[29] In these two examples of coronation, Solomon and David are enthroned, crowned, and flanked by attendants. They, and other enthronements like them, have striking artistic parallels to the central image of the Enthroned Mockery of Jesus, discussed above (Figure 27). Jesus too sits enthroned on a similar seat, is crowned, flanked, and holds the reed while giving a gesture of blessing with his other hand. The

---

[25]Jean-Michel Leniaud and Françoise Perrot, *The Sainte Chapelle* (Paris: Ed du patriomine, Centre des monuments nationaux, 2007), 51.
[26]For detailed information on the construction of the Sainte-Chapelle see especially: Leniaud and Perrot 2007: 97–119; Bony 1983: 357–377; Bottineau 1966: 67–79; Gordecki 1960: 5–30; Weiss 1998: 16–30.
[27]Leniaud and Perrot, *The Sainte Chapelle,* 83.
[28]For suggestions on the significance and purpose of Sainte-Chapelle's artistic program, see especially: Leniaud and Perrot *The Sainte Chapell,* 89; Alyce Jordon, *Visualizing Kingship in the Windows of the Sainte Chapelle* (Turhout: Brepols, 2002), 18–26; Daniel Weiss, *Art and Crusade in the Age of Saint Louis* (Cambridge: Cambridge University Press, 1998), 33–74.
[29]The series of enthronements is situated in the northern window of the chevet. The entire right-side window begins with a similarly Enthroned Christ, who carries a cross in his left hand.

coronation and enthronement of the kings and their similarity to the enthroned Christs throughout the chapel may intentionally be drawing parallels between the coronations of ancient kings, Christ, and the French king. The multitude of crowned and enthroned ancient kings in the stained glass program all culminate to the Enthroned Mockery, depicted just above the relic Crown of Thorns itself. The Crown of Thorns, as it epitomizes humility, patience, victory, and eternal rule, may serve to emphasize and legitimize Louis IX's connection to Christ-like kingship. Its physical presence, surrounded by other prestigious coronations, solidifies these ideals. As stated above and outlined in detail above, coronations played a large role in propagating the ideologies of kingship. It seems that the idea of coronations, as a reminder of the king's supreme, Christ-like rule, persisted into the thirteenth century.

From this brief examination of the Sainte-Chapelle, it is likely that the royal associations to the Crown of Thorns probably lie behind the resurgence of the Enthroned Mockery in this period. The above demonstrates that the revival of the Enthroned Mockery, and its centuries of regal and Christ-like associations, coincides with the arrival of the Crown of Thorns.

The relic of the Crown of Thorns was squirreled away in the holy shrines of Jerusalem from at least the fifth century. At some point it made its way to Constantinople at the earliest by the ninth century, and definitively by the mid-eleventh century. This is tentatively confirmed by the popular legends of Charlemagne in the *Descriptio qualiter*, which mention pieces of the Crown of Thorns as constituting a reward for Charlemagne's fictitious exploits in Jerusalem. The *Descriptio qualiter*, written in the late eleventh century, is also the first hint of interest in, popularity of, and kingly associations with, the relic of the Crown of Thorns in the West. Prior to this, the Crown of Thorns, its theology, politics, and imagery, developed independently from Byzantium.

It is only in the thirteenth century that the relic plays a possible role in the development of the imagery of the Mockery and Crown of Thorns. During the thirteenth century there is a sudden resurgence of the Enthroned Mockery scene, where Jesus is mocked and crowned while seated, regally, on a throne. The associations with royalty and kingship inherent in the Enthroned Mockery have not disappeared. They likely gained renewed focus by King Louis IX's acquisition of the relic of the Crown of Thorns in the mid-thirteenth century. The construction of the Sainte-Chapelle to house the relic additionally served to promote the Crown and the ideology of kingship with which the Crown of Thorns had become associated. This brief examination of the relic of the Crown of Thorns and its eventual influence over the popularity and artistic dominance of the Mockery scene provides a glimpse into the continual progression of the Crown of Thorns. It also demonstrates how the themes established in the West in Christianity's first eleven centuries consistently accompany its depiction. And, as we will discover, these themes carry on for hundreds of years into our own modern art and psyche.

6

Medieval or modern? The Crown of Thorns today

We have seen that, unlike most elements of the Passion cycle, the depiction of the Crown of Thorns was a long time in the making. But by the fourteenth century, the Crown had already become ingrained in the Passion iconography, staying with Jesus throughout the rest of his trial and into the Crucifixion. Anyone with cursory knowledge of this imagery could recognize that the painful, thorned crown adorning Jesus' head, is meant to be the Crown of Thorns.

Throughout the following centuries, imagery around the Passion, especially the Mockery and Crucifixion, begin to exhibit more pathos, more obvious pain, suffering, and blood—and the Crown of Thorns features heavily in these scenes.

One need not look far. Stumble through any esteemed museum's late Medieval, Renaissance, or early Modern galleries and you will likely see room after room of paintings from the masters across Europe carefully, even lovingly, depicting Christ's suffering with, inevitably, the addition of the Crown. From Dirk Bouts' *Christ Crowned with Thorns* painted around 1470 with the deep blue bruises under Christ's eyes and blood dripping from his crowned brow down to his bare chest; to Caravaggio's *The Flagellation of Christ*, 1607, that sheds an eerie glow on the spines of the Crown of Thorns upon a slumped, suffering Jesus; and even Rembrandt's 1631 *Christ on the Cross*, with his quintessential dark, looming shadows encasing an open-mouthed Jesus, screaming in pain and frustration, adorned with a thick plait of thorns.

In each of these images—and countless others up to the twenty-first century—the Crown of Thorns seems in its place. Indeed, such Passion scenes at this point would seem to be missing some crucial component without the Crown. And they are all similarly rendered with sharp, horrifyingly large thorns, woven into a crude circlet.

This style of the Crown of Thorns, as we know, is the popular way to render it. It is immediately recognizable as part of most scenes that form the Passion cycle.

But what of those themes that developed alongside the Mockery and Crown of Thorns? Into the fourteenth century the ideas of humility, patience, endurance, kingship and, of course, triumph, were inseparable from the Crown's depiction. And now? While the image has shifted slightly from our eleventh-century manuscripts, has the modern, twentieth- and twenty-first-century artist, in the inexhaustive artistic methods now available, maintained these ideas?

Looking briefly at three media will help elucidate whether the Crown of Thorns and the sentiment it provokes remains constant to this day: film, fine art, and literature.

The Crown of Thorns makes it to the big screen

In March 2004, the headlines and critics blared a paradoxical combination of horror and praise. The religious, the secular and the curious in equal measure flocked to watch, maw agape, at the most violent rendition of Jesus' story ever portrayed.

Mel Gibson's *The Passion of the Christ* provoked both awe and ire. Considered by many factions to be antisemitic in its overt villainization of the Jewish elite, in the same breath, they were dumb-founded by the superb cinematic quality, the spectacular acting and the fascinating use of Aramaic and Latin for the entire dialogue. The movie follows the last twelve hours of Jesus' life—the Passion—during which he is arrested in the Garden of Gethsemane, dragged before the high priests for condemnation, brought to trial before Pontius Pilate, flogged, mocked, forced to carry his cross through the streets of Jerusalem and finally crucified.

The violence, though perhaps gratuitous on screen for those of us who have never known such brutality, was steeped in historical accuracy. Indeed, this would have been the most pain Jesus would have likely suffered during his entire life, and that is before he was crucified. The Romans were cruel. Their punishments swift and memorable for survivors or witnesses.

The movie's official poster is also memorable. It defines the movie. In a dim light, we see a close-up profile of an unmistakable Jesus during his Passion. How do we know it is Jesus during the Passion? He is wearing a bloody, sharp, Crown of Thorns. It is an iconic image and sticks in the mind—and in one picture tells the viewer exactly what this movie will be about.

Throughout *The Passion of the Christ* the Crown of Thorns represents Jesus' suffering. After Jesus is scourged nearly to death, he is brought aside to be mocked by the vicious Roman soldiers. They fashion the Crown and deliberately press the spines into his head (accompanied by apt sound effects), causing even more pain and bleeding. They drape a scratchy red cloak over his shoulders, place one of the reeds they had recently used to flog him into his hand and mock him cruelly, bowing down and call him "king of the worms." They spit on him and continue to beat him.

This scene is interspersed with another scene—and with one of the many flashbacks that occur throughout the movie. We shift from Jesus in the midst of his Mockery, to Mary the mother of Jesus and Mary Magdalene, a follower of Jesus, in the praetorium where Jesus was tortured. They are on their knees cleaning Jesus' blood from the soaked floor. While cleaning, Mary Magdalene recalls her own experience of Jesus' salvation. We see her remember Jesus bending down and writing in the sand in front of Jewish priests, stones in their hands. When he has finished writing, they toss away their stones and turn their backs on Jesus. Mary Magdalene, curled in the dirt, dressed then as a wealthy woman, reaches slowly for Jesus' feet. He crouches down and raises her up.

The movie conflates Mary Magdalene with the woman taken in adultery. In this story, the elders and Pharisees bring a woman who has been caught in the act of adultery to Jesus and ask him what should be done with her. The law says she should be stoned—does Jesus agree? Jesus bends down to write in the sand, and, with the greatest sympathy for this woman, says to the men, "let anyone among you who is without sin throw the first stone." Confounded—and put smartly in their place—the priests retreat. Jesus tells the woman gently to go on her way, and sin no more.[1]

The juxtaposition of this flashback to the Mockery is significant. Being paraded before this well-known righteous man after being caught in adultery was undoubtably the most humiliating moment of this woman's life. Jeered at, probably physically harmed, and on the brink of the further humiliation of a public death by stoning, she is saved. The message is clear—in the midst of Jesus' greatest humiliation and on the threshold of his own demise, we see that he saves another from humiliation and death.

The Crowning and Mockery of Christ, even in the twenty-first-century religious rendering, is still seen as an abject humiliation. It is not just a painful experience of

---

[1] Jn. 8:1–11.

being mocked, it is deeply shameful. We cringe at this scene while also amazed at Jesus' kindness for a stranger. Now, as in the medieval art, this scene evokes a sense of the viewer's own humility—their own rock bottom.

The portrayal has become bloodier and more distant from the leafy wreath of the original Greek, but the sentiment remains: the Crown evokes in the modern viewer both humiliation and hope, defeat and victory. As Mary was saved from her shame, so too will Jesus' followers be victorious in the end and conquer all humiliation and torment.

Even unto the penultimate scene of the film, the Crown of Thorns remains a fixed point, reminding the viewers of extreme suffering. While the two Marys and Jesus' followers take him down from the cross, eventually gracefully taking up the famous pose of Michelangelo's *La Pietà*, we see flashes of a large stone upon which rest the nails and Crown of Thorns—the Instruments of the Passion. They remind the viewer of Jesus' suffering, pain, and humiliation, which is now at an end for him, and for his believers.

All is transitory—the modern artist's Crown of Thorns

Only a year into Britain's entry into World War II, a little-known artist paints his own tragic feelings about the war on a small canvas. In the painting, a pure white cloth is roughly draped over a hard brown surface against a dark back drop. The cloth contains several objects. On the far left sits a silver chalice with a cover, closed over a stained cloth. A kerchief, lightly discolored by blood, is tied in a knot and balances on top of both chalice and cloth. Next to the cup lie a pair of iron pliers—thick, strong, solid, and menacing. To the far right, set almost feather light and entirely atop the white cloth, are vicious looking thorns crudely woven into a wreath. It casts a shadow as sharp as the thorns themselves—shadows which elongate as they approach the viewer.

It is this unmistakably recognizable object that gives the painting its name: *Crown of Thorns* (Figure 28).

The piece bleeds emotion. Its creator, Albert Houthuesen, was transplanted from Amsterdam to London after a dramatic end to his childhood. His father, a piano-maker turned painter was said to have been "unintentionally" cudgeled to death by his mother. His mother, who was frustrated not only with his father selfishly pursuing his non-lucrative passion of art, but also encouraging their eldest son Albert to practice art as well, struck her husband over the head with the heel of her shoe, penetrating his skull

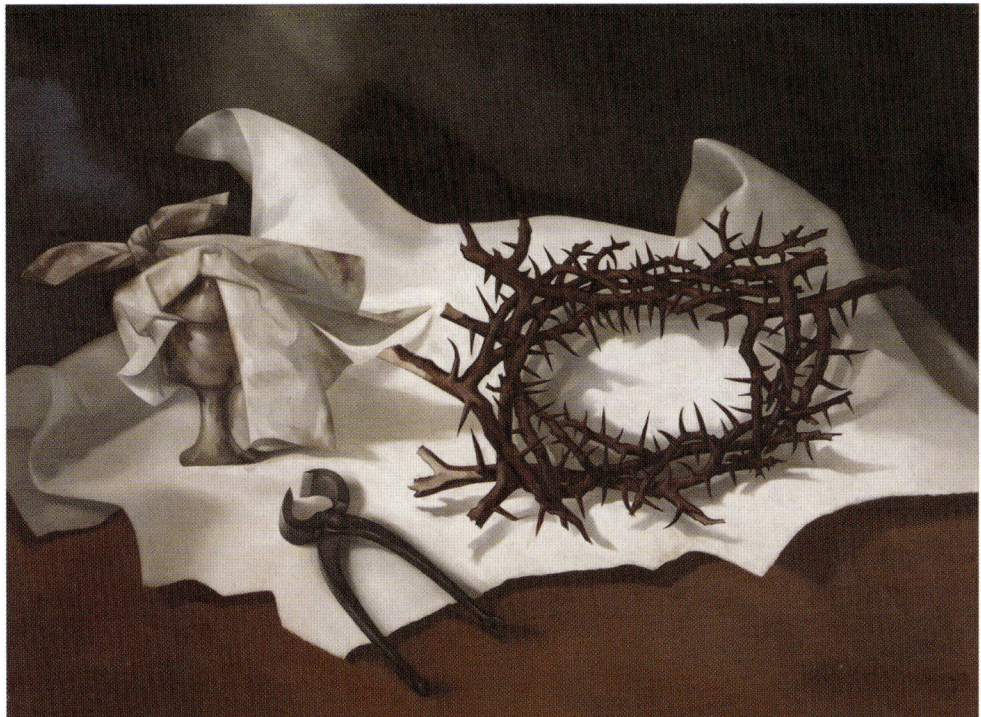

Figure 28 *Crown of Thorns, 1939, Albert Houthuesen 1903–1979.*

in the process. Needless to say, Houthuesen's father did not last long after this attack.[2] The remnants of the family promptly left Amsterdam and headed to London in 1912.

Houthuesen's life was haunted by this event. He was acutely aware of the precariousness and transitory nature of everything around him. His life in the early twentieth century was marred by disappointment and false hope. He was largely an unrecognized artist until the 1960s, the decade before his death; he signed up to fight for his adopted country, but was rejected on medical grounds which eventually led to a nervous breakdown; his London home, along with many of his early paintings, were destroyed by a bomb during the Blitz; and his mother repeatedly tried to thwart his work when he was young—including "accidently" burning a drawer full of his and his father's first portraits.[3]

And yet Houthuesen continued to hope. His unadulterated admiration for Jesus' teachings and endurance inspired some of his best work—including the *Crown of*

---

[2] John Rothenstein, *Modern English Painters,* vol. 3 (London: Macdonald and Jane's Publishers, 1976), 70–71.
[3] Rothenstein, *Modern English Painters,* 74–76.

Thorns. Another religiously influenced piece, *The Supper at Emmaus*, largely displays hope and gentleness. In this painting, completed as part of his diploma for the Royal Academy of Arts from 1926–1929,[4] a softly glowing Jesus enters a yard, reminiscent of a small English garden. The table, which takes up most of the canvas, is carefully laid. What is intended to be Jesus' seat, appears more like a high-backed throne. It also softly shines, as Jesus does, while creeping roses grow gently around it, as if it were a wreath encasing the warmth of the glow. On the surface, it is a graceful, idyllic image that appears to be beyond pain.

However, we also see evidence of suffering. Jesus' feet are clearly pierced, he walks with a stick, the trees above the scene are rough and sharp, and the roses, while indeed bright and soft are also, we know, full of thorns. Many of Hauthuesen's paintings, as with both these pieces, have rough edges. There is a constant sense of vulnerability, even amidst the tenderness.

His *Crown of Thorns* was born during a time of fear and tragedy, but there are rounded edges within the piece as well. The cloth appears almost as silk, the Crown of Thorns is nearly weightless: the pain, while evident through the Crown of Thorns, is fading as the blood already does in the knots of the kerchief. It is an image expressing hope that sorrow will end.

Even for Houthuesen, it seems that the Crown of Thorns evokes unmistakable suffering—a persistent prickly sense of chaos and pain just around the corner—but also a sense that this pain does, eventually, cease. As it is likely that his hope was not only for the war Europe was enduring, but for his own physical pain. Houthuesen thought that all humanity should try and emulate Jesus as much as possible—through his endurance of humiliation and pain, kindness, and commitment to stating the truth.[5]

As the Ottonian kings saw that the path to peace and power was through emulating and experiencing humiliation and suffering like Christ, so we witness that same idea too in modern art: with the endurance of suffering there is hope of victory.

It is important to remember as well that there were other elements that first brought a recognizable Crown of Thorns together with the Mockery scene. In the eleventh century, this fully-fledged scene is born from the near identical scene of the enthroned king. The Ottonian kings came into their power only through enduring suffering and humiliation, just as Jesus had. Their coronations paralleled his mock crowning. It is only

---

[4]Rothenstein, *Modern English Painters*, 74.
[5]Jonathan Evens, "The Spirituality of the Artist-Clown; the significance of the clown in the life and work of Albert Houthuesen," retrieved April 24, 2023, https://artway.eu/content.php?id=1025&lang=en&action=show.

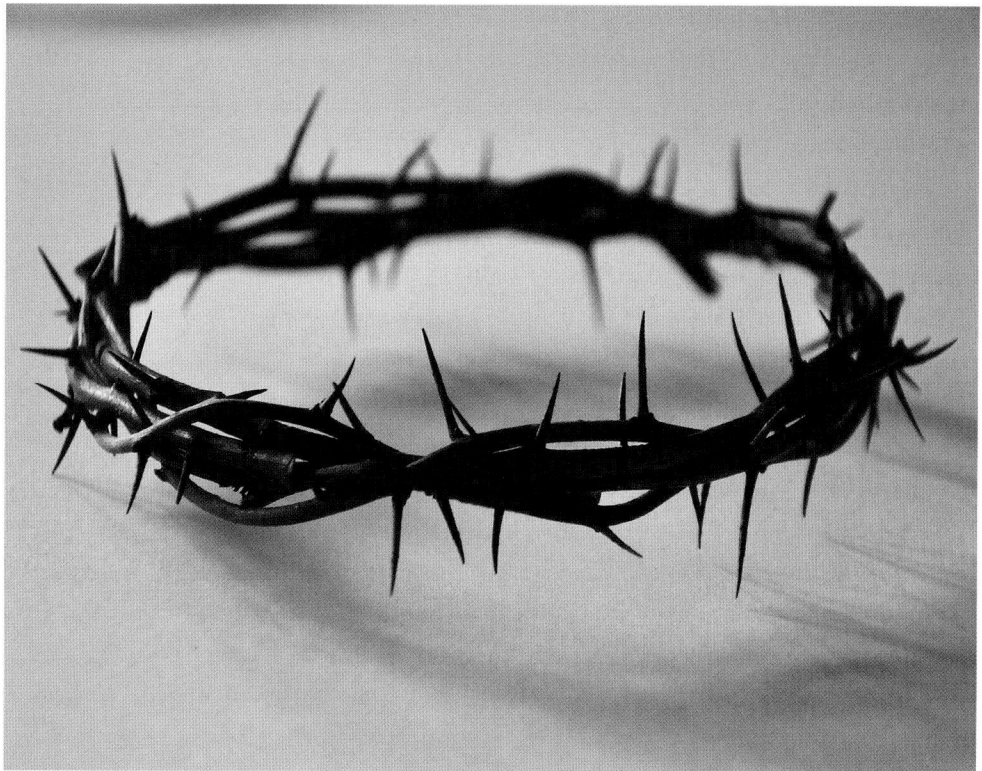

Figure 29 *Crown of Thorns, 2012, Jane Morgan.*

through imitating Christ's humility and suffering, so the medieval kings believed, that they could be victorious and claim their kingdom as Jesus also did.

Shockingly, these medieval associations with the Crown of Thorns and kingship, perhaps even subconsciously, persist into even the twenty-first century.

We must turn once again, as Houthuesen did for inspiration and education, to the Royal Academy. The Royal Academy of Arts' Summer Exhibition in 2012, among the many fine, bizarre, and inspired pieces in the exhibition, displayed a small bronze sculpture.[6] Two intertwining brambles weave delicately around one another with gigantic, sharp, solid thorns jutting out in all directions. It is, perhaps predictably, entitled *The Crown of Thorns* (Figure 29). Though diminutive, measuring just 17 centimeters wide, the familiar, piercing object immediately—and purposefully—resonates with the viewer.

---

[6]Royal Academy of Arts Summer Exhibition 2012, retrieved February 4, 2023, https://www.royalacademy.org.uk/art-artists/exhibition-catalogue/ra-sec-vol244-2012.

The artist, Jane Morgan, who is established in the United Kingdom, understands the image of the Crown of Thorns, albeit through her modern, secular eye, to be a "globally identifiable object" and one that provokes a wide range of dialogue: from pain and suffering to kingship.[7]

Several years before casting her bronze *Crown of Thorns*, Morgan experimented with casting objects in nature. She found that the solid twigs or leaves invited viewers to question what is real, to contemplate—as Houthuesen did—the transitory state of nature.[8]

In the same vein, she chose to render the image of the Crown of Thorns as a stimulus with which to invite the viewer to question reality. Though Morgan and her studio insist any religious connotation can be stripped from the image of the Crown of Thorns,[9] it is still unmistakably "a conventional iconographic symbol and intended to pose questions of kingship, and power," particularly to question their genuine nature.[10]

While the medieval depictions are unobjectionably and inherently religious, there is a continuity of symbolism. Even for the modern rendering, the connection of the Crown of Thorns to royalty instinctively permeates through hundreds of years of depicting the image.

It has transcendent meaning. The modern artist, while depicting the more conventional image of sharp thorns, still understands that it parallels kingship—though humbly begotten. Indeed, even Morgan, in crafting the brambles found the process "inherently physical, injurious, with bodily pain and suffering. Lacerations became common afflictions in the making of these works."[11] One can easily envision the frustration of the artist, struggling to weave this crown just so, consistently thwarted by the unyielding thorns. There is humility in this frustration, her endurance to persevere, and her eventual triumph.

From medieval kings to modern twentieth- and twenty-first-century artists, success, victory, and power come only through humility, trial, and pain.

A story for the ages—the Crown of Thorns in literature

In any form of storytelling, from film to fine art, Jesus, as a character, is undoubtably fascinating. There is enough detail and drama in the Gospels to weave a good tale.

---

[7]Jane Morgan, Artist Proposal, *Eva International Ireland's Biennieal,* Limerick City 2014.
[8]Jane Morgan Studio, "A Crown of Thorns—Follow-up," received by author, March 23, 2023 (email).
[9]Jane Morgan Studio, interview by author, February 17, 2023.
[10]Jane Morgan's Studio, "A Crown of Thorns—Follow-up," received by author, March 23, 2023 (email).
[11]Jane Morgan, Artist Proposal, *Eva International Ireland's Biennieal,* Limerick City 2014.

Taken at face value, the story of Jesus' life is a rich creative seam: A child of a god is born to a poor, unexpecting family living in a world recently swallowed up by one of the strongest, fiercest nations around. The family must flee to another land to avoid the murder of their newborn god-child who grows to be an intelligent, philosophical, loving man, swept up in the messianic fervor of the day. He causes blind men to see, lepers to heal, turns water into wine, makes dangerously pithy ripostes towards the extremely powerful religious leaders. He even occasionally loses his cool and physically whips a temple full of tradesmen, just to prove a point. And in the end, he is shockingly, dramatically, arrested as a terrorist and executed for the things he said.

It is hard to deny—this is a gripping story.

No wonder then that novels concerning the life and times of Jesus are innumerable. And they span an even wider breadth of genres. Many carefully follow the life of Jesus laid out in the Gospels, while others take a single character or a moment in Jesus' ministry and expound upon it—searching through the historical records of the time to reveal a new angle, a new insight. There are those with a more subtle take on Jesus' life and teachings, using fantastical worlds with different characters to tell the story. Some are for children, some are humorous, some are philosophical, some are critical.

But do they all see the Crown of Thorns the same way? Do they, as we have seen in the previous two artistic media, understand the Crown of Thorns as the medieval audience did?

One novel that is often recalled immediately when people think of "Jesus novels" will suffice to demonstrate the point. It is one that not only follows the Gospel story of Jesus, but also portrays him as a very human character. It looks at his time and place outside the Gospel story, is occasionally humorous, but is fully steeped in philosophical questions, and, of course, raised the indignation and interest of the world: Nikos Kazantzakis' *The Last Temptation of Christ*.

Published in Greek in 1955 and translated into English in 1960, Kazantzakis' novel follows Jesus as a young man as he struggles with his destiny to suffer and be sacrificed for the sake of the world. He contends with human emotion, temptation, and the politics of the time before coming to embrace his mission. The climax of the book portrays Jesus, dying on the cross, suddenly finding himself in another life—a vision of a life married to Mary Magdalene, with many children, experiencing a normal, human life of happiness, pain, contentment, and disappointment. The vision is, of course his last temptation, manufactured by Satan, from which Jesus eventually forces himself to wake, victorious in the knowledge that he is still on the cross and will save humanity.

Throughout the entirety of the novel, the Crown of Thorns comes up more often than one might expect—and features prominently in the book's opening.

In the very first chapter, we find Jesus dreaming. It is a wretched dream full of demon-like creatures that are hunting him down to force him into his divine calling. The creatures carry with them the tools of the Passion, including implements of torture, nails and an unwieldy cross. One of the creatures, "the vilest of the lot," a "skinny, crossed-eyed hunchback" carries the Crown of Thorns.[12] In this nightmare, we are made fully and immediately aware that the Crown of Thorns foreshadows the visceral nature of the suffering ahead. There is no doubt for the reader what the dream is about: Jesus' pain and death. The presence of the Crown of Thorns confirms it.

A few pages later, the Crown of Thorns comes up again. Jesus, having awoken from his dream, begins his day as a carpenter supporting his family. But not just any carpenter, one of the few who (deliberately ironic for our character) makes crosses for the Romans. He is accosted by Judas Iscariot who attempts to convince him not to make this particular cross because it is for a Zealot who has been deemed to be the messiah. Judas Iscariot argues that, if they rush to his rescue, this man "will throw off his rags and the royal crown of David will shine on his head."

Jesus refuses. He murmurs his defense, explaining that this is not how the messiah will come:

> No, the Messiah will not come in this way. He will never renounce his rags or wear a royal crown. Neither men nor God will ever rush to save him, because he cannot be saved. He will die, die, wearing his rags; and everyone—even the most faithful—will abandon him. He will die all alone at the top of a barren mountain, wearing on his head a Crown of Thorns.[13]

Judas Iscariot believes the Messiah should wear a royal crown. However, before this happens, Jesus prophesizes that he must first be adorned and abandoned in rags and a mock crown. That is, humiliation before triumph. A stark differentiation is drawn between the hopeful, determined belief of Judas Iscariot that their salvation will be crowned in glory, and the reality of rags and the Crown of Thorns. Once again, the Crown of Thorns swiftly encompasses both the suffering and humiliation of Jesus within the first twenty pages of the novel.

---

[12] Nikos Kazantzakis, *The Last Temptation of Christ*, trans. Peter A. Bien (New York: Simon and Schuster, 1955), 8–9.
[13] Kazantzakis, *The Last Temptation of Christ*, 17.

The Crown of Thorns comes up regularly in Jesus' dreams—which often prefigure (or cruelly remind him of) his impending suffering and death.[14] In one such dream, the Crown takes a slightly different, though now familiar, tack.

Again, Jesus dreams of his Crucifixion. This time, however, he is a heavenly beast, who is briefly taken away from his torment by Mary Magdalene who leads him out of the city. There they meet Jesus' mother. "When she saw the wounds, the blood all over him and crown of thorns in his hair" she throws her arms in the air, deeply upset and ashamed by his appearance, and curses Jesus for bringing so much embarrassment on her and their people.[15]

The Crown causes Mary the mother of Jesus deep shame. Thus, we find the Crown representing pain and suffering, but now also humiliation.

In another significant—though by no means the last[16]—reference, the Crown of Thorns comes full circle. Approaching the final hours of Jesus' life, he is with his disciples at the Last Supper. Once they all get up to leave for prayer in the Garden of Gethsemane, several of the disciples "sense complications" and slink away. Once what remains of the group arrives in Gethsemane, Jesus queries where three of them went off to. One of his followers, Andrew, angrily answers that they have left and abandoned him. Jesus smiles in response:

"Do not condemn them, Andrew. You will see: one day all three shall return, and each will be wearing a crown made of thorns, which is the most royal of crowns—and unwithering!"[17]

The Crown of Thorns, which has haunted Jesus' life and nightmares is now something he revels in—and encourages his disciples to do so as well. It is a crown of royal, undying triumph.

Thus, we see the qualities of the Crown, first established thousands of years ago from the earliest representations of wreaths through to the first recognizable Crown of

---

[14]See also Kazantzakis, *The Last Temptation of Christ*, 142–144.
[15]Kazantzakis, *The Last Temptation of Christ*, 386.
[16]Kazantzakis, *The Last Temptation of Christ*, Other examples include: (427–430) We find the Crown again during the actual Mockery, though in this rendition, it is Pilate's idea to dress him in a robe, give him a reed and put a Crown of Thorns on his head, in order, he hopes, to provoke pity and release for Jesus (462–463). In a conclusion which is redolent of Shakespeare's Lady Macbeth, within his "other life" vision, Jesus is told by Simon of Cyrene that Pilate went mad. Every night he wakes, asking for a basin to wash his hands, but he cannot get the blood off. He then continually fashions a crown from thorns for himself, presses it into his brow, and asks his servants to whip him—repenting for the pain he caused Jesus. Eventually Pilate crucifies himself (465–471). Still within the vision, an elderly Jesus encounters Paul, to whom he reveals his identity, determined not to allow Paul to spread the lie that he died on the cross and was resurrected. Paul refuses, saying he will continue to tell the story so that when anyone, anywhere in the world looks up at a crucifixion of Jesus and sees the Crown of Thorns, it "will cleanse their souls of all their sins."
[17]Kazantzakis, *The Last Temptation of Christ*, 421–422.

Thorns itself, fulfilled in Kazantzakis' book. Just mentioning the Crown fills characters and readers alike with dread of impending suffering. It is an object that elicits shame and humiliation amongst followers and family, but, eventually, is also triumphant—a wreath for a royal victor. Even on the last pages of the novel, Jesus wakes on the cross from his revery and feels that the Crown still pierces him. It brings him joy as its presence undeniably confirms his ultimate victory and fulfilment of purpose.[18]

The range and scale of modern representations of the Crown of Thorns could easily fill another book. Religious and secular, fine art or cinematic, artists return again and again to depictions of this object that elicits enduring resonance for central aspects of Christian philosophy. Humiliation and suffering are key to the Crown of Thorn's modern renditions. The imagery inspires us to reflect on our own humiliation, while also remaining hopeful that the pain will end in triumph. Deliberate nods to kingship and ultimate power did not stop with Louis IX and the Sainte-Chapelle, but echo even into modern sculptures that seek to be areligious.

The Crown of Thorns is not only a distinguished element of Passion art but stirs nearly identical ideologies over lengthy periods of time: humiliation, pain, hope and triumph. The themes surrounding the Crown of Thorns were full of meaning and were carefully unfolded over the early centuries of the medieval world.

They continue to reverberate in our society today.

---

[18]Kazantzakis, *The Last Temptation of Christ*, 487.

Conclusions

This study has followed for the first time the complicated evolution of the imagery of the Crown of Thorns. In doing so it sought to accomplish two primary tasks. First, to document how the imagery of the Crown of Thorns and Mockery of Jesus developed to the point where not only the Crown and Mockery came together as one scene, but when it was established as a recognizable and repeated motif. Specifically, this study has demonstrated the late arrival of the Crown of Thorns and its slow development and inclusion of the Mockery scene into the Passion cycle. In doing so, this research has contributed a more in-depth understanding of the visualization of a curiously overlooked episode of the Passion in the early Middle Ages.

We were also able to demonstrate how and why each significant stage of development occurred. Art does not progress in a vacuum, it evolves and is reinvented, influenced by the political culture, art, and ideologies of the time in which it was made. While my research undertakes a detailed consideration of potential artistic influences on the Crown of Thorns and Mockery, it also considers the influence of the world surrounding or viewing it. Previous scholarship has done excellent work in elucidating what images such as the Crucifixion, the Cross, and other moments of the Passion may have evoked or implied to the Medieval viewer; this book has now brought to light the richness and complexities of Jesus' Mockery and his Crown of Thorns.

The Crown of Thorns took some time to become a universally recognized image and one that is closely associated with Jesus' Passion: a thorny plant braided into a wreath-like shape brutally forced onto the head of a battered Jesus. This image evolved many centuries after the Gospel event and independently of the physical relic, even though it was preserved in Jerusalem and later in Constantinople. The Crown of Thorns did not have a truly identifiable artistic presence until the eleventh century. The imagery started out in the fourth century as a wreath-crown, following the specific vocabulary and connotations of the Greek Gospel text and the Roman concept of military wreaths. The

Crown then disappears almost entirely from the sixth to the tenth centuries. It is detached from its narrative context of the Mockery, a narrative which develops congruently with contemporary theological exegeses. The Crown appears for the first time within the Passion imagery only in the next century. It occurs in several different forms, until finally the wreath-like crown with visibly protruding thorns is derisively placed on Jesus' head in the eleventh century. Thus, despite this long progression, it is only within the brief timeframe of the eleventh century that many of the precedents and familiar associations with the Crown of Thorns are established.

This circuitous journey began with two words: wreath and acanthus. Pilate's soldiers wove for their victim a wreath intended to mock Jesus' failures: his failure to save his people; his failure to militarily defeat the Romans; his failure to escape death. For Jesus' followers, however, the acanthus wreath represented their own truth: that Jesus had indeed been victorious over his enemies and had saved his people from destruction through his triumphant conquest of death. Victory over death or victory over enemies, this "wreath of acanthus" represented eternal triumph, and anyone who followed Jesus' example too could win such a wreath for themselves in heaven. Jesus' wreath, whether made of leaves or of thorns, from the fourth century onward, would retain in some form this initial understanding of victory.

It is therefore possible to conclude from this analysis that the imagery of the Crown of Thorns, from the fourth to the eleventh centuries, exemplifies Christian ideologies that permeate the development of the faith. The concept of the Crown of Thorns, even before it was recognizably a crown made of thorns in the eleventh century, was quickly established as representative of triumph over evil by the practice of humility, patience, and endurance. Such actions not only lead to Jesus' own triumph, but also that of his true and righteous imitators. It is possible to see this idea threaded through each of the eras under discussion and is indelibly represented in their art.

The martyrs are first depicted with their victory wreath-crowns as reward for emulating Christ's endurance. By suffering in their own lives and deaths as Jesus suffered during the Mockery, they gain a similarly representative wreath. Their wreath-crowns, as was Jesus' wreath-crown, though conceived in mockery, proclaimed their successfully fought battle against a tormenting enemy and against sin. Similarly, Jesus' humility during the Mockery is considered the greatest example of how one must oppose duplicity and evil. The Carolingian commentaries and depictions of the Mockery illustrate ideal patience. It is the Mockery of Christ, the theologians expound, that all the faithful look to and imitate as a paradigm for how to defeat adversaries.

Later, the king is meant to encompass all Christly attributes as Jesus' greatest imitator to the point where the king is artistically and literarily comparable to Jesus. To gain the initial kingship and be crowned as a true and worthy king, the Ottonian and Salian rulers had to endure a life of suffering and humiliation. This suffering was an essential demonstration of their likeness to Jesus; as Jesus had endured the pinnacle of suffering and humiliation during the Mockery, so too did the kings. As a result, both were crowned. Indeed, even as late as the thirteenth century, the image of the Crown is still associated with kingly worth and humble piety, a link which was further strengthened by the presence of the physical relic of the Crown of Thorns. The relic of the Crown of Thorns unquestioningly helped legitimize and sanctify Louis IX, which prompted an enduring association between king, Christ, and worth.

Humility, patience, endurance, imitation, pain, and victory are visually invoked by the Crown of Thorns. The visual representations of the Mockery and the Crowning, even within the variation they develop through the centuries up to the modern day, are instantly associated with these fundamental concepts of the Christian faith.

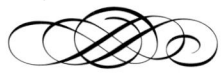

Bibliography

Ambrose of Milan. *Political Letters and Speeches.* Translated by J. Liebeschuetz. Liverpool: Liverpool University Press, 2005.
Antonius Martyr. *Of the Holy Places Visited by Antonius Martyr.* Translated by Aubrey Stewart. London: Palestine Pilgrims' Text Society, 1887.
Bagge, Sverre. *Kings, Politics, and the Right Order in German Historiography c. 950–1150.* Leiden: Brill, 2002.
Belting, Hans. "An Image and Its Function in the Liturgy: The Man of Sorrows in Byzantium." *Dumbarton Oaks Papers,* 34/35 (1980): 1–16.
Belting, Hans. *Likeness and Presence; A History of the Image before the Era of Art.* Translated by Edmund Jephcott. Chicago: University of Chicago Press, 1994.
Berg, K. "A Contribution to the Early Iconography of the Crowning with Thorns." In *Miscellanea Bibiothecae hertzianae*, edited by Leo Bruhns, Franz Graf Wolff Metternich, and Ludwig Schudt, 37–44. Galway: MW Books, 1961.
Beyreuther, Gerald. "Die Osterfeier als Akt königlicher Repräsentanz und Herrschaftsausübung unter Heinrich II. (1002–1024)." In *Feste und Feiern im Mittelalter; Paderborner Symposion des Mediävistenbandes*, edited by Detlef Altenburg, Jörg. Jarnut, and Hans-Hugo Steinhoff, 245–253. Sigmaringen: Thorbecke, 1991.
Bielowski, A., ed., *Monumenta Poloniae Historica*, vol. 1, Lwow: Nakladem Wlasnym, 1864.
Bond, Helen. *Pontius Pilate; In History and Interpretation.* Cambridge: Cambridge University Press, 1998.
Bottineau, Yves. *Notre-Dame de Paris et la Sainte-Chapelle.* Paris: B. Arthaud, 1966.
Bovini, Giuseppe. *Ravenna Mosaics.* Greenwich: New York Graphic Society, 1966.
Brenk, Beat. "The Imperial Heritage of Early Christian Art." In *Age of Spirituality: A Symposium.* Edited by Kurt Weitzmann, 39–52. New York: Metropolitan Museum of Art, 1980.
Brown, Peter. *The Rise of Western Christendom; Triumph and Diversity, AD 200–1000.* West Sussex: Wiley-Blackwell, 2013.
Campbell, Brian. *The Roman Army, 31 BC–AD 337; A Sourcebook.* London and New York: Routledge, 1994.
Castelli, Elizabeth. *Martyrdom and Memory; Early Christian Culture Making.* New York: Columbia University Press, 2004.
Ciggaar, Krijna. "Une description de Constantinople traduite par un pèlerin anglaise." *Revue des études byzantines*, 34 (1976): 211–268.
Ciggaar, Krijna. *Western Travellers to Constantinople; The West and Byzantium, 962–1204: Cultural and Political Relations.* Leiden: E.J. Brill, 1996.
Chazelle, Celia. *The Crucified God in the Carolingian Era; Theology and Art of Christ's Passion.* Cambridge: Cambridge University Press, 2001.

Chazelle, Celia and Burton Van Name Edwards. "The Study of the Bible and Carolingian Culture." In *The Study of the Bible in the Carolingian Era*, edited by Celia Chazelle and Burton Van Name Edwards. Turnhout: Brepols, 2003.

Clement of Alexandria. *Christ the Educator*. Translated by Simon Wood. Washington D.C.: Catholic University Press, 1954.

Cohen, Meredith. *The Sainte-Chapelle and the Construction of Sacral Monarchy*. Cambridge: Cambridge University Press, 2015.

Contreni, John. "Carolingian Biblical Studies." In *Carolingian Learning, Masters and Manuscripts*, edited by John Contreni, 71–98. Hampshire: Variorum, 1992.

Coon, Lynda. "Gendering Dark Age Jesus." *Gender & History*, 28:1 (2016): 8–33.

Corrigan, Kathleen. *The Ninth Century Byzantine Marginal Psalters*. PhD dissertation. University of California, Los Angeles, Ann Arbor: University Microfilms International, 1984.

Corrigan, Kathleen. *Visual Polemics in the Ninth Century Byzantine Psalter*. Cambridge: Cambridge University Press, 1992.

Corrigan, Kathleen. "Early Medieval Psalter Illustration in Byzantium and the West." In *The Utrecht Psalter in Medieval Art; Picturing the Psalms of David*, edited by Koert van der Horst, et al., 85–103. Tuurdijk, Netherlands: HES, 1996.

Costambeys, Marios, Matthew Innes, and Simon Maclean. *The Carolingian World*. Cambridge: Cambridge University Press, 2011.

Coupland, Simon. "Carolingian Arms and Armor in the Ninth Century." *Viator*, 21 (1990): 29–50.

Croix, Geoffrey de Ste. *Christian Persecution, Martyrdom, and Orthodoxy*. Oxford: Oxford University Press, 2006.

Cruz, Joan. *Relics; The Shroud of Turin, the True Cross, the Blood of Januarius . . . History, Mysticism and the Catholic Church*. Huntington: Our Sunday Visitor, 1984.

Cushing, Kathleen. *Reform and Papacy in the Eleventh Century; Spirituality and Social Change*. Manchester: Manchester University Press, 2005.

Dodwell, Charles. *The Pictorial Arts of the West, 800–1200*. New Haven: Yale University Press, 1993.

Deliyannis, Deborah. *Ravenna in Late Antiquity*. Cambridge: Cambridge University Press, 2010.

Derbes, Anne. *Picturing the Passion in Late Medieval Italy*. Cambridge: Cambridge University Press, 1996.

Elsmann, Thomas. "Das Evangelistar (Perikopenbuch) Kaiser Heinrich III. (msb 0021)," *Staat-und Universitätsbibliothek Bremen*, 2014. https://m.suub.uni-bremen.de/app/webroot/uploads/cms/files/Evangelistar_SuUB_Bremen.pdf. Retrieved February 19, 2016.

Elsner, Jas. *Art and the Roman Viewer*. Cambridge: Cambridge University Press, 1995.

Evens, Jonathan. "The Spirituality of the Artist-Clown; The Significance of the Clown in the Life and Work of Albert Houthuesen." Retrieved April 24, 2023. https://artway.eu/content.php?id=1025&lang=en&action=show.

Faller, Otto and Michaela Zezler. *Ambrosius, Epistulae et acta; Corpus Scriptorum Ecclesiasticorum Latinorum*, 82, vol. 3. Vienna: Austrian Academy of Sciences Press, 1968–1996.

Forstner, Karl. "Die Schreibschule von St. Peter." In *St. Peter in Salzburg. Das älteste Kloster im deutschen Sprachraum. 3. Landesaustellung, 15 Mai-26. Okt. 1982. Schätze europäischer Kunst und Kultur. Red. Heinz Dopsch und Roseitha Juffinger*, 182–186. Salzburg: Druckhaus Nonntal, 1982.

Franz, Gunther and Franz Ronig. *Codex Egberti; Teilfaksimile-Ausgabe des Ms. 24 der Stadtbibliothek Trier*. Wiesbaden: Reichert, 1983.

Freeman, Charles. *A New History of Early Christianity*. New Haven: Yale University Press, 2009.

Freeman, Charles. *Holy Bones, Holy Dust; How Relics Shaped the History of Medieval Europe*. New Haven: Yale University Press, 2011.

Gabriele, Matthew. "Frankish Kingship, Political Exegesis and the Ghost of Charlemagne in the Diplomas of King Philip I of Francia." In *The Charlemagne Legend in Medieval Latin Texts*, edited by William Purkis and Matthew Garbriele, 9–32. Cambridge: Boydell & Brewer, 2016.

Gaehde, J. "Treasury; Aachen." In *The Dictionary of Art*, vol. 1, edited by Jane Turner, 1–5. New York: Grove, 1996.

Garrison, Eliza. *Ottonian Imperial Art and Portraiture: The Artistic Patronage of Otto III and Henry II*. Farnham, Surrey: Ashgate, 2012.

Gilliver, Kate. "The Augustan Reform and the Structure of the Imperial Army." In *A Companion to the Roman Army*, edited by Paul Erdkamp, 183–200. Oxford: Blackwell, 2007.

Gilsdorf, Sean., translated by. *Queenship and Sanctity; The Lives of Mathilda and the Epitaph of Adelheid*. Washington, D.C.: The Catholic University of America Press, 2004.

Goldsworthy, Adrian. *The Complete Roman Army*. London: Thames & Hudson, 2011.

Goldsworthy, Adrian. *Pax Romana*. New Haven: Yale University Press, 2016.

Grebe, Anja. *Codex Aureus; Das Golden Evangelienbuch von Echternach*. Darmstadt: Wissenschaftliche Buchgesellschaft, 2007.

Head, Thomas. "Art and Artifice in Ottonian Trier." *Gesta*, 36:1 (1997): 65–82.

Hellemo, Geir. *Adventus Domini; Eschatological Thought in 4th-Century Apses and Catecheses*. Translated by E. Waaler. Leiden: Brill, 1989.

Henderson, George. "Emulation and Invention in Carolingian Art." In *Carolingian Culture: Emulation and Innovation*, edited by Rosamond McKitterick, 248–274. Cambridge: Cambridge University Press, 1994.

Henten, Jan Willem van and Friedrich Avemarie. *Martyrdom and Noble Death; Selected Texts from Graeco-Roman, Jewish and Christian Antiquity*. London: Routledge, 2002.

Hermann, Friedrich. "Salzburg, St. Peter." In *Die Benediktinischen Mönchs- und nonnenklöster in Osterreich und Südtirol*, edited by Ulrich Faust and Waltraud Krassnig, 263–408. St. Ottilien: EOS Verlag, 2002.

Hermann, Karl. *Geschichte der erzabtei St. Peter zu Salzburg, Band: Frühgeschichte 696–1193*. Salzburg: Salzburger Druckerei, 1996.

Hinks, Roger. *Carolingian Art; A Study of Early Medieval Painting and Sculpture in Western Europe*. Ann Arbor: University of Michigan Press, 1966.

Holter, Kurt. "Hauptwerke der Buchkunst aus St. Peter in Salzburg." In *St. Peter in Salzburg. Das älteste Kloster im deutschen Sprachraum. 3. Landesausstellung, 15 Mai-26. Okt. 1982. Schätze europäischer Kunst und Kultur. Red. Heinz Dopsch und Roseitha Juffinger*, 154–165. Salzburg: Druckhaus Nonntal, 1982.

Horsely, Richard. "Popular Prophetic Movements at the Time of Jesus; Their Principal Features and Social Origins." *Journal for the Study of the New Testament*, 8:3 (1986): 4–11.

Horst, Koert van der, William Noel, and W. Wüstefeld (eds.). *The Utrecht Psalter in Medieval Art*. Tuurdijk, Netherlands: HES, 1996.

Hourihane, Colum. *Pontius Pilate, Anti-Semitism, and The Passion in Medieval Art*. Princeton: Princeton University Press, 2009.

Hourihane, Colum. "Echternach." In *The Grove Encyclopedia of Medieval Art and Architecture*, edited by Colum Hourihane, 408–409. Oxford: Oxford University Press, 2012.

Jensen, Robin Margaret. *Understanding Early Christian Art*. New York: Routledge, 2000.

Jordan, Alyce. *Visualizing Kingship in the Windows of the Sainte Chapelle*. Turhout: Brepols, 2002.

Josephus, *Jewish Antiquities*. Translated by L. Feldman. Loeb Classical Library, vol. 10. London: Heinemann, 1965.

Josephus, *The Jewish Wars*. Translated by H. Thackeray. Loeb Classical Library, vol. 2. London: Heinemann, 1965.

Justin Martyr. *The First and Second Apologies*. Translated by Leslie Barnard. New York: Paulist Press, 1997.

Kahsnitz, Rainer. "Echternach und Trier zur Entstehungszeit des Goldenen Evangelienbuches." In *Das Goldene Evangelienbuch von Echternach*, edited by Rainer Kahsnitz, Ursula Mende, Elisabeth Rücker, 19–37. Frankfurt am Main: S. Fischer Verlag GmbH, 1982.

Kantorowicz, Ernst. *The King's Two Bodies: A Study in Mediaeval Political Theology*. Princeton: Princeton University Press, 1957.

Kasperson, Søren and Erik Thunø. *Decorating the Lord's Table: On the Dynamics between Image and Altar in the Middle Ages*. Copenhagen: Museum Tusculanum Press, 2006.

Karwasinksa, H., edited. *Monumenta Poloniae Historica, Series Nova, vol. 4.3*. Warsaw: Panstowowe Wydawnictow Naukowe, 1973.

Kazantzakis, Nikos. *The Last Temptation of Christ*. Translated by Peter A. Bien (1960). New York: Simon and Schuster, 1955.

Kessler, Herbert. *The Illustrated Bibles from Tours*. Princeton: Princeton University Press, 1977.

Lawrence, Marion. *The Sarcophagi of Ravenna*. Rome: L'Erma di Bretschneider, 1945.

Ławrynowicz, Olgierd. "The Iconography of Weapons of Western Slavs in the Early Middle Ages; Some Notes on the Example of the So-Called Group of Vysehrad Codex." *Acta Universitatis Lodziensis, Folia Archaeoligica*, 29 (2012), 123–144.

Le Bohec, Yann. *The Imperial Roman Army*. London: Batsford, 1994.

Leemans, Johan, et al. *"Let us Die that we May Live"; Greek Homilies on Christian Martyrs from Asia Minor, Palestine and Syria (c. AD 350–AD 450)*. London: Routledge, 2003.

Leniaud, Jean-Michel and Françoise Perrot. *The Sainte Chapelle*, Paris: Ed du patriomine, Centre des monuments nationaux, 2007.

Leonardi, Claudio. "Intellectual Life." In *The New Cambridge Medieval History, Vol. III, c. 900–1024*, edited by Timothy Reuter, 186–211. Cambridge: Cambridge University Press, 1999.

Levine, Lee. *Jerusalem; Portrait of the City in the Second Temple Period*. Philadelphia: The Jewish Publication Society, 2002.

Leyser, Karl. *Communication and Power in Medieval Europe; The Carolingian and Ottonian Centuries*. Vol. 1. London: Hambledon Press, 1994.

Leyser, Karl. *Rule and Conflict in an Early Medieval Society; Ottonian Saxony*. Bloomington and London: Indiana University Press, 1979.

Logan, F. Donald. *The History of the Church in the Middle Ages*. London: Routledge, 2002.

Lowden, John. "The Beginning of Biblical Illustration." In *Imaging the Early Medieval Bible*, ed. by John Williams, 9–60. University Park: Pennsylvania State University Press, 1999.

Lynch, Joseph and Phillip Adamo. *The Medieval Church*, London: Routledge, 2014.

Mackie, Gillian. "New Light on the So-Called Saint Lawrence Panel at the Mausoleum of Galla Placidia, Ravenna." *Gesta*, 29:1 (1990): 54–60.

Malbon, Elizabeth. *The Iconography of the Sarcophagus of Junius Bassus*. Princeton: Princeton University Press, 1990.

Marenbon, John. "Carolingian Thought." In *Carolingian Culture: Emulation and Innovation*, edited by Rosemond McKitterick, 171–192. Cambridge: Cambridge University Press, 1994.

Maas, Walter. *Der Aachener Dom*. Köln: Greven, 1984.

Mathews, Thomas. *The Clash of Gods*. Princeton: Princeton University Press, 1993.

Maxfield, Valerie. *The Military Decorations of the Roman Army*. Berkeley: University of California Press, 1981.

Mayr-Harting, Henry. *Ottonian Book Illumination; An Historical Study*. London: Harvey Miller Publishers, 1999.

Mayr-Harting, Henry. *Church and Cosmos in Early Ottonian Germany; The View of Cologne*. Oxford: Oxford University Press, 2007.

McClendon, C. "Aachen: Buildings; Palatine Chapel." In *The Dictionary of Art*, vol. 1, edited by Jane Turner, 2–24. New York: Grove, 1996.

McKinnon, James. "The Book of Psalms, Monasticism, and the Western Liturgy." In *The Place of the Psalms in the Intellectual Culture of the Middle Ages*, edited by Nancy van Deusen, 43–58. Albany, NY: State University of New York, 1999.

McKitterick, Rosamond. "Continuity and Innovation in Tenth-Century Ottonian Culture." In *Intellectual Life in the Middle Ages*, edited by Lesley Smith and Benedicta Ward, 15–24. London and Rio Grande: The Hambledon Press, 1992.

McKitterick, Rosamond. "Text and Image in the Carolingian World." In *The Frankish Kings and Culture in the Early Middle Ages*. Collected Studies Series, edited by Rosamond McKitterick, 297–318. Aldershot: Variorum, 1995.

McKitterick, Rosamond. *Charlemagne; The Formation of a European Identity*. Cambridge: Cambridge University Press, 2008.

McLynn, Neil. *Ambrose of Milan; Church and Court in a Christian Capital*. Berkeley: University of California Press, 1994.

Metz, Peter. *The Golden Gospels of Echternach*. Translated by Ilse Schrier and Peter Gorge. New York: Frederick A. Praeger, 1957.

Milburn, Robert. *Early Christian Art and Architecture*. Aldershot: Scolar Press, 1988.

Migne, Jacques Paul. ed. (1841–1865a), *Patrologiae Curusus Completus; Series Latina*, Paris: Garnier online edition, http://patristica.net/latina Last retrieved in June 2018.

Migne, Jacques Paul. ed. (1841–1865b), *Patrologiae Curusus Completus; Series Graeca*, Paris: Garnier online edition, https://web.archive.org/web/20140608080824/http://graeca.patristica.net/. Last retrieved in June 2018.

Monumenta Germaniae Historica, online edition, http://www.dmgh.de, Last retrieved June 2018. Series and sub-series cited in thesis are in the form given in the website menu.

"Annales Regni Francorum," *Scriptores, Scriptores Rerum Germanicarum in Usum Scholarum Separatim Editi (SS rer. Germ)*, vol. 6.

Thietmar, "Chronicon", *Scriptores, Scriptores Rerum Germanicarum, Nova Series (SS rer. Germ. N.S.)*, vol. 9.

"Vita Mathildis Reginae Posterior," *Scriptores, Scriptores Rerum Germanicarum in Usum Scholarum Separatim Editi (SS rer. Germ)*, vol. 66.

Widukind, "Rerum Gestarum Saxonicarum," *Scriptores, Scriptores Rerum Germanicarum in Usum Scholarum Separatim Editi (SS rer. Germ)*, vol. 60.

Wipo, "Gesta Chuonradi II Imperatoris," *Scriptores, Scriptores Rerum Germanicarum in Usum Scholarum Separatim Editi (SS rer. Germ)*, vol. 61.

Morgan, Jane. Artist Proposal, *Eva International Ireland's Biennieal*. Limerick City, 2014.

Morgan, Jane. Jane Morgan Studio, interview by author, February 17, 2023.

Morgan, Jane. Jane Morgan Studio. "A Crown of Thorns – Follow-up." Received by author, March 23, 2023 (email).

Morrison, Karl. *The Two Kingdoms; Ecclesiology in Carolingian Political Thought*. Princeton: Princeton University Press, 1964.

Moss, Candida. *The Other Christs; Imitating Jesus in Ancient Christian Ideologies of Martyrdom*. Oxford: Oxford University Press, 2010.

Müller-Mertens, Eckhard. "The Ottonians as Kings and Emperors." In *The New Cambridge Medieval History, Vol. III c. 900–1024*, edited by Timothy Reuter, 233–266. Cambridge: Cambridge University Press, 1999.

Minucius Felix. *Octavius*. Translated by G. Rendall. Loeb Classical Library. Vol. 1. London: Heinemann, 1960.

Netzer, Nancy. *Cultural Interplay in the Eighth Century; The Trier Gospels and the Making of a Scriptorium at Echternach*. Cambridge: Cambridge University Press, 1994.

Netzer, Nancy. "Willibrord's Scriptorium at Echternach." In *St. Cutherbert, his Cult and his Community*, edited by Gerald Bonner, David Rollason and Clare Stancliffe, 203–212. Woodbridge: Boydell Press, 1989.

Noel, William. "Psalters." In *Leaves of Gold; Manuscript Illuminations from Philadelphia Collections*, edited by James Tanis. Philadelphia: Philadelphia Museum of Art, 2001.

Oltrogge, Doris and Robert Fuchs. *Die Maltechnik des Codex Aureus Aus Echternach; Ein Meisterwerk im Wandel*. Nuremberg: Verlag des Germanischen Nationalmuseums, 2009.

Origen. *Contra Celsum*. Translated by Henry Chadwick. Cambridge: Cambridge University Press, 1965.

Origen. *Contra Celsum, Libri VIII*. Edited by M. Marcovich. Leiden: Brill, 2001. 109–110; 505–506.

Panayotova, Stella. "The Illustrated Psalter; Luxury and Practical Use." In *The Practice of the Bible in the Middle Ages*, edited by Susan Boynton and Diane Reilly, 247–271. New York: Columbia University Press, 2011.

Pastan, Elizabeth. "Charlemagne as Saint? Relics and the Choice of Window Subjects at Chartres Cathedral." In *The Legend of Charlemagne in the Middle Ages; Power, Faith, and Crusade*, edited by Matthew Gabriele and Jace Stuckey, 97–135. New York: Palgrave Macmillan, 2008.

Pataki-Hundt, Andrea. "Conservation Treatment and Stabilization of the Ninth-Century Stuttgart Psalter." *Journal of the Institute of Conservation*, 35: 2 (2012), 152–164.

Philo. *Legatio Ad Gaium*. Translated by F. H. Colson. Loeb Classical Library, vol. 10. London: Heinemann, 1962.

Pierpont Morgan Library, "Saint Peter Gospels MS M. 781," Curatorial Description, corsair.morganlibrary.org/msdescr/BBM0781a.pdf Retrieved April 2017, 1–7.

Pierpont Morgan Library, "Saint Peter Gospels MS M. 781," CORSAIR Collection Catalogue, corsair.themorgan.org. Retrieved April 2017.

Pliny. *Naturalis Historia*. Translated by W. Jones. Loeb Classical Library, vols. 6 and 10. London: Heinemann, 1961.

Pollini, John. "The Acanthus of the Ara Pacis as an Apolline and Dionysiac Symbol of Anamorphosis, Anakyklosis, and *Numen Mixtum*." In *Von Der Bauforschung Zur Denkmalpflege*, edited by Martin Kubelik and Mario Schwarz. Vienna: Phoibos, 1993.

Rauschen, Gerhard edited by. "Incipit Descriptio, qualiter Karolus magnus clavum et coronam domini a Constantinopoli Aquisgrani detulerit qualiterque Karlus calvus hec ad sanctum Dyonisium retulerit." In *Die Legende Karls des Grossen im 11 und 12 Jahrhundert*, 103–25. Leipzig: Verglan von Duncker & Humblot, 1980.

Reuter, Timothy. *Germany in the Early Middle Ages, c. 800–1056*. London and New York: Longman, 1991.

Ronig, Franz. "Erläuterungen zu den Tafeln. Ikonographie." In *Codex Egberti; Teilfaksimile-Ausgabe des Ms. 24 der Stadtbibliothek Trier*, edited by Franz Gunther and Franz Ronig, 47–142. Wiesbaden: Reichert, 1983.

Rothenstein, John. *Modern English Painters*. Vol. 3. London: Macdonald and Jane's Publishers, 1976.

Rutgers, Leonard. *Subterranean Rome; In Search of the Roots of Christianity in the Catacombs of the Eternal City*. Leuven: Peeters, 2000.

Royal Academy of Arts, 244th Summer Exhibition (2012). *Summer Exhibition List of Works 2012*. Retrieved February 4, 2023. https://www.royalacademy.org.uk/art-artists/exhibition-catalogue/ra-sec-vol244–2012.

Sadler, Donna. "The King as Subject, the King as Author: Art and Politics of Louis IX." In *European Monarchy: Its Evolution and Practice from Roman Antiquity to Modern Times*, edited by Heinz Duchhardt, 53–68. Stuttgart: Steiner, 1992.

Schiller, Gertrud. *Iconography of Christian Art*. Vol. 2. Translated by Janet Seligman. London: Lund Humphries, 1972.

Schutz, Herbert. *The Carolingians in Central Europe, Their History, Arts and Architecture; A Cultural History of Central Europe, 750–900*. Leiden: Brill, 2004.

Smallwood, Mary. *The Jews under Roman Rule: from Pompey to Diocletian*. Leiden: Brill Academic Press, 2001.

Soper, Alexander. "The Latin Style on Christian Sarcophagi of the Fourth Century", *The Art Bulletin*, 19:2 (1937), 148–202.

Stansbury, Mark. "Early Medieval Commentaries, Their Writers and Readers." *Frühmittelalterliche Studien*, 33 (1999), 49–82.

Stoll, Oliver. "The Religions of the Armies." In *A Companion to the Roman Army*, edited by Paul Erdkamp, 451–476. Oxford: Blackwell, 2007.

Tacitus. *The Annals*. Translated by J. Jackson. Loeb Classical Library. Vol. 5. Cambridge: Harvard University Press, 1956.

Tertullian. *Ad Nationes Libri Duo*. Translated by J. Borleffs. Leiden: Brill, 1929.

Tertullian. *Apology, De Spectaculis*. Translated by G. Rendall. Loeb Classical Library. Vol. 1. London: Heinemann, 1960.

Tertullian. *Christian and Pagan in the Roman Empire; The Witness of Tertullian*. Translated by Robert D. Sider. Washington, D.C.: Catholic University Press, 2001.

Tertullian. *De Corona*. Edited by Jacques Fontaine. Paris: Presses Universitaires de France, 1966. From https://tertullian.org/latin/de_corona.htm. Retrieved July 2016.

Thietmar of Mersburg. *Ottonian Germany; The Chronicon of Thietmar of Merseburg*. Translated by David Warner. Manchester and New York: Manchester University Press, 2001.

Throop, Priscilla, translated by. *Hrabanus Maurus; De Universo*, Charlotte, VT: Medieval MS, 2009.

Van der Horst, Koert. *The Utrecht Psalter in Medieval Art*. Tuurdijk, Netherlands: HES, 1996.

Van Liere, Frans. "Biblical Exegesis Through the Twelfth Century." In *The Practice of the Bible in the Middle Ages*, edited by Susan Boynton and Diane Reilly, 157–178. New York: Columbia University Press, 2011.

Verkerk, Dorothy. "Biblical Manuscripts in Rome 400–700 and the Ashburnham Pentateuch." In *Imaging the Early Medieval Bible*, edited by John Williams, 97–120. University Park: Pennsylvania State University, 1999.

Vitruvius. *De Architectura*. Translated by F. Granger. Loeb Classical Library, vol.1. London: Heinemann, 1962.

Volbach, Wolfgang Fritz. *Early Christian Art*. London: Thames and Hudson, 1961.

Volbach, Wolfgang Fritz. "Sculpture and Applied Art." In *Carolingian Art*, edited by Jean Hubert, et al., 207–260. London: Thames and Hudson, 1970.

Wagner, Stephen. "Establishing a Connection to Illuminated Manuscripts Made at Echternach in the Eighth and Eleventh Centuries and Issues of Patronage, Monastic Reform and Splendor." *Peregrinations: Journal of Medieval Art and Architecture*, 3:1 (2011), 49–82.

Weinfurter, Stefan. *The Salian Century: Main Currents in an Age of Transition*. Philadelphia: University of Pennsylvania Press, 1999.

Weiss, Daniel. "Architectural Symbolism and the Decoration of the Ste.-Chapelle." *The Art Bulletin*, 77:2 (June 1995), 308–320.

Weiss, Daniel. *Art and Crusade in the Age of Saint Louis*. Cambridge: Cambridge University Press, 1998.

Widukind. *Deeds of the Saxons*. Translated by Bernard Bachrach and David Bachrach. Washington D.C.: The Catholic University of America Press, 2014.

Wolfram, Herwig. *Conrad II 990–1039: Emperor of Three Kingdoms*. Translated by Denise Kaiser. University Park: Pennsylvania State University Press, 2006.

Wollasch, Joachim. "Monasticism: The First Wave of Reform." In *The New Cambridge Medieval History, Vol. III c. 900–1024*, edited by Timothy Reuter, 163–185. Cambridge: Cambridge University Press, 1999.

Wormald, Francis. "The Miniatures in the Gospels of St. Augustine, Corpus Christi College, Cambridge, MS 286." In *Collected Writings; Studies in Medieval Art from the Sixth to the Twelfth Centuries*, edited by J. Alexander, et al., 13–35. New York: Oxford University Press, 1984.

Wormald, Francis. "The Utrecht Psalter." In *Collected Writings; Studies in Medieval Art from the Sixth to the Twelfth Centuries*, edited by J. Alexander, et al. London: Harvey Miller, 1984.

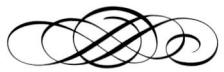

Index

Aachen
    Cathedral 99, 126, 148
    city 127, 147–8, 116–17
Abbey of St. Peter at Salzburg, and scriptorium
    96, 96 n. 15, 128–9, 140–1
Abraham 114
Agnellus, Archbishop 47
Alcuin of York 65, 69, 78, 84, 86
Ambrose of Milan, bishop 45, 49–51, 50 n. 53,
    53–4
Amiens 153
Anglo-Saxon 131
Annales Regni Francorum 147
Anonymous Pilgrim of Piacenza, see Antonius
    of Piacenza
Anonymus Mercati 149
Antonius of Piacenza 146–7
Apollo 16
Apostles, general 26, 37, 45–7, 52, 55, 57, 74, 132
Ara Pacis 17
Archelaus 5–6
Arcosolium 26, 44, 47
Asklepios 16
Assassins 8
Athlone Crucifixion 81
Augustine of Hippo 52–3, 53 n. 61, 63–4, 67,
    69–70, 95
Augustus, Emperor 5–6, 17, 19 n. 45
Augsburg Gospels 129–31
Aureus of Diocletian 40

Baldwin II 149, 156
Bamberg Apocalypse 104, 118, 120
Bamberg Bible 86
Barabbas 8, 13, 22–3, 93–4
Bartholomew, Apostle 136

Beauvais Psalter 153
Bede 68
Bernard the Monk, see Bernard the Wise
Bernard the Wise 146–7
Boleslav the Brave 108, 113
Bruno of Querfurt 108
Bulgarians 149
Byzantine 67 n. 23, 74–5, 79–80, 105, 147, 150–2

Caesarea 6–7, 10, 12–13
Caiaphas, Joseph 9, 90, 152–4
Canticle of Habbacuc 75
Carolingian
    Empire 56, 137, 139 n. 108
    art 2, 57–66, 70, 75–6, 76 n. 51, 78, 81–2,
        84–8, 92, 106
    literature 60–1, 61 n. 7, 63–5, 67–71, 73–4,
        76, 78–9, 84, 87–8, 110, 114 n. 54, 174
Cassiodorus, Magnus Aurelius 67–8, 70, 95, 146
Catacombs of Domitilla 47
Catacombs of San Severo 44
Certosa Sarcophagus 37–9, 42, 47
Chapel of St. Peter Martyr 79
Charlemagne 57, 61 n. 7, 126, 147–50, 158
Chartres Cathedral 148
Christ in Majesty 100 n. 19, 101, 126–7
Christ-like 52, 107–9, 142, 158, see also
    Christo-Mimesis
Christo-Mimesis 107–8, 114, 127
Chthonic 16, 24
Church of Holy Mary the Mother of Christ,
    Constantinople 149
Church of Sant' Apollinare Nuovo 38, 46–7
Christian of Stavelot 65–6, 78, 84, 87, 140
Christ as philosopher 37–8
Chrysostom, John 35–6, 42, 69 n. 32

Clement of Alexandria 32–3
Cluniac reform 138–9
Cluny 138
Codex Aureus of Echternach 90–2, 94, 98–9, 103, 106, 121–3, 127, 132–6, 140, 156
Codex Egberti 93–6, 98, 100, 103, 118, 122–4, 127–8, 137, 140
Codex Eyckensis 129, 131–2, 134, 136
Conrad I 118–19
Conrad II 90, 107, 109, 113, 117, 121
Constantinople 40, 147–9, 152, 158, 173
Contra Celsum 35–6
Coponius, governor of Judaea 7
Corinthian, columns 17
Corona Graminea 18–19, 19 n.43, 23, 28
Coronation, ceremony 101–6, 103 n. 24 and 25, 109, 113, 115–21, 124, 126–7, 142, 157–8, 166
Crucifixion 1–2, 9, 22, 26, 60, 70, 74–6, 79–83, 85–6, 88, 92, 94–5, 126, 150, 161, 171, 173
Curule chair 3, 41
Cyril of Jerusalem 33–4

Daniel, prophet 86
David, King 73, 114, 157, 170
De Bello Judaico 103, 105, 117–18, 120
Decius, Emperor, 48
De Corona 31–3
Descriptio qualiter 147–8, 158
Diocletian, Emperor 40, 44, 48, 49 n.50
Dirk Bout 161
Drogo Gospels 82–3, 76 n. 51

Ecclesia 82, 85–6
Echternach, abbey and scriptorium 90, 105, 122–3, 128–35, 137, 139–40
Egbert, Archbishop of Trier 93–4, 128, 140
Enthroned Christ 25, 37–9, 42, 46, 52, 55, 101 n.21, 127, 158
Enthroned Mockery 96, 98–106, 101 n. 21, 115–21, 123–7, 142, 145, 152–8
Epidaurus 16
Epiphany 135
Eusebius 27
Evangelist
    general 45, 53, 66, 84
    in art 59, 86–7, 130–2, 134–6
Ezekiel, prophet 86

Fadus, Cuspius, governor of Judaea 7
Felix, Antonius, governor of Judaea 8
Felix, Martyr 49–50
Flagellation of Christ
    in art 70, 74–9, 87, 90, 94, 98, 126, 146, 153–4
    by Caravaggio 161

Galerius 49
Galilee 5, 6 n. 5
Gaul 6, 45
Gesta Chuonradi see Wipo of Burgundy
Gethsemane, Garden of 22, 76, 126, 162, 171
Gibson, Mel 162
Golden Altar 96, 99–103, 105, 126–7, 141, 156
Gorze reform 138, 140
Gospel Book of Otto III 102, 105, 118
Gospels of St. Augustine 58–60, 65, 74, 92 n. 7
Gratus, Valerius, governor of Judaea 9

Haymo of Halberstadt 67–8, 73–4
Henry I 109–10, 119
Henry II 90, 100, 100 n. 19, 103, 103 n. 25, 104, 104 n. 26, 105, 108–9, 109 n. 37, 111–15, 113 n. 48, 117–18, 120–1, 126, 140
Henry III 113, 121–4, 135, 140
Henry of Bavaria, Duke 109 n. 37, 110–11, 113 n. 47
Henry the Fowler 137
Henry, Margrave 113
Herod the Great 5–6, 5 n. 5, 7–8, 13
Hildebert, archbishop 116, 119
Holy Lance 118–19
Houthuesen, Albert 164–6
Hrabanus Maurus 65–6, 69, 76, 84, 87
Humbert, abbot 140
Huth Psalter 154

Imperial Crown 118–19
Instruments of the Passion 2, 57, 70–5, 79, 84–9, 119 n. 68, 164
Irene, Empress 147
Irish Evangelary, St Gall 80
Isaiah, prophet 86

Jeremiah, prophet 86
Jerome of Stridon 15, 67
Jerusalem 5–8, 10–11, 13–14, 16, 20, 78, 79 n. 59, 90, 145–9, 158, 162, 173

John
    Apostle and Evangelist 76 n. 51, 82, 150
    the Baptist 20
    Gospel of 15, 43, 54, 59, 65, 69, 72, 84, 90,
        93–5, 124
Josephus, Flavius 9, 9 n. 20
Judaea 3–10, 13, 15, 20, 22–4, 41
Judaea Capta 29
Judas, disciple 22, 63–5, 153, 170
Judas of Galilee 7, 20
Jupiter 28, 40

Kazantzakis, Nikos 169–72

Lamb, as Christ 86–7
La Pietà, Michelangelo 164
Le Mans 45
Laurentius 129–30
Lectionary of Henry III 122–4, 132, 135–6
Legion
    the demon 21–2
    Roman 5–6, 22, 27, 42
Leistas 9
Liber Peritephanon 44
Libri Carolini 61
Life of Christ, in art 75, 79, 100
Litany of Saints 45–6, 153
Longinus, spear bearer 79–86
Louis IX, King 145, 149, 152, 156–8, 172, 175
Louvre Ivory 76, 82–3
Luke
    Apostle and Evangelist 59
    Gospel of 22, 43, 59–60, 70, 76 n. 51, 152

Mainz 117
Majestas Agnus 87
Mark
    Apostle and Evangelist 21–2, 130
    Gospel of 15, 22, 43, 52, 54, 59, 65–6, 152
Mary Magdalene 163, 169, 171
Mary, mother of Jesus 82–3, 101, 150, 171
Martyr, Justin 28
Matilda, Queen 109–12, 113 n. 47
Matthew
    Apostle and Evangelist 131, 134–6
    Gospel of 1, 15, 36, 42–3, 65–6, 98, 152
Mausoleum of Galla Placidia 43–5
Maximus, Fabius 19

Merovingian 130, 130 n. 93
Messiah 4, 18–23, 170
Messianic 4–5, 8, 18, 20–3, 169
Milan 45, 49, 51, 53
Ministri 59–60, 65, 94
Minucius Felix 28
Mithreaum 47
Monastery of the Pantocrator 149
Morgan, Jane 167–8
Mosaic of Saint Lawrence 43
Moses 5
Mount Gerizim 5, 12
Mount of Olives 8, 20

Naples 44, 49
Nero, Emperor 48
Nola 45, 146

Octavian 19, see also Augustus, Emperor
Origen 35–6, 69 n. 32
Otto I 116, 119
Otto II 93, 109 n. 37, 117
Otto III 90, 93, 102–3, 102 n. 23, 103 n. 25,
    104 n. 26, 109 n. 37, 117
Ottonian
    empire and rulers 89–90, 101, 106–10,
        116–2, 126–7, 137–40, 166, 175
    art 88–90, 93–4, 96, 101, 105–6, 115, 141–2,
        145, 149–52
    theology 114 n. 54

Palatine Chapel, Aachen 99, 126 n. 81
Paludamentum 4
Passion sarcophagi 26, 29, 37
Passion Sarcophagus, Vatican 14, 24, 26, 34, 36,
    41, 105
Passover 5, 13–14, 93
Paulinus of Nola 146
Pavia 45
Pax 17, 40
Pericopes of Henry II 82–3, 85
Pharisees 163
Philo of Alexandria 12
Pilate, Pontius 1, 3–5, 7, 9–14, 22, 26, 41, 53,
    53 n. 61, 57–9, 60, 65, 67, 69–70, 73,
    76, 76 n. 51, 78, 88, 92, 93–5, 99, 110,
    114, 118, 122, 142, 152–4, 156, 162,
    171 n. 16, 174

Pilgrimage 5, 146
Pliny the Elder 18–19, 23
Poppo of Stavelot 140
Prudentius 44

Rabula Gospels 79–80
Ravenna 43, 44, 46
Reichenau 93, 128
Reims 72, 82
Rembrandt 161
Republic, Roman 41
Res Gestae Saxonicae see Widukind of
 Corvey
Resurrection 16–17, 25, 27, 29, 68, 73, 146
Rinaldo Sarcophagus 39–40, 46
Roma 40
Romano-Christian
 culture 15–6, 48, 56, 145
 art 1, 25, 31, 33–4, 37, 41–2, 47, 55, 57
Rome 5–8, 12–14, 19–20, 19 n. 23, 39, 40, 43, 47,
 51, 80
Rule of Benedict 138
Rouen 45

Sabinus, procurator of Syria 5
Sainte-Chapelle, Paris 152, 155–8, 172
Saint Catherine's Church, Maaseik 131
St. Catherine Monestary, Sinai 150
Saint-Denis 157
Saint Gauzelin Gospel 87
Saint Gervasius 45–6, 49–51, 53–5
Saint Jerome, see Jerome of Stridon
Saint Lawrence 43–5
Santa Maria Antiqua 80
Saint Martin 47
Saint Peter, Apostle 26, 38, 42, 45–6, 48, 76, 76 n.
 51, 90, 105, 118, 152
Saint Peter Gospel 96, 98–106, 121, 124–5,
 127–8, 137, 141, 153–4
Santa Prisca, church 47
Saint Protasius 45–6, 49–51, 53–4
San Severo, catacombs 44
Saint Stephen 45, 146
Saint Vincent of Saragossa 44
Salian
 art 88–9, 119, 121–2, 125, 137, 141, 152
 empire and rulers 90, 101, 106–8, 113, 116,
  121, 127, 138–9, 142, 175

Samaritan 4, 7, 12–13
Sarcophagus with Victories 29
Satyrus, Uranius 51
Shrine of Charlemagne 148
Sicarii 8
Simon of Cyrene 4, 92, 171 n. 16
Sion Basilica, Jerusalem 147–8
Soissons 45
Solium 40
Solomon 157
Speyer Cathedral 123, 136, 139–40
Speyer Gospels 123–4, 132, 135–6, 140
Standards, roman military 10–11, 10 n. 20,
 27–8, 31
Stephaton, sponge bearer 79–82
Strabo, Walafrid 73–4
Stuttgart Psalter 56 n. 70, 61–70, 72, 74–6, 83,
 88, 93–6, 99–100, 123–4
Supper at Emmaus, Houthuesen 166
Syria 5–7, 12, 79

Tertullian 28, 31–3
The Passion of the Christ 162–4
Theodulf of Orleans 61
Theodotus, chapel of 80
Theophanu, Empress 90
Theudas 7, 20
Thietmar 107, 112–13, 113 n. 47, 116,
 118
Tiberieum 12
Tiberius, Emperor 9 n. 20, 11–13
Titus, Emperor 29
Tours 86
Tree Sarcophagus 26, 41
Trial, of Jesus 2, 8, 13, 18, 22, 41, 57, 70, 74, 145,
 153, 161–2
Trier, city 93, 128–31, 139–40
Trier Gospels 129–31, 135–6
Triumphal Wreath 25–9, 31, 36–7, 55
Triumph Sarcophagus of Married Pair 37
Tropaeum 27–9, 37
Twelve Apostles Sarcophagus 38–9, 42,
 46–7

Utrecht Psalter 56 n. 70, 71–2, 74–5, 84, 88

Valerian, Emperor 48
Varus, Publius Quinctilius 5–6, 5 n.3

Venetian 149
Vespasian, Emperor 29
Vexillum 27, 27 n. 6, 29
Vita Mathilda Posterior (*VMP*) 109–14
Vitellius, Lucius, legate of Syria 12–13
Vitruvius 17
Vratislaus II 124
Vysehrad Codex 124–5

Widener 9 Psalter 153
Widukind of Corvey 116–19
Willibrord, Saint and founder 129–30
Wipo of Burgundy 107, 113–14, 117–18
Wreath-crown 25, 33–4, 42, 48, 55–7, 105, 149, 173–4

Zealot 170